ANGELS & URCHINS

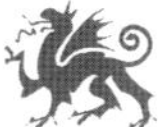

ACKNOWLEDGMENTS

Many people have contributed in different ways towards making this exhibition possible. I am grateful for the efforts of the administrative and curatorial the staff of English Heritage: Julius Bryant, Roger Carr Jones, Wayne Casey, Sue Coventry, Julie Ehlan, Trish Jones, Alex Saint, Sarah Whitbread, and Robin Wyatt. I also owe a particular debt of gratitude to Ian Dejardin, Chris Higgs, Tori Petfield, Cathy Power, Hazel Sutherland, Sue Worsey, and Amina Wright. Thank you also to Jeremy Richards, who travelled the length and breadth of the country photographing works specially for the exhibition. At Nottingham I would like to thank Matt Cambridge, Stuart Dilks, Liz O'Neill, Maureen Probert and Fran Shipley. I am also deeply indebted to Joanne Wright, who first encouraged me to go ahead with this project and who has continued to provide enthusiastic support and expertise throughout. Tracey Isgar, too, must be singled out for the manner in which she has patiently carried out a whole range of tasks, with a dedication which goes way beyond the call of duty. Friends and colleagues up and down the country have contributed their expertise and assistance. My particular thanks, in no particular order, go to Anthony Griffiths, Sheila O'Connell, Kim Sloan, Elizabeth Einberg, Peter Cannon-Brookes, John Coleman, Ann Sumner, James Lomax, Jane Wallis, Ron Clarke, Margaret Rylatt, William Vaughan, Raymond Chapman, Lois Potter and Dan Cruickshank. I am also eternally grateful to Richard Green at York City Art Gallery for agreeing to loan to us at very short notice. Thanks also to Hugh Belsey at Gainsborough's House, Sudbury, not only for assisting with loans but for his help and expert guidance over the entries on Gainsborough. I would like to express my profound gratitude to David Alexander for the entries on prints he has contributed to the catalogue (those initialled 'DSA') and for the generous loans he has made from his own collection. Finally, I would like to thank Draig Publications for their dedication and professionalism, especially designer David Hodgson and editor Robin Simon.

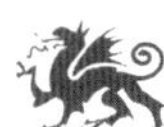

Catalogue edited, designed and produced by Draig Publications 1998
Printed by Aldridge Print Group, London

Catalogue published by The Djanogly Art Gallery in association
with Lund Humphries Publishers Ltd.

© Djanogly Art Gallery, 1998

British Library Cataloguing-in-Publication Data
A Catalogue record for this book is available from the British Library

Djanogly Art Gallery ISBN: 1 900809 45 1
Lund Humphries ISBN: 0 0835331 761 5

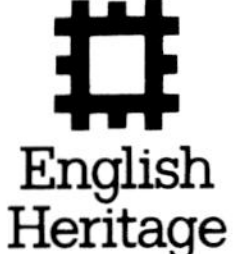

English
Heritage

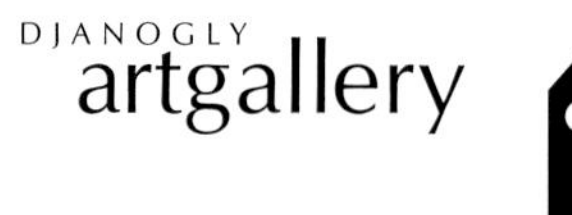

An exhibition organized by English Heritage and the Djanogly Art Gallery, University of Nottingham, with additional grants from the Paul Mellon Centre for Studies in British Art and the University of Delaware, USA

ANGELS & URCHINS

The Fancy Picture in 18th-Century British Art

MARTIN POSTLE

Djanogly Art Gallery, University of Nottingham
28 March-4 May 1998

Kenwood House, Hampstead, London
14 May-9 August 1998

CONTENTS

Cover Illustration
Boy Flying a Kite (detail) by Hugh Robinson (cat. 35)

FOREWORD

*A*ngels and Urchins is the first exhibition ever to be mounted on the subject of the 'fancy picture', a category of art which has been oddly neglected by generations of art historians studying British art. For the fancy picture was one of the most popular types of painting produced during the eighteenth century. The genre is complex to define because it can encompass such a broad range of subjects, from a child reading or playing a game to an old beggar selling baubles, from a maid performing domestic duties to the portrayal of an historical or literary character or even an infant saint. The common element is the notion of a character study of an individual, or small group of individuals presented in the format of a portrait, an idea which finds its origins in the seventeenth-century European tradition. The genre quickly became established in Britain after its import in the 1730s by the French Huguenot emigré Philip Mercier and found favour with such distinguished and diverse artists as William Hogarth, Joshua Reynolds, Thomas Gainsborough, Francis Wheatley, Joseph Wright of Derby, Johan Zoffany and Thomas Lawrence. But, as is amply demonstrated by this exhibition, fancy pictures are often less straightforward than they at first appear. They respond to a deeper level of interpretation and show themselves to be rich in meaning, allegory and innuendo while presenting the acceptable face of drudgery, indigence, underprivileged childhood, old age and sexual promiscuity to fashionable eighteenth-century society.

The exhibition has been devised and curated by Dr Martin Postle of the University of Delaware, with whom both English Heritage and the University of Nottingham have worked in our previous collaboration of 1991, 'The Artist's Model: its Role in British Art from Lely to Etty'. Dr Postle has brought to 'Angels and Urchins' the same combination of expertise and enthusiasm that made 'The Artist's Model' such a successful and enriching experience. This catalogue will give his project a life long beyond the exhibition itself and surely become a standard text for all students of eighteenth-century British Art.

The success of an exhibition of this scale and complexity depends on a large number of individuals and institutions being willing to lend their valuable works of art. The Djanogly Art Gallery and English Heritage would like particularly to thank David Alexander (not only as a lender but as a contributor to the catalogue), the Earl of Halifax, Sir Reresby Sitwell, Bt, and all the other private lenders who wish to remain anonymous. Public institutions to whom we are indebted both for their willingness to lend and for their co-operation with all the administration that lending works entails are the Ashmolean Museum, Oxford; the British Museum (Department of Prints and Drawings); Cannon Hall Museum, Barnsley; Gainsborough House, Sudbury; the Herbert Art Gallery, Coventry; Holburne Museum, Bath; Leeds City Art Galleries; The National Gallery, London; The National Galleries of Scotland; The Royal Academy of Arts, London; The Tate Gallery, London; the University of Manchester (Tabley House Collection); and the York City Art Gallery. The Djanogly Art Gallery is further indebted to our collaborators at English Heritage who have lent to the Nottingham show a number of treasures from the permanent collection at Kenwood House. Both venues are also immensely grateful for the financial support of the Paul Mellon Centre for Studies in British Art and the University of Delaware, USA.

Much of the preparatory work on the administration of this exhibition was done by Ian Dejardin, Senior Curator at English Heritage until taking up his new position at Dulwich College Picture Gallery in January this year. We thank him for his vital contribution which we have greatly missed in the final stages of the show's preparation.

Joanne Wright
Directory of Visual Art
University of Nottingham

Julius Bryant
Director of Collections
English Heritage

Introduction

Angels, Urchins, Oyster Sellers and Old Beggars

The 'fancy picture' was among the most original, popular, and self-consciously modern art forms to have emerged in Britain during the eighteenth century. Its subject-matter consisted of life-sized portrayals of cherubic children, ragged street urchins, winsome market women, and poor old beggars. They are works which remain visually accessible and pleasing. The term 'fancy picture' was coined in the eighteenth century, when the word 'fancy' was more akin to 'fantasy'. Today it retains a meaning only to a handful of individuals with a specific interest in the art of the period. Indeed, one of the principal tasks in the early planning stages of the present exhibition was to come up with a title which would convey some idea of the subject-matter in hand to a wider audience. Eventually, 'Angels and Urchins' was adopted because, although it by no means encompasses everything which we might call a fancy picture, it was felt to be apt, evocative, and it has a nice alliterative ring to it. Far more is involved, however, in defining the fancy picture than mere semantics.

The fancy picture emerged as a recognisable genre in its own right in Britain during the first half of the eighteenth century. More than any other single artist, it was promoted by the efforts of the French émigré painter Philip Mercier, who arrived in England in 1716 following an apprenticeship in Berlin and sojourns in France and Italy. Although Mercier was never a painter of the first rank, his familiarity with a range of European styles and genres, including notably the fêtes galantes of Watteau and Dutch seventeenth-century genre painting and portraiture, placed him in an ideal position to introduce new pictorial forms and ideas. Significantly (in terms of what we will have to say about the role of the market in shaping the ethos of the fancy picture), it was following his estrangement from the court patronage of Frederick, Prince of Wales, that Mercier turned his hand to the more 'democratic' sphere of the fancy picture – portrayals on the scale of life of anonymous children, pretty street vendors, domestic servants, musicians and courtesans (Fig. 1). On some of these works Mercier used a reversed signature, '*Reicrem*', an indication, perhaps, of his determination to make a new start in his art and his life (Ingamells and Raines, 1976-78, p. 4). Among others, these pleasing pictures caught the eye of George Vertue, artist, engraver and assiduous chronicler of the Georgian art world. In 1737 Vertue recorded in his diary Mercier's 'pieces of some figures of conversation as big as the life: conceited plaisant Fancies and habits: mixed modes really well done – and much approved of' (Vertue,

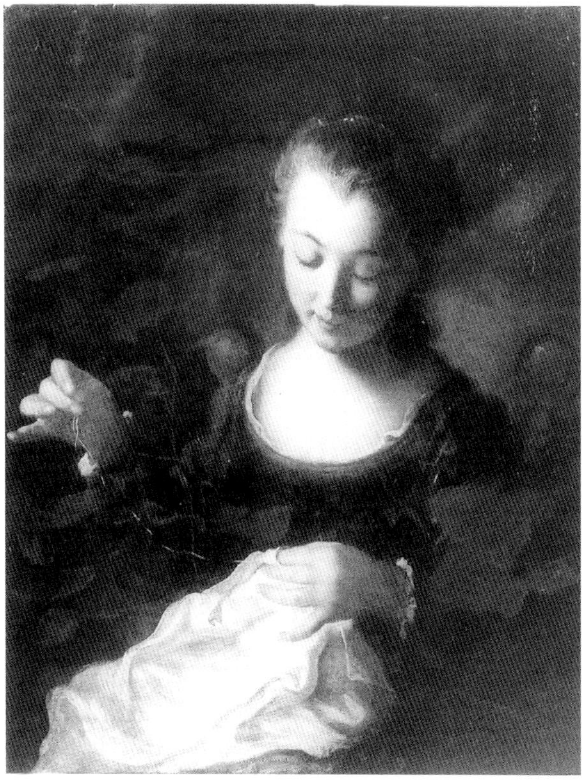

1 *The Seamstress* by Philip Mercier (?1689-1760). Oil on canvas, 74.5 x 62 cm. Private Collection

2 *La Jeune Laboreuse* by Alexis Grimou (?1678-1733). Oil on canvas, 83.7 x 69.7 cm. Private Collection

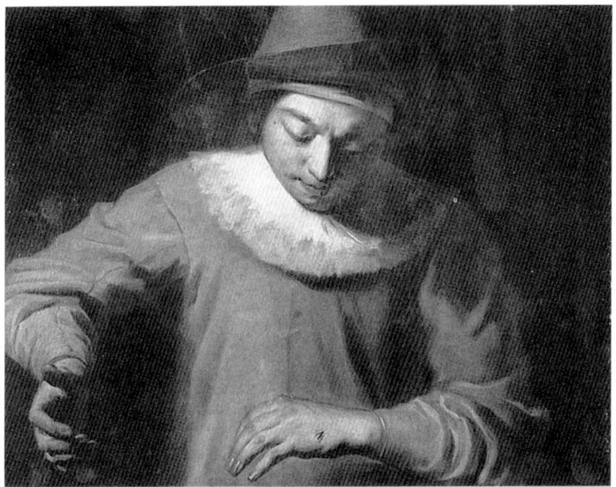

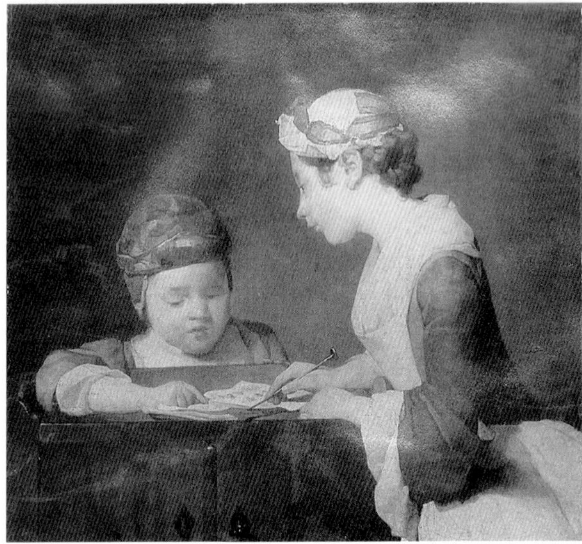

3 *Pantaloon Catching a Fly* by Antoine Watteau (1684-1721). Oil on canvas, 78.4 x 73.6 cm. The Art Institute of Chicago. Bequest of Mrs Sterling Morton

4 *The Young Schoolmistress* by Jean-Baptiste Simeon Chardin (1699-1779). Oil on canvas, 61.5 x 66.5 cm. The National Gallery, London

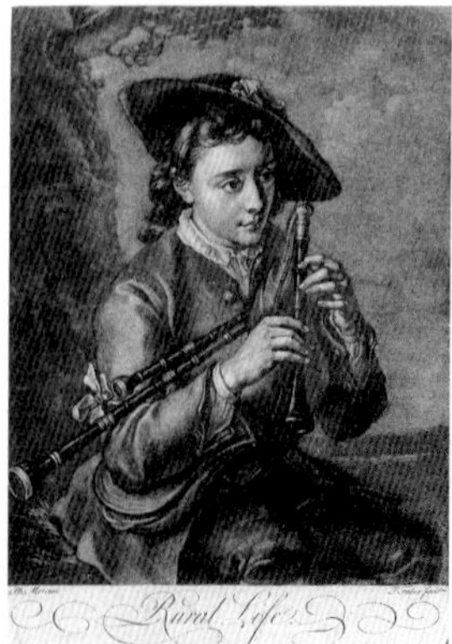

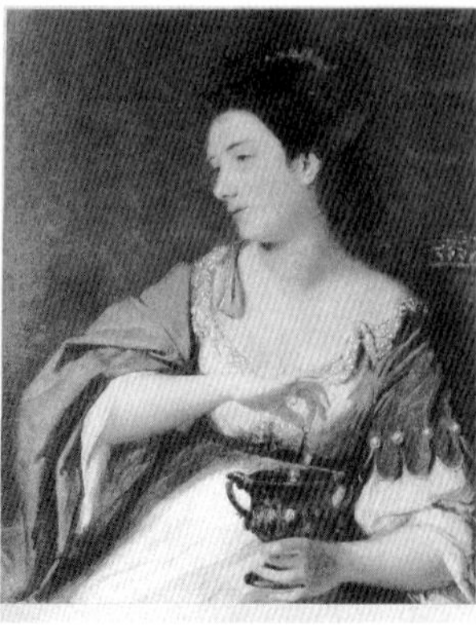

5 *Rural Life* by John Faber II, after Philip Mercier (?1689-1760). Mezzotint engraving. The Trustees of the British Museum

6 *Kitty Fisher as Cleopatra* by Sir Joshua Reynolds (1723-92). Oil on canvas, 76.2 x 63.5 cm. The Iveagh Bequest, Kenwood

1934, p. 82). Indeed, the 'mixed mode' of Vertue's own slightly confused response tells us that he was witnessing something new in British art.

The immediate source of Mercier's inspiration was the art of his French contemporaries, engravers such as Charles-Nicolas Cochin père and François-Bernard Lépicié père, and painters, notably Alexis Grimou (Fig. 2) – known in his own day as 'le Rembrandt français' – and, of course, Watteau (Fig. 3). It is worth stressing that the fancy picture was always truly European. Only a few artists, notably Chardin (Fig. 4), were capable of transforming the fancy picture into something quite profound, but there were many like Mercier whose efforts entertained generations of picture- and print-buyers. Even so, Mercier's own particular contribution ought not to be understated. Through his fancy pictures Mercier introduced to the British public an art form based purely upon the pleasure principle. 'He was,' as Ingamells and Raines observe, 'never instructing... only entertaining, and in this spirit of domestic, affecting, sentimentality he was a pioneer' (op. cit., p. 5).

Mercier's success in promoting the fancy picture was linked to its translation into print form, at first by the mezzotinter John Faber Jr (Fig. 5), and later by James

McArdell, Richard Houston and Richard Purcell. Mercier's financial interest in these pictures was geared to the print market as much as the paintings themselves, and he was no doubt encouraged by the recent success of Hogarth in marketing prints after his own 'Progresses', which he ensured by the passage of the Engravers' Copyright Act of 1735. The prints, which sold for two shillings and sixpence, were also available via subscription in London, and in York, where Mercier was living at the time (Ingamells and Raines, op. cit., p. 5). The close working partnership between artist and engraver, pursued so effectively by Mercier, had by the mid-eighteenth century become the norm. Portraits as well as custom-made fancy pictures were also adapted to suit the demands of this new market, especially those of young women and children. Thus, for example, Reynolds's portrait of Kitty Fisher (Iveagh Bequest, Kenwood) was engraved by Edward Fisher as *Cleopatra* (Fig. 6), eliding the persona of the most notorious prostitute of her age with the libidinous Egyptian queen. Similarly, endless portraits of small children reappeared in print form as emblems of 'Innocence', 'Simplicity', 'Sprightliness', and the 'Age of Bliss'.

Increasingly printmakers also made fancy pictures from their own designs and even from the work of enthusiastic amateurs (see cats. 29 and 46). John Dean, who engraved a number of Reynolds's fancy pictures, made one of a small girl holding a cat by a well. This print , although of limited artistic merit, is memorable as much as anything else for its title or titles. Presumably in an attempt to maximise the potential for pathos Dean entitled an early proof *Fatal Friendship* (Fig. 7). He later had a change of heart and opted instead for '*Puss in Danger*' – allowing the cat an escape clause. Marketing, as much as making the image, was a key component in the success, or otherwise, of the fancy picture. It is for this reason that the fancy picture must be viewed within the context of the vagaries of the British print market, and one reason also why prints as well as paintings feature so much in the present exhibition.

Already widely available in print form, the fancy picture also became a favoured art form at the annual exhibitions of the Society of Artists during the 1760s, notably through the efforts of Henry Morland who began to exhibit his popular nocturnes of young women by candlelight (Fig. 8). The popularity of the fancy picture also made an impression upon those artists who aspired to loftier genres such as history and portraiture, but who also wished to cash in on the vogue. In 1767, for example, in excusing Reynolds's unwillingness to exhibit at the Society of Artists, Edmund Burke wrote that his friend 'having no piece of fancy sends in nothing this time' (Postle, 1995, p. 8). Reynolds's fancy pictures were quite unlike those of Mercier and Morland, being largely clever and amusing 'companions' to Old Master paintings, designed to appeal to his own intellectual circle, and allied to his own mode of portraiture, as in, for example, his *Careful Shepherdess* of 1775, so reminiscent of *Miss Bowles* (Wallace Collection) of the same period. In 1774 Reynolds's *Montgomery Sisters, Three Ladies adorning a Term of Hymen*, was said to possess 'an elegant design and fancy', a compliment that emphasised the imaginative qualities of the design which lifted it above 'mere' portraiture towards the level of subject painting.

Gainsborough's interest in the fancy picture, on the other hand, evolved out of his landscapes, and the subject-matter was closely allied to the lives and activities of ordinary rural characters, exemplified by his superlative *Girl with Pigs* (Fig. 10), a picture so admired by Reynolds that he at once purchased it. In his fourteenth *Discourse* to the Royal Academy of 1788, Reynolds explained what he found so attractive in these works: 'In his fancy-pictures, when he had fixed on his subject of imitation, whether it was the mean and vulgar form of a wood cutter, or a child of an interesting character, as he did not attempt to raise the one, so neither did he lose any of the natural grace of the other; such a grace, and such an elegance, as are more frequently found in cottages than in courts' (Wark, 1975, p. 254).

Increasingly in the eighteenth century, for many artists, and not just Gainsborough, the fancy picture focused upon the 'mean and vulgar'. For younger artists, those reaching maturity during the 1780s, the fancy picture became the most popular vehicle for advertising their burgeoning skills. Works also became larger in scale and more ambitious, as one can see through the work of Hugh Robinson, Richard Morton Paye and John Opie – whose reputation as the 'Cornish Wonder' was founded upon a series of accomplished character studies of old beggar men, women and children. The ways in which the presentation of such individuals was accommodated within a genre originally designed to amuse and entertain is significant in the evolution of the fancy picture.

In terms of subject-matter, children were the most popular and widespread subjects in fancy pictures: the ragged beggar child; the innocent child at play; and even the child transformed into a infant saint or deity. But the fancy picture had always extended much farther than children, to a whole range of 'colourful' characters whose lives and labours were not conditioned by the mores of polite society. Exactly how one can identify these people in terms of a social class or grouping is by no means straightforward, not least because the word 'society' was as meaningless in the eighteenth century as the term 'fancy picture' is to most people today. Yet attempts were made in the visual sphere to categorize people according to rank and occupation. In 1793, for example, Henry Bromley published an extensive *Catalogue of British Engraved Portraits* from 'Egbert the Great to the Present Time'. The modern period comprised ten sections or classes, beginning with royalty, aristocracy , artists, 'the female sex', gentry and clergy, for example, and concluding with 'Class X. Phaenomena, Convicts, and Persons otherwise remarkable'. This category included subjects such as Nathaniel Hone's

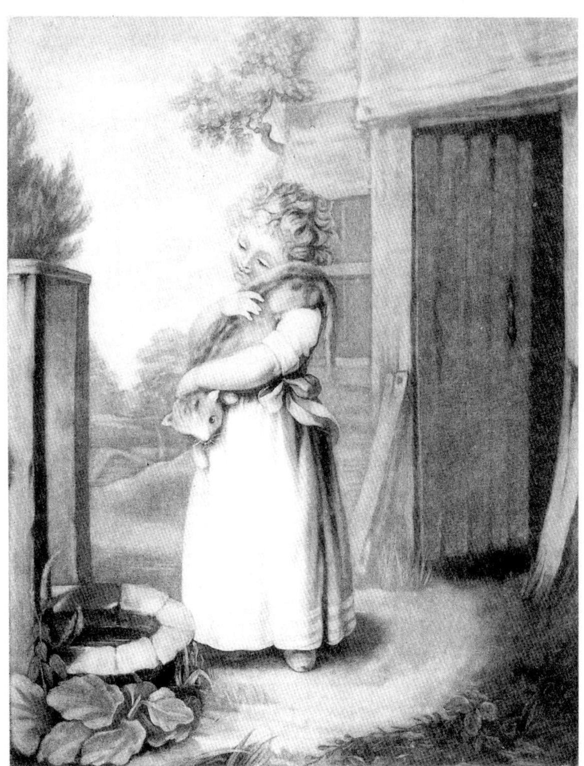

7 *Puss in Danger* by John Dean (1750-98). Mezzotint engraving. The Trustees of the British Museum

Brickdust Man and Nathaniel Dance's *Beggar Man* (cats. 58 and 92), both of whom were no doubt well-known characters in their own right, rather than anonymous 'types'. Alongside a host of other 'celebrity' beggars, fruit vendors, pedlars, ballad singers and rat-catchers, were various outlaws, rapists, murderers, arsonists and 'idiots', as well as those poor creatures whose physical deformities classed them in the eyes of the consumer as outsiders: the very stuff of their nightmares.

When adults were the focus of attention, the fancy picture clearly embraced identifiable individuals acting out familiar household tasks. Models were used in imaginative roles appropriate to their form and features. So, for example, Reynolds would recast his street-wise urchins as fortune tellers, imps, and shepherds while his famous old model George White (a street pavior-cum-beggar) took on successively the role of an Italian count, a bandit, a renaissance pope, and sanctified sages (Fig. 11). At the time, Reynolds's fancy pictures were feted by fashionable society and fetched higher prices than his portraits of comparable size. After his death they were criticized by those outside the charmed circle of Reynolds's friends and admirers. William Hazlitt, for instance, observed that the care-worn features of George White, far from reflecting the aura of a saint or a medieval Italian count, were all too clearly those of 'a common mendicant at the corner of a street, waiting patiently for some charitable donation' – which is exactly what he was before he took up a modelling career with Reynolds (see Allen, 1995, p. 135).

While the fancy picture traded in both fact and fable, in imps and urchins, beggars and saints, only rarely were 'factual' figures portrayed as they must have appeared in life. Gainsborough's urchins were recast in the rose-tinted light of Spanish seventeenth-century art (Fig. 12), while Mercier's oyster sellers and Morland's laundry maids were

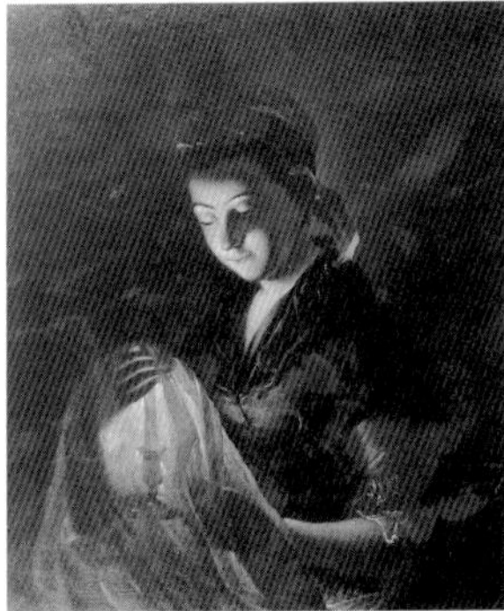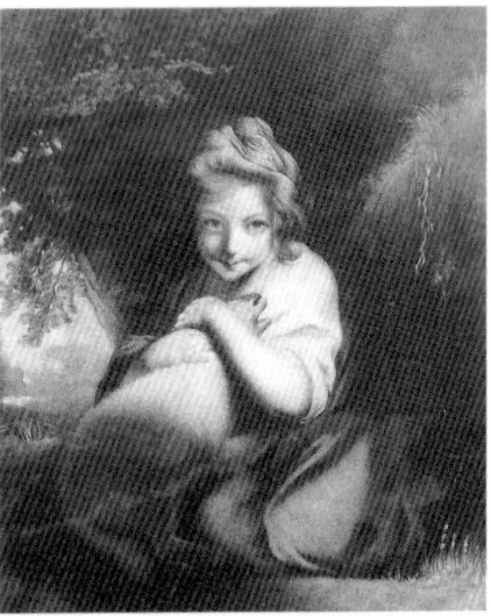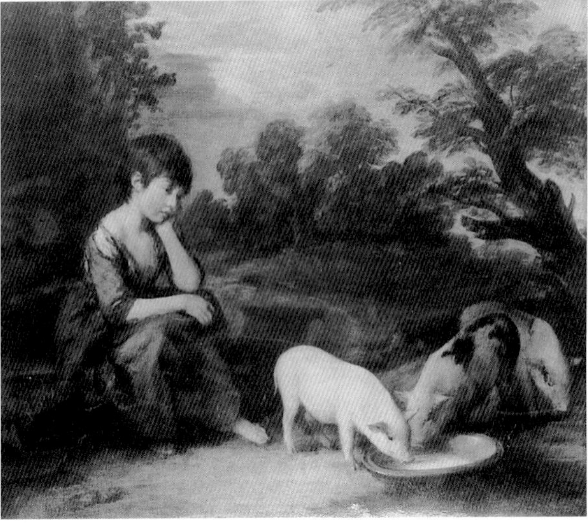

8 *A Servant Girl with a Candle* by Philip Mercier (?1689-1760). Oil on canvas, 74.2 x 61.5 cm. Private Collection

9 *The Careful Shepherdess* by Elizabeth Judkins, after Sir Joshua Reynolds (1723-92). Mezzotint engraving. The Trustees of the British Museum

10 *Girl with Pigs* by Thomas Gainsborough (1727-88). Oil on canvas, 129.5 x 152.4 cm. The Hon. Simon Howard, Castle Howard

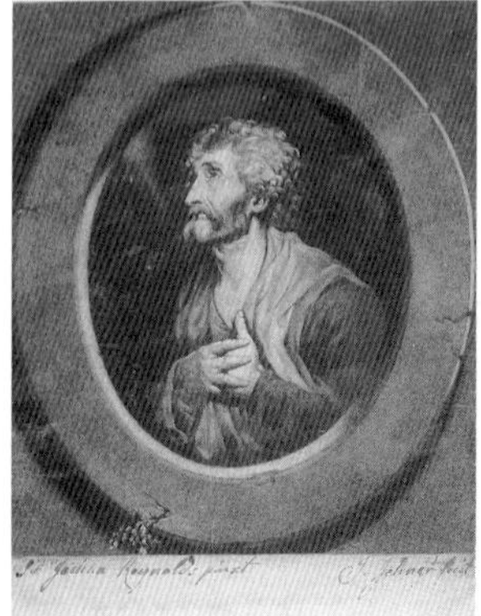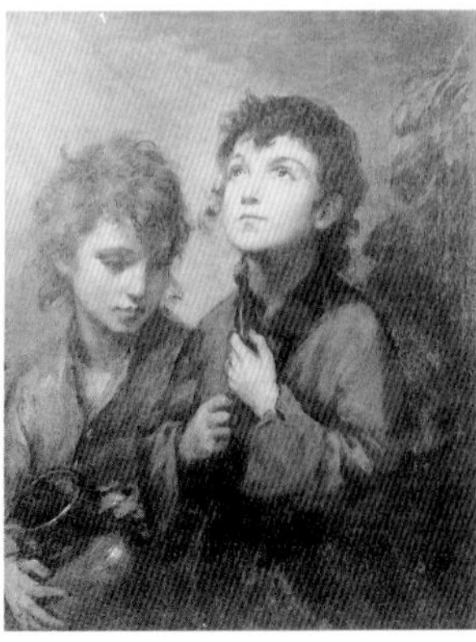

11 *Dionysius Areopagites* by John Jehner, after Sir Joshua Reynolds (1723-92). Mezzotint engraving. David Alexander

12 *Beggar Boys* by Thomas Gainsborough (1727-88). Oil on canvas, 73.6 x 63.5 cm. Private Collection

connotation, and they are quite literally works of fancy' (Waterhouse, 1953, p. 132). This is true up to a point. The artists who made them were not concerned about making statements about the condition of working people, or the roles of children or the aged in society. And for the most part the people who purchased these paintings and prints did so primarily because they were pleasing and undemanding to look at. They were just one manifestation of the emergence of a sense-driven culture, individuals who were collectively enticed, as John Brewer has recently revealed, by the 'pleasures of the imagination' (see Brewer, 1997, passim.) Yet, that does not mean that fancy pictures are trivial or devoid of meaning: like much of the so-called ephemera which reflect popular taste they often tell us more about the manners and mores of a society than the high-flown histories and allegories advocated by the arbiters of high taste.

conceived as figures of male fantasy and objects of covert desire, a point which emerges more clearly in France where such images were termed 'figures de fantaisie'. Even Zoffany's painstaking depiction of *Beggars on the Road to Stanmore* (see cat. 89) was carefully stage-managed, not simply to expose the realities of indigence but to exalt the generosity and beneficence of the Drummond family of bankers on whose land the beggars now (fictionally) trod. The Drummonds commissioned the picture to hang on the wall of their country house, alongside portraits of themselves. Fancy pictures were made to please – even when they depicted subjects who were clearly in distress. In order to succeed they had, above all else, to submit to the strictures of a consumer society. Where morality reared its head, it was the morality of the market-place, where hard cash was a reward for industry and its distribution was as much a panacea for the donor as relief for the recipient of charity.

In commercial terms, the fancy picture's success was grounded firmly upon the emergence in eighteenth-century Britain of a bourgeois culture of consumption. It was an art form which was led and controlled by market forces. According to Sir Ellis Waterhouse, who made a particular study of Gainsborough's fancy pictures, 'The subjects are intended only to please and have no moral or satirical

The material in the exhibition has been set out in four interrelated sections. The first section explores the historical links between the eighteenth-century fancy picture and the old master tradition. It includes engravings by British print-makers after Old Master paintings, a copy of a Murillo by Gainsborough and a very curious 'collaboration' by Reynolds with an unknown seventeenth-century master. Children, the most popular subject-matter for the fancy picture, are the subject of the second section. The third section, entitled 'Love Songs and Matches', after the title of a pastel painting by John Russell, examines the role of the fancy picture within the world of commerce and the ambiguities which emerge in the various depictions of characters who are themselves transformed through the pictorial image into marketable, desirable, objects. Poverty and its corollary, charity, form the final section of the exhibition, with images dating mainly from the last quarter of the century, a period in which there was not only an increased awareness of the plight of the poor but a self-absorbed sense of collective guilt and repressed anxiety over their very existence.

I

The Old Master Tradition

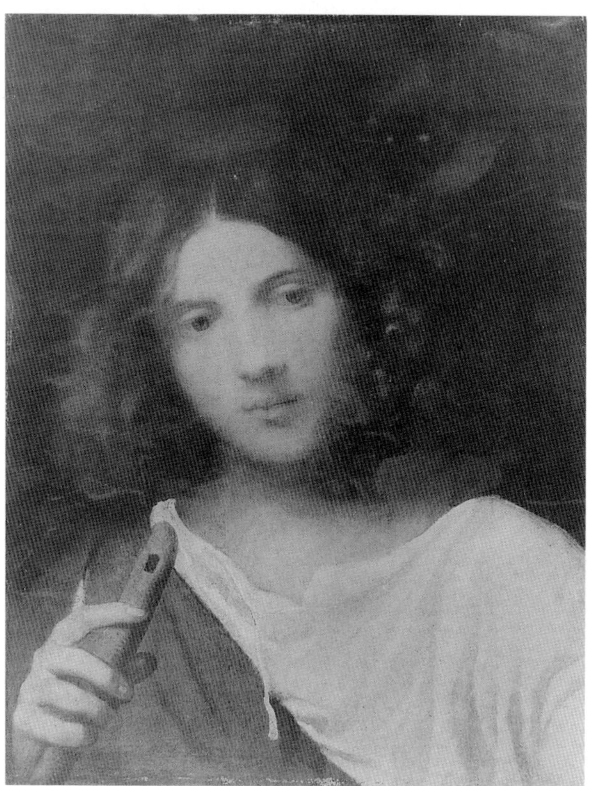

The fancy picture was a nebulous, multifaceted and ambiguous genre, inhabiting a hinterland between real and ideal, fact and fantasy, high art and common life. Pictorially, it is possible to trace its roots right back to the art of the Italian Renaissance, to the piping shepherds of Giorgione and Titian (see Fig. 13), dreamy courtesans, courting couples by Paris Bordone, or any number of 'character' studies which lie outside the customary art-historical categories and hierarchies of subject-matter. Yet the starting point – if there is one – is to be found not perhaps in the art of sixteenth-century Venice but that of early seventeenth-century Rome and Naples, in the revolution fomented by Caravaggio and those followers of his who spread the radical message of his art across Italy, Spain, and northern Europe.

What separated Caravaggio from previous artists who had made character studies of shepherds and courtesans was the decision to take his inspiration not from the rarefied realm of the court but the city streets. Into secular and sacred art he injected a new sense of realism (Fig. 14). Saints and apostles were drawn without concession to current protocol, their features misshapen, their clothes ragged, their feet caked in dust, their gestures often awkward, their settings stark. Street urchins were invested with the aura of angels, and angels and saints were invested with the spirit of everyday life. Caravaggio's art laid bare a fundamental ambiguity in art, namely its very artifice, the tension between the real world and the imaginary one inhabited by the artist's imagination. Though without a single pupil, his impact on Western art was immense, inspiring legions of 'Caravaggisti', including Luca Giordano, Artemesia Gentileschi and Jusepe De Ribera. It was, however, the Northern followers of Caravaggio, such as Hendrick ter Brugghen (Fig. 15) and Dirck van Baburen who, with their lusty portrayals of musicians, revellers and procuresses, most fully exploited the secular aspect of the Caravaggio's legacy. Even in Italy it was a Danish-born artist, Bernhard Keil ('Monsu Bernardo'), who most enthusiastically devoted his attention to the single figures of street urchins and old beggars in the same manner as others treated characters from the Bible and mythology.

In the history of Western art Caravaggio is a colossus. But in eighteenth-century Britain he remained a remote figure. Sir Joshua Reynolds, the country's leading artist and art theorist, does not mention him once in any of his *Discourses on Art*. Nor did he pay him more than a cursory glance during his three-year Italian sojourn from 1749 to 1752. We

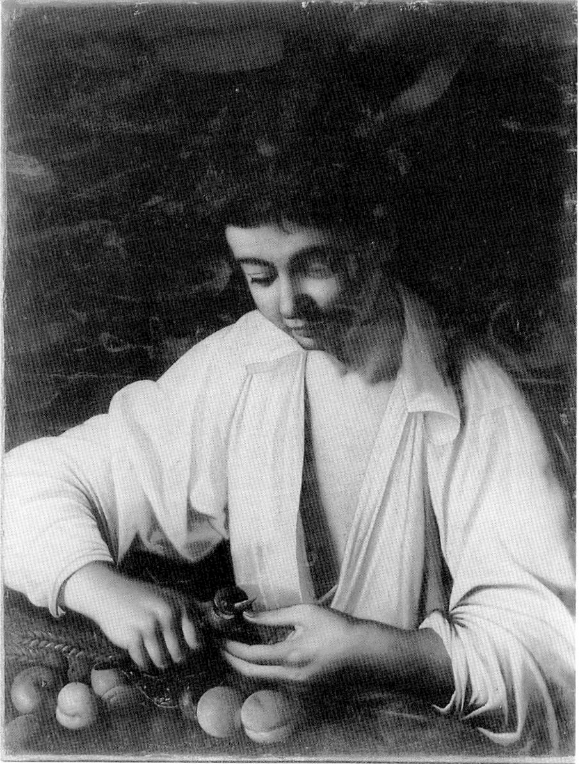

13 *Shepherd with a Pipe* attributed to Titian (*c* 1488-1576). Oil on canvas, 61 x 51 cm. Her Majesty The Queen

14 *A Boy Paring Fruit* by Caravaggio (1573-1609/10). Oil on canvas, 64 x 51.5 cm. Private Collection

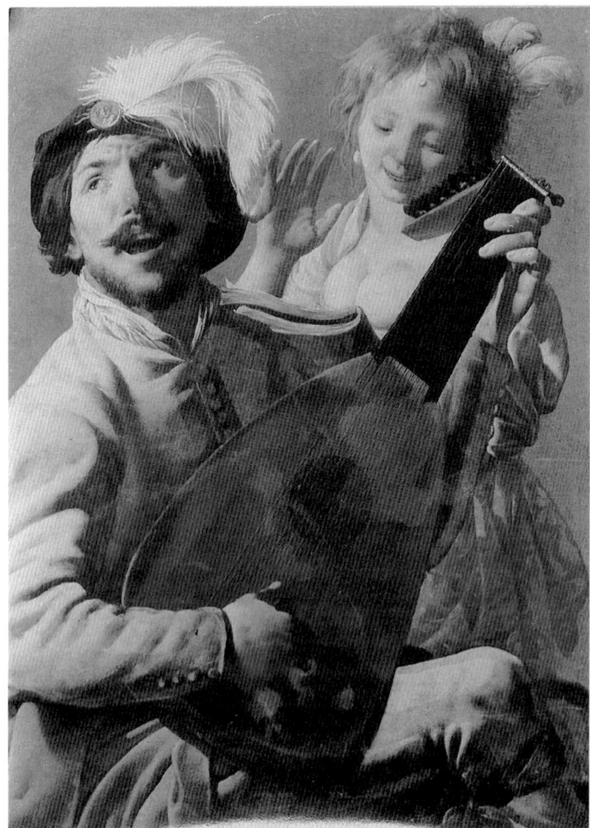

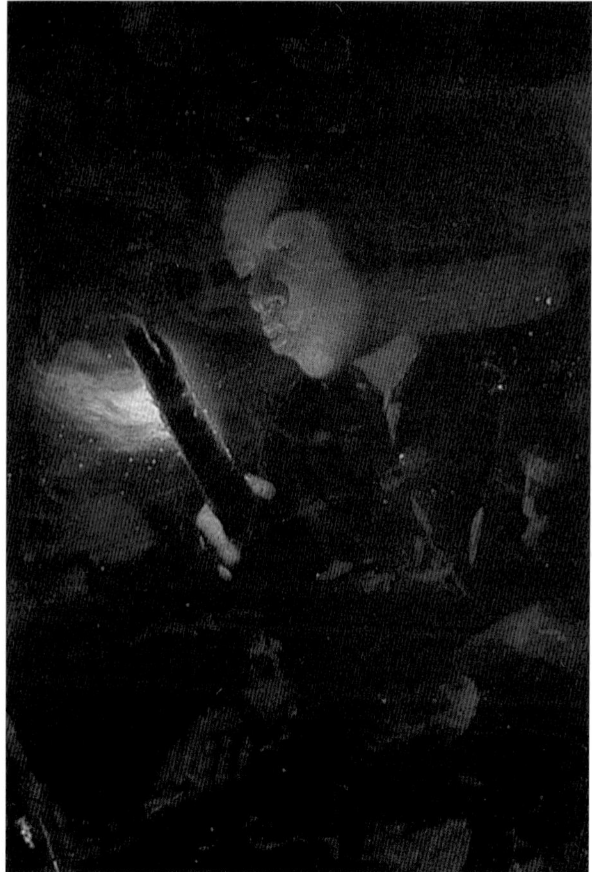

18 *A Boy Blowing on a Firebrand* by Godfried Schalcken (1643-1706). Oil on canvas. National Gallery of Scotland, Edinburgh.

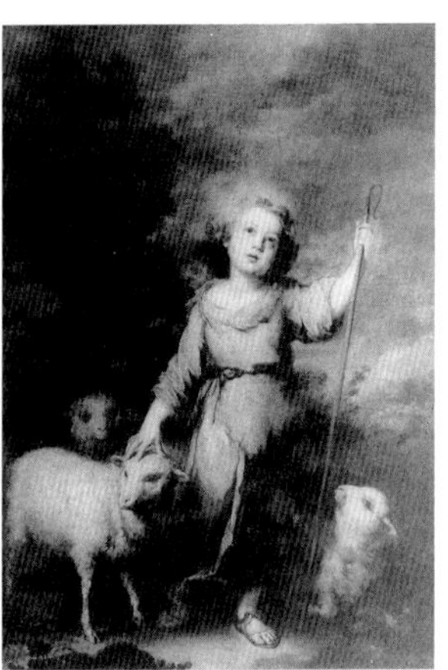

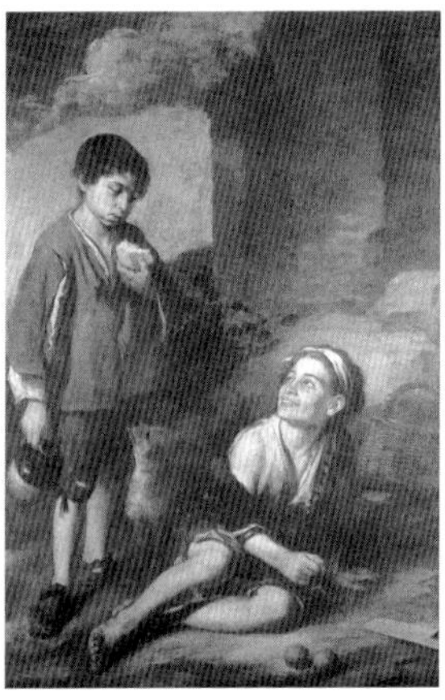

15 *Lute Player and Singer* by Hendrick ter Brugghen (1588-1629). Oil on canvas. Musée du Louvre, Paris

16 *The Good Shepherd* by Alexis Grimou, after Bartolomé Murillo (1617-82). Oil on canvas, 162.5 x 114.3 cm. Private Collection

17 *Invitation to the Game of Pelota* by Bartolomé Murillo (1617-82). Oil on canvas, 165 x 110.5 cm. Dulwich College Picture Gallery

cannot here speculate as to why so little heed was taken of Caravaggio (which is all the odder since this was self-consciously the age of the Grand Tour, when more artists and aesthetes than ever before travelled to Italy). Suffice it to say that Caravaggio's art, which was anti-academic, lay beyond the parameters of officially endorsed taste. Even so, although he was completely unaware of the fact, Reynolds owned a version, or perhaps even the original, of one of Caravaggio's earliest 'fancy' pictures, *Boy Paring Fruit* (see Fig. 14). This painting was then believed to be by the Spanish seventeenth-century painter Murillo, who,

according to the sales catalogue of Reynolds's posthumous studio sale, 'was not only elegant in his historical compositions, but imitated rustic characters with minute attention to Nature' (Broun, 1987, vol. 2, p. 334).

Although Murillo's reputation declined steadily during the the nineteenth century, he was one of the most popular and sought-after artists with eighteenth-century collectors. The mainstay of Murillo's art was the large altarpieces painted for the churches and chapels of Seville. Later in his career he began to paint small-scale devotional pictures of the infant St John the Baptist and 'Christ as the Good Shepherd' (see cats. 7 and 12). At this time (during the 1660s and '70s) he also made a series of pictures of street urchins – occasionally even combining the two genres as in his *St Thomas of Villanueva as a Child Dividing his Clothes among the Beggar Boys* (Cincinnati Art Museum). In the late seventeenth century, Seville, despite the decline of the Spanish economy, remained a thriving port. It was also a city of stark contrasts: at once the resort of wealthy traders and merchants and what J.H. Elliott has described as 'a vast, poverty-stricken sub-world of unemployed and under-employed – vagabonds, rogues, street urchins, casual labourers, dock-workers, pedlars, water sellers, all of them anxiously wondering how and where to get a square meal' (in Murillo, 1982, p. 45). In Seville, Murillo's angelic boyhood saints decorated chapels sponsored by wealthy Catholic patrons. Pictures like these and more especially their secular equivalents also appealed to visiting merchants who took them to Antwerp, Rotterdam and London.

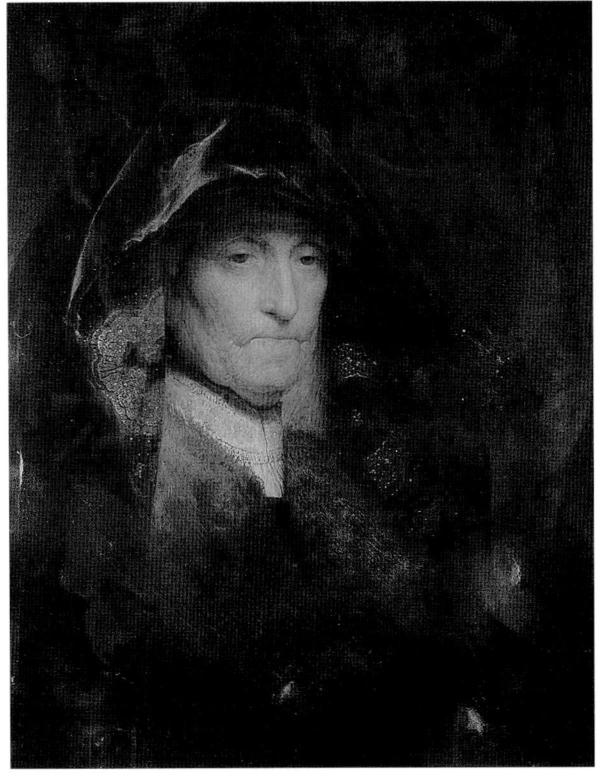 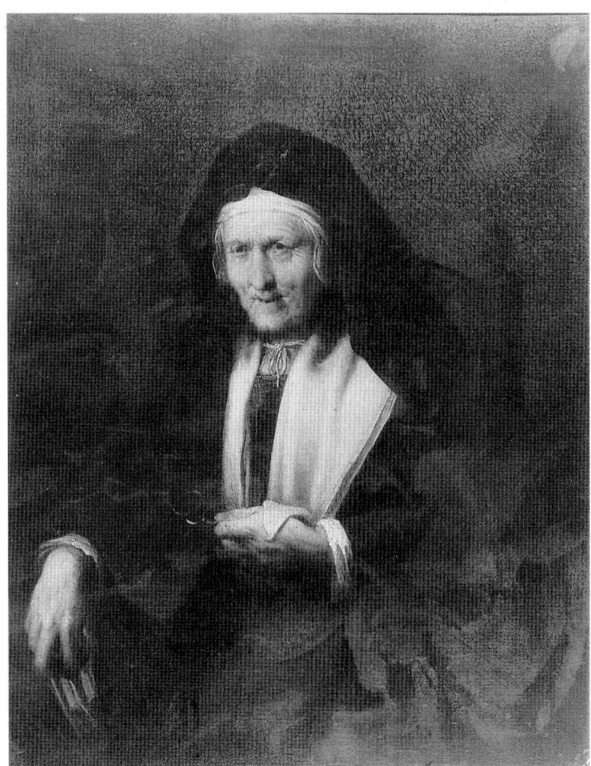

19 *The Artist's Mother* by Rembrandt van Rijn (1603-69). Oil on panel, 61.3 x 47.3 cm. Her Majesty The Queen

20 *An Old Woman* by Thomas Worlidge (1700-66). Oil on canvas, 97.7 x 88.8 cm. Private Collection

Murillo's popularity beyond his native Spain was fanned by the winds of trade, and by the fact that his art was eminently adapted to suit a secular market, for even the devotional paintings had a strong vein of realism artfully combined with a tug on the heart strings, key ingredients in the burgeoning secular cult of sensibility. Long before Gainsborough made his copy of Grimou's version of Murillo's *Good Shepherd* (Fig. 5) in the late 1770s (cat. 7), a taste for his art had been established in England, as is demonstrated by Pieter van Bleeck's engraving of two children with a rabbit (cat. 11). Notable among those works which had been in English private collections since at least the mid-eighteenth century were an *Infant St John* (now in the collection of the Duke of Buccleuch) and what was then Sir Sampson Gideon's *Flight into Egypt* (The Institute of Arts, Detroit), a picture which Gainsborough must surely have known quite well, owing to his friendship with Gideon (later Lord Eardley). He certainly had looked closely at the pair of paintings bought by the dealer Noel Desenfans, *Invitation to the Game of Pelota* (Fig. 17) and the *Three Boys* (Dulwich Picture Gallery), a figure in the former serving as a model for Gainsborough's celebrated *Shepherd Boy* (see cat. 6) .

The taste for Murillo in eighteenth-century England was an example of the way in which an individual artist could achieve cult status within a culture which was fundamentally different from his own. By way of contrast, the manner in which the art of the Low Countries infiltrated British aesthetic life, and in turn impacted upon the development of the fancy picture, stemmed from common cultural and economic ties shared by the two nations. Simon Schama has revealed close links between the Dutch culture of consumption and arts of the country (see Schama, 1991, passim). Although Schama focuses solely upon the Dutch Republic, traits and attitudes which emerge in the Low Countries must, he concedes, be apparent elsewhere. In the case of Britain, those 'traits and attitudes' were quite deliberately imported in the later seventeenth century, more especially in the period following the Glorious Revolution and the establishment of a constitutional monarchy – and a Dutch King, William III.

Prior to the 1690s, continental cultural influence had been dominated by Flemish- and German-born painters, notably Van Dyck, Lely, and Kneller. Among those Dutch artists to have an immediate impact upon British art towards the end of the century was Godfried Schalcken, who in 1692 travelled to London. In addition to several portraits of William III, Schalcken also painted *A Boy Blowing on a Firebrand* (Fig. 18), later engraved by Richard Purcell (cat. 21). Although Schalcken remained in London only until 1698, and died in 1706, his art was to have a lasting impact on British painters, notably on Joseph Wright and Henry Morland, who both experimented with his technique for painting nocturnes from the 1760s onwards. Both Wright and William Tate (who made a painting of girls blowing on a firebrand, see cat. 22) were surely influenced by Schalcken's painting illustrated here.

Another artist to have a significant impact upon the fancy picture was Frans Hals (and this was long before he gained celebrity as the creator of *The Laughing Cavalier*). Hals – or 'Frank Halls' as he was then known – commanded considerable respect, which earned him qualified praise in Reynolds's *Discourses* (see Wark, 1975, p. 109). His work was collected and engraved, even though (see cat. 2) it was at times confused with that of other painters. Significantly, Lely's *Boy Playing a Jew's Harp* (cat. 1), the earliest picture

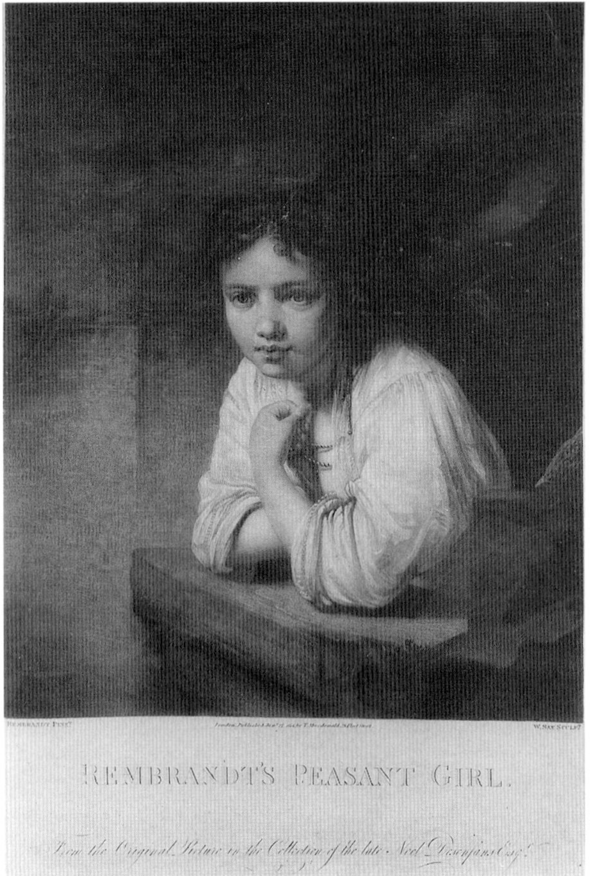

21 *Rembrandt's Peasant Girl* by W. Say, after Rembrandt (1603-69). Mezzotint engraving. Private Collection

Matthew Peters, John Opie, and Thomas Worlidge (Fig. 20), among others. Yet of all those artists who emulated Rembrandt through their fancy pictures, the most thoughtful and cultured disciple was Joshua Reynolds. As early as 1747, in his *Boy Reading* (private collection) Reynolds had paid tribute to Rembrandt. Again in the 1770s he used Rembrandt as the basis of fancy pictures, including *The School Boy* (see cat. 44) and the so-called *Laughing Girl* (cat. 33), which may have been originally conceived as a playful pendant to Rembrandt's celebrated *Girl at a Window* (Fig. 21, see Dulwich, 1993, passim; Postle, 1995, pp. 104 ff.). Reynolds was, however, deliberately eclectic and, although Rembrandt was an important influence, he was happy, as in his *Calling of Samuel* (cat. 14), to combine Rembrandtesque chiaroscuro with a vein of sentiment quarried from Murillo.

Both Gainsborough and Reynolds couched their fancy pictures in the language of the Old Masters, although the manner in which they did so was quite different. As in his portraiture, Gainsborough responded instinctively to artists whom he admired: Watteau, Van Dyck, Rubens, and Murillo. He had a deep distrust of allegory, and avowed that he 'never could have patience to read Poetical impossibilities' (Woodall, 1961, p. 53). He seldom took the fancy picture into the realm of high art, except in the most oblique manner – as in the *Cottage Girl with a Dog and Pitcher* (cat. 25) or his *Shepherd Boy* (see cat. 6), where the debt to Murillo is undisguised. Reynolds, on the other hand, was always eclectic, and liked to flaunt his familiarity with a whole range of historical schools and styles.

Later in their careers, Reynolds and Gainsborough each renewed his interest in the art of Flanders and Holland. Reynolds made trips to Flanders in 1781 and again in 1785. His remarks at the time make it clear that, while he admired the technical skill of Dutch painters such as Gerrit Dou, their ability was confined primarily to 'the mechanical parts of the art' (Malone, 1819, vol. 2, p. 371). His preference was for the broader sweep and beguiling colour of Rubens, whose influence can be seen in Reynolds's fancy pictures of the 1780s, notably his *Infant Academy* and *Nymph and Cupid* (see cat. 19). Gainsborough too became increasingly entranced by Rubens during the same period, and he was prompted to make at least one journey to Flanders in 1783. It was his love of Flemish art that inspired his most ambitious fancy pictures, *Two Shepherd Boys with Dogs Fighting* (cat. 8) and *The Woodman* (see cat. 86), works which in their heroic scale and dazzling bravura allowed the genre for the first time to compete with High Art.

In the summer of 1788, when Gainsborough lay dying, he invited Reynolds to his home to look over his paintings, and specifically asked him to view *The Woodman*, which had not yet been seen in public. This final meeting no doubt spurred Reynolds to devote his next *Discourse* to Gainsborough's memory. Here Reynolds praised the portraits and landscapes, but particularly the fancy pictures of Gainsborough – the 'interesting simplicity and elegance of his little ordinary beggar-children' – and allowed them a greater place in the history of art than the combined efforts of the rank-and-file contemporary continental history painters. 'If ever,' Reynolds continued, 'this nation should produce genius sufficient to acquire to us the honourable distinction of an English School, the name of Gainsborough will be transmitted to posterity' (Wark, 1975, p. 248).

in this exhibition, and one which acts as a visible link between Flemish seventeenth-century art and that of the British eighteenth century, was considered to be by Hals until the present century.

Finally, it was not just the example of individual painters that influenced British eighteenth-century artists, but the whole range of symbols and emblems employed in domestic Dutch seventeenth-century art. And while the various meaning and interpretation of such symbols must in both cultures be treated with caution, Jacob Cats's emblem book, for example, not only informed the work of seventeenth-century Dutch artists but also played an integral part in shaping Joshua Reynolds's early visual vocabulary (he book was in his father's well-stocked library).

While many individual artists were influential on the evolution of the fancy picture, the most important role-model for many British artists and engravers was Rembrandt. An appreciation of Rembrandt's art was already well established by the early eighteenth century. It was reflected in the widespread vogue for collecting his pictures and etchings and in the emulation of his style and technique (see White *et al.*, 1983, passim). Admiration for Rembrandt was not unqualified: praise was reserved for his portraits and character studies, notably the *Old Woman Plucking a Fowl* (cat. 23) and the *Old Woman: the Artist's Mother*, versions of which belonged to the King (Fig. 19) and the Earl of Pembroke (Wilton House). This latter picture in particular acted as a talisman for British artists, serving as a prototype for portrayals of old women by

II

Innocence and Experience

It is generally agreed by historians that the eighteenth century witnessed some sort of watershed in the evolution of attitudes towards childhood, which was regarded increasingly as a distinct phase of life in its own right rather than a period of preparation for adulthood. A key to this change, argues Hugh Cunningham, was the 'secularization' of childhood, within the context of a decline in the power of the Christian Church to legislate morality. 'With that decline,' he states, 'children were transformed from being corrupt and innately evil to being angels, messengers from god to a tired adult world' (Cunningham, 1995, p. 62). These remarks occur in the course of a discussion of a 'middle-class ideology of childhood'. If this 'transformation' did indeed take place – and there are those who would question such an argument – what bearing did it have on the fancy picture, which was concerned not just with children who were a product of this middle-class ideology but those who belonged to the so-called 'lower orders' of society?

In pictorial terms the fancy picture owed a great deal to a culture of childhood nourished in the seventeenth-century Dutch republic. It was here, according to Simon Schama, that the visualization of the child was couched in the language of everyday life – the 'putto' supplanted by 'the little perisher' (Schama, 1995, p. 484). Dutch society was unusually sensitive to the value of play, both for its sheer enjoyment value, and the way in which it taught lessons for future life: what he refers to as the 'tutorial and the satirical voices' (ibid., p. 504). These values were reflected in art, although, as Schama notes, nothing is to be gained in attempting to decide which 'voice' emerges in any one image, ambiguity being, as it were, the name of the game. The same can be said of the fancy picture, grounded as it was on the shifting sands of commerce and consumption.

It was in the Low Countries too that a type of child, familiar later within the iconography of the fancy picture, emerges, the 'leering ragamuffins' of Judith Leyster and Adrian Van der Werff (Fig. 22). 'To the truly fearful,' states Schama, 'they seem to be literally little demons. Their opposites, then, must be what adults dream of: little angels' (op. cit., p. 546). This was precisely the kind of fantasy that underpins a picture such as Joseph Wright's deeply unsettling yet compelling picture, *Dressing the Kitten* (cat. 27), where dear little angels, left alone with their pet by adoring parents, rapidly revert to sadistic demons. Wright's picture, although it features two children from a distinctly bourgeois background, belongs to the world of the fancy picture. As Marcia Pointon has observed, the distinction between portraits of children (and women too) and those who modelled for fancy pictures was far less cut and dried than images of their male adult counterparts. Children, regardless of their station in life were, like their pets, little creatures (see Pointon, 1993, pp. 177ff.). Children, whether they appear in fancy pictures or portraits, are passive objects, and how they appear is invariably 'the result of negotiated

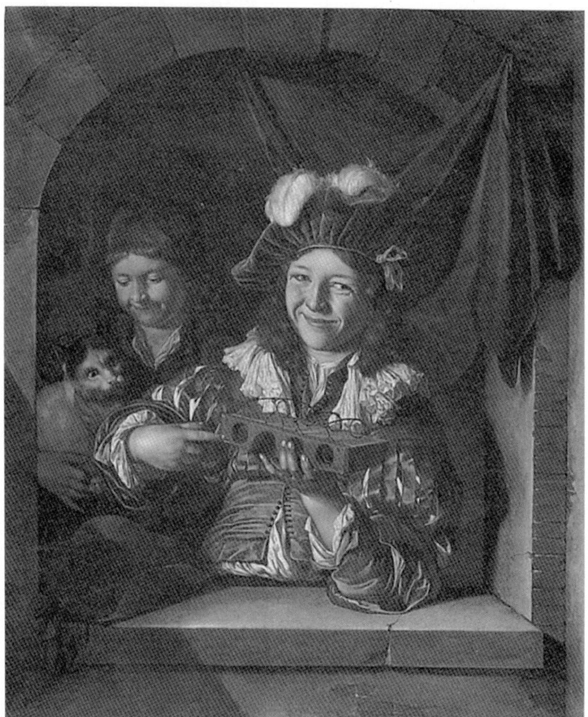

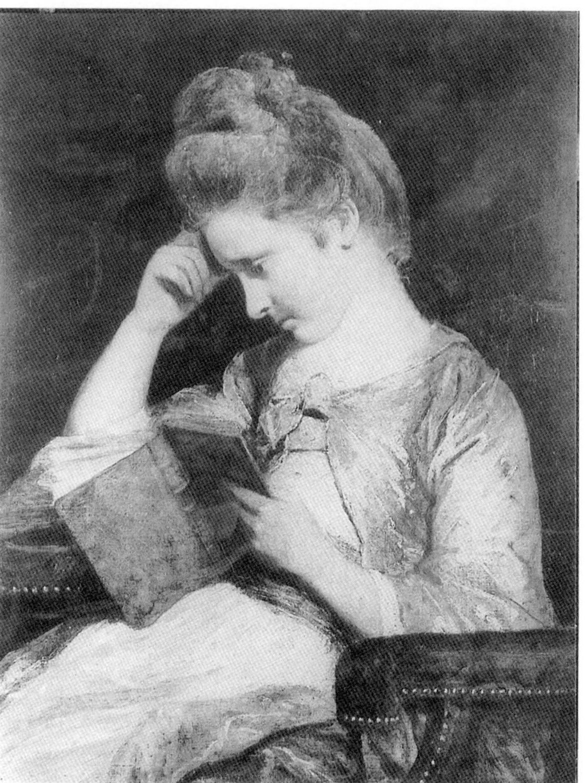

22 *Boy with a Mousetrap* by Adriaen van der Werff (1659-22). Oil on panel, 38.1 x 32 cm. Private Collection

23 *A Girl Reading* by Sir Joshua Reynolds (1723-92). Oil on canvas. Lady Hillingdon

relationships in the adult world designed, consciously and unconsciously, to produce a set of explicit and implicit meanings' (Pointon, 1993, p. 178).

One area where the elision of portraiture and the fancy picture becomes particularly evident is where artists paint their own offspring, or young relatives, as one can readily see in the various depictions by Gainsborough of his young daughters, or Reynolds's portrayals of his various nieces.

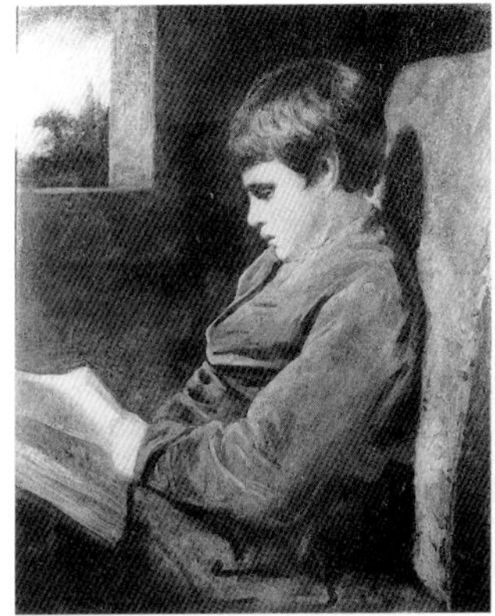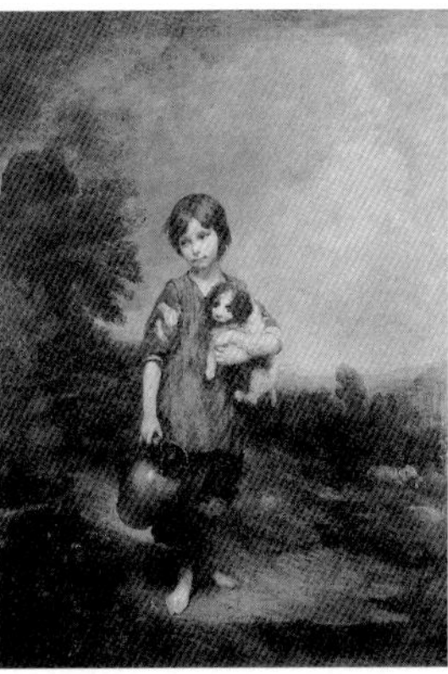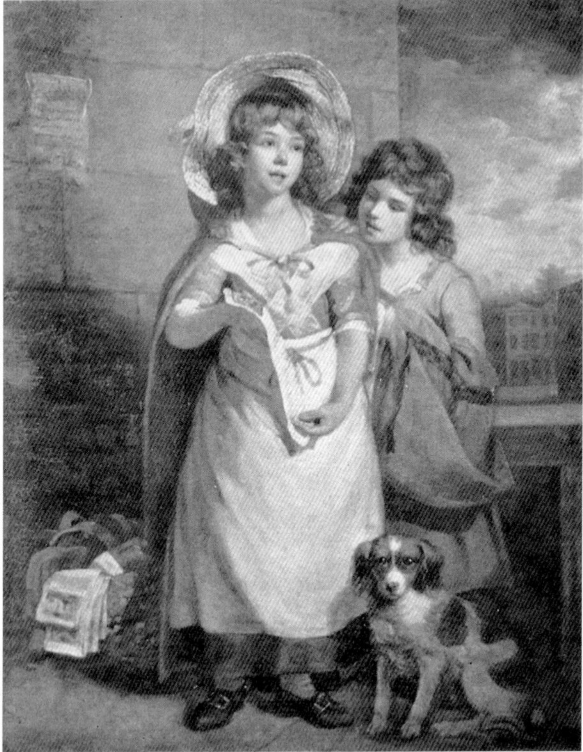

24 *A Boy Reading* by Sir Joshua Reynolds (1732-92). Oil on canvas. Private Collection

25 *Girl with a Dog and Pitcher* by Thomas Gainsborough (1727-88). Oil on canvas, 174 x 124.4 cm. The National Gallery of Ireland

26 *The Ballad Singers* by John Rising (1753-1817). Oil on canvas, 139.7 x 110.5 cm. Private Collection

During the late 1760s and early seventies Reynolds painted several pictures based upon his niece Theophila ('Offie') Palmer. Reynolds teased her, 'Don't be vain my dear, I only use your head as I would that of any beggar – as a good practice' (Postle, 1995, p. 58). Among the works for which Offie sat to Reynolds was *A Girl Reading* (Fig. 23), exhibited at the Royal Academy in 1771. Apparently the title offended her. 'I think,' she said, 'they might have put *A Young Lady*' (loc. cit.). As she knew, the title suggested that this was not a polite 'fancy' portrait but a 'fancy picture', and that she was being viewed primarily as a mere vehicle for the artist's conception of childhood. Yet, unlike Reynolds's *Boy Reading* (Fig. 24) or his *School Boy* (both figures modelled by a child who made cabbage nets for a living, see cat. 44), Offie was quite capable of reading and understanding the book in her arms. Her displeasure therefore was based not merely on being judged a little girl

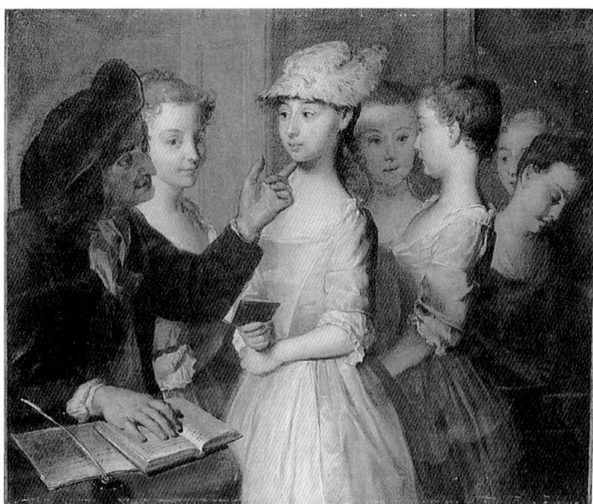

27 *School for Girls* by Philip Mercier (?1689-1760). Oil on canvas, 92 x 109 cm. Private Collection

28 *A Lady Reading by Candle-Light* by Henry Robert Morland (?1719-1797). Oil on canvas, 74.2 x 61.5 cm. Private Collection

rather than a young lady, but a fictive child rather than a real, sentient being. Even so, there were clear instances when the status of children in fancy pictures was less liable to be confused.

Patricia Crown has noted the disparity between the way in which the cosseted offspring of the wealthy were depicted in portraits compared to the children of the poor who acted as hired models, these 'neglected mendicant children, who seem to appear at random, like weeds outside of conservatories and gardens' (Crown, 1984, p. 161). Behind the facade created by the artist, Crown perceives genuine expressions of sorrow and deprivation. The character Gainsborough creates in his *Cottage Girl with Dog and Pitcher* (Fig. 25), she notes, 'is isolated, vulnerable and passive... performing listlessly the dreary task of carrying water'. She also notes how contemporary critics failed to perceive in such children real people, couching their appreciation instead within a 'pattern of picturesque aesthetic interpretation' (ibid.). It is an attitude which Crown sees also in the work of some modern scholars preoccupied only with pictorial roots and source-spotting. It was not until the nineteenth century, she argues, that urchins stopped being 'random aesthetic forms, but began to be depicted as fully human' (ibid., p. 165). Yet, while we have cause to feel sympathy for these children, or to castigate the elitist attitudes of contemporary art critics or patrician art historians, we can also turn to two fundamental issues which help to account for the appearance of these poor children: their position in society beyond the studio, and within current social and sexual hierarchies.

Those children, lured into artists' studios by the promise of a few coins and temporary respite from the elements, were not isolated ragamuffins but part of a large, and continually growing, child population. In cities these poor children formed part of a seething mass, a plague, 'lousing like swarms of locusts', as one contemporary put it, 'in every corner of the streets' (Cunningham, 1991, p. 22). They were vulnerable, but they were also often unemployed and potentially threatening. Certainly, they could not be ignored. Moreover, it was the rise of private philanthropy in the seventeenth and eighteenth centuries that caused street urchins to appear less as a blot on the landscape than

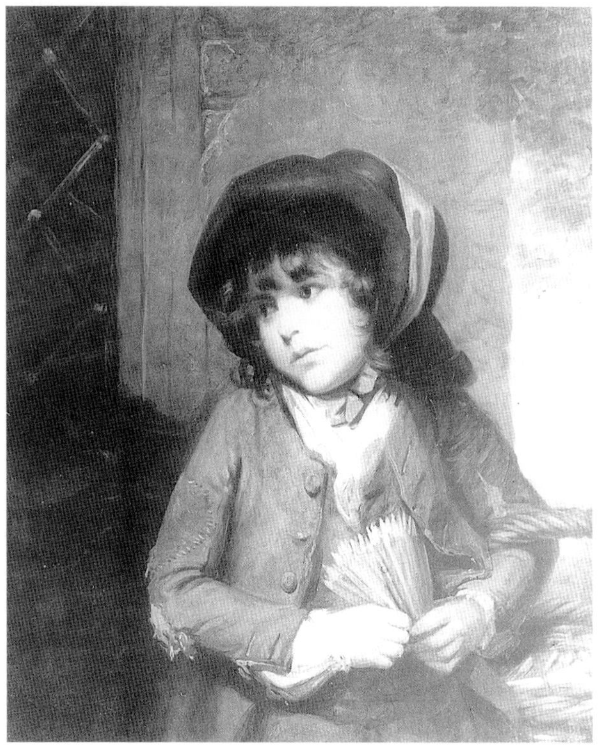
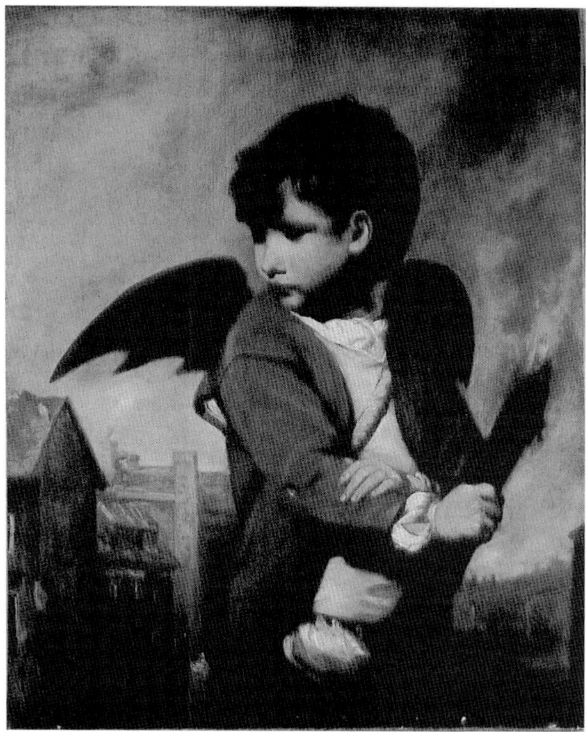

29 *A Match Girl* by Edward Penny (1714-91). Oil on canvas, 72.4 x 58.4 cm. Private Collection

30 *Cupid as a Link Boy* by Sir Joshua Reynolds (1723-92). Oil on canvas, 76 x 63.2 cm. Albright-Knox Art Gallery, Buffalo New York

a collective social problem. In the public imagination they threatened urban disorder, and later in the century, rural disorder. In this light Gainsborough's unusually violent *Two Shepherd Boys with Dogs Fighting* (cat. 8) perhaps presented a more accurate mental picture of the energy which the populace feared may be unleashed upon themselves by an untamed and unaccountable youth.

Yet the fancy picture, in its own fanciful way, was designed to reassure. Its success depended upon its ability to confirm prejudices and reinforce clichés. It represented ragged children in small numbers, in ones and twos, going about useful chores (Fig. 26). And even if they did not always look entirely happy they never present a threat. Yet beneath the veneer of a picture such as that of the cheery little ballad-sellers and their dog represented by John Rising and John Russell (cat. 65) was the eerie nocturnal spectacle, witnessed by William Cowper, of 'children of seven years of age [who] infest the streets every evening with curses and with songs' (Cunningham, 1991, p. 23). If they were to be rescued from such a situation it was not to be through education but labour, through 'Schools of Industry', sweatshops making pins, lace, and matches. Images of little street vendors selling these items may have served as a hopeful reminder of the success of such schemes,even if that was not their aim.

In turning to the issue of sexuality in the child fancy picture, we can look again at Reynolds's painting of *A Girl Reading*. As the lettering on book's spine indicates, the girl is reading a volume of Samuel Richardson's *Clarissa Harlowe* which, although it is now regarded a classic work of fiction, would have been deemed unsuitable for consumption (as would the majority of novels) for young women in less liberal households. According to Peter Pawlowicz, who has looked at Reynolds's *Girl Reading* in the context of attitudes towards female literacy and sexuality, this image of the girl, who exposes herself to the imaginary world of love and deceit contained in the novel's pages, could herself be 'read' by the viewer as a vulnerable object of desire (in Brewer and Bermingham, 1995, p. 47). This may be so. Certainly, it is significant that images of girls or young women reading are associated with sexual licence. We see it in Mercier's *School for Girls* (Fig. 27), where young school girls are easy prey for an old man's lusts, and later in the nocturnes of Joseph Wright and Henry Morland, where young women pursue their own secret, candle-lit fantasies (Fig. 28), or are pursued by young men ready to take advantage of their vulnerability.

While the level of sexuality remains open to debate in a bourgeois image such as *A Girl Reading*, it is less open to question in those works by Reynolds purporting to feature the lower orders. In *A Strawberry Girl* (see cat. 66), a painting for which Offie Palmer also served as the original model, we are presented with a small vulnerable girl in the guise of a strawberry seller, a character readily associated with the market place and with the appetites of the consumer. Nor was this an isolated instance, as we can see by comparing the image with, for example, Edward Penny's *Match Girl* of the same period (Fig. 29). The sense of challenged innocence in these pictures, rendered by the girls' air of wide-eyed apprehension, is enhanced by the very hostile environment in which they are placed. And just as these girls are emblematic of the sexual vulnerability and innocence of the working child, so Reynolds's *Cupid as a Link Boy* (Fig. 30) and *Mercury as a Cutpurse* (see cats. 39 and 40) represent sexual, predatory, experience made incarnate in the form of two familiar creatures of the city's underworld, the link boy and the thief. Their menacing presence is, however, mitigated by their transformation into mischievous infant gods.

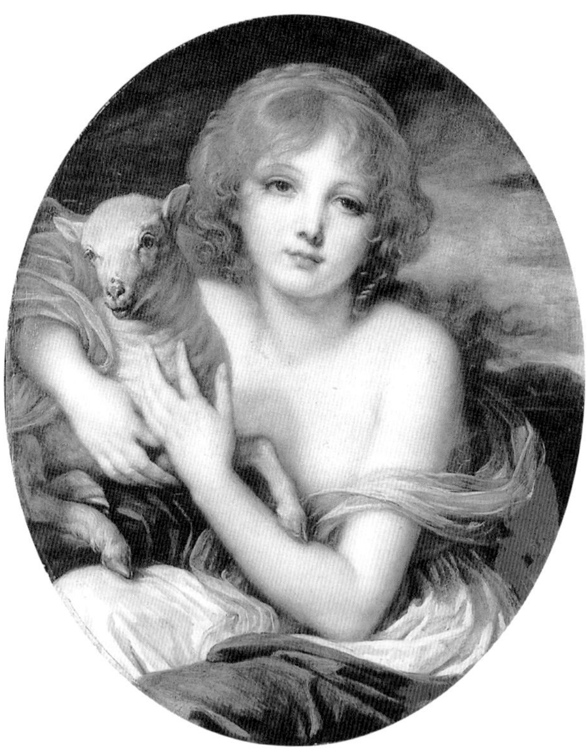

31 *Innocence* by Jean-Baptiste Greuze (1725-1805). Oil on canvas, 63 x 53 (oval). The Trustees of the Wallace Collection, London

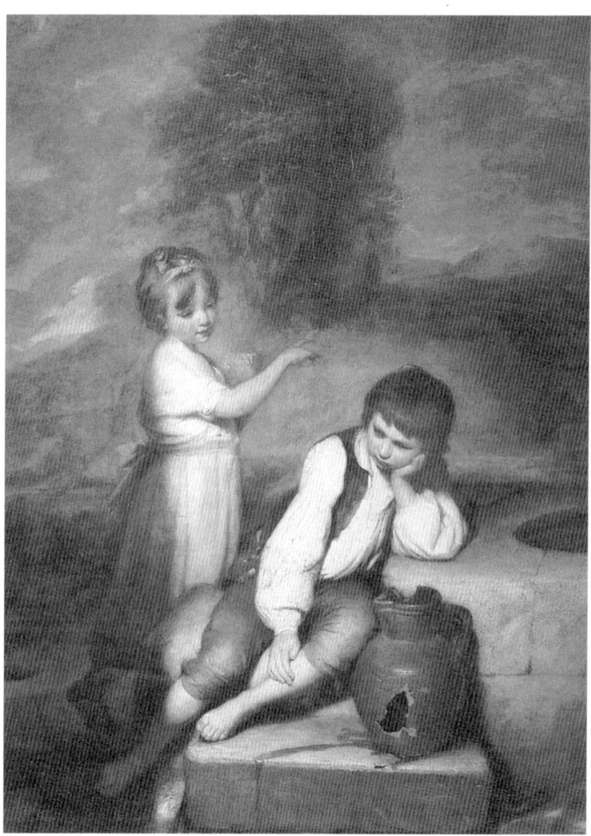

32 *The Sulky Boy* by Richard Morton Paye (*fl* 1773-?1821). Oil on canvas, 181 x 132 cm. Private Collection

The reality for poor children in the city was quite at odds with the artistic image, except perhaps that both involved the manipulation of childhood sexuality to serve the needs and desires of adults. 'Necessity,' noted a guide to London of 1761, 'makes them prostitutes, even before their passions can have any share in their guilt. Among these unhappy objects very agreeable features are frequently seen amidst dirt and rags and this exposes them to greater hazards... ' (quoted in Crown, 1984, p. 164). The real physical danger for children has been noted by Antony Simpson, who has highlighted the alarming rate of prostitution and venereal disease among London's poor children, a result of perversion and also of a popular mythology that intercourse with children was a means of curing the disease itself (in Rousseau and Porter, 1987, pp. 193ff.). It would be a gross distortion to suggest that fancy pictures were conceived or peddled as sexual playgrounds for voyeuristic adults, but there is sufficient evidence to suggest that they were at times fodder for jovial male fantasy. *Muscipula*, for example, Reynolds's painting of a girl holding a caged mouse was purchased in 1785 by the French Ambassador, prompting one critic to observe that a 'trap baited with a girl, is surely sufficient to catch the Viceroy of the kingdom of gallantry' (Postle, 1995, p. 117).

Another prominent courtier in 'the kingdom of gallantry' was the sybaritic 3rd Duke of Dorset, English Ambassador to the court of Louis XVI. He was an avid admirer of Reynolds's child fancy pictures, including the pendant *Cupid* and *Mercury* and of several other paintings featuring Reynolds's favourite boy model. These pictures were hung together in a special 'Reynolds room' at the Duke's seat, Knole, in Kent, where he lived with the rest of his menagerie, including his exotic Italian mistress, Giovanna Baccelli, whose naked body, sculpted by Locatelli in the form of the Borghese *Hermaphrodite*, still adorns the entrance to his apartments.

Reynolds was, of course, not alone in painting images of children designed to appeal to sophisticated adult tastes. It was the stock in trade of his French contemporary Jean-Baptiste Greuze (Fig. 31). It had also been the norm in Dutch seventeenth-century art, where any object or situation, or so we are told, was capable of submitting to some sort of sexual innuendo. Even here, however, the symbolism so graphically spelt out by iconographers did not always transfer directly into the work of artists. Allusions are often to be read in the most circumspect manner, making, as Schama has stated, 'the dichotomy between a descriptive and a prescriptive interpretation unnecessary' (Schama, 1987, p. 413). The same principle holds for the majority of eighteenth-century fancy pictures, which do not carry the same clear allegorical intention as Reynolds's infant saints and sinners. More typical are those pictures which refer obliquely to states of childhood innocence and vulnerability, such as Richard Morton Paye's masterpiece *The Sulky Boy* (Fig. 32), where the boy seated by the broken pitcher may be taken as an emblem either of lost innocence or mere clumsiness, just as the intact pitcher in the hand of Gainsborough's *Cottage Girl* or Opie's *Peasant Family* (cat. 87) may be viewed simply as a vessel for transporting milk or water or, if one prefers, an emblem of virginity. The same criteria apply to any number of children tugging at kite strings, blowing up bladders, or teasing kittens. Unlike the clearly prescriptive function of history painting, or even the fancy images belonging to the adult world – where appended verses could force particular meanings – images of childhood, 'the age of innocence', often remained elusive, lingering in the eye and the mind of the beholder.

III

Love Songs and Matches

The success of Britain as a world power in the eighteenth century was built on trade. Yet, as the historian Paul Langford has observed, 'Commerce was not just about exchange but more fundamentally about consumption' (Langford, 1989, p. 3). As Langford stresses, English consumers were deeply concerned not merely with the acquisition of material goods for their own ends but the manner in which they marked out their position within an advanced, sophisticated, progressive, and above all else 'modern' culture. This trait was shared with other leading commercial cultures, notably France and the Netherlands. Indelibly linked to this emerging culture was the idea of 'politeness', which in essence connoted an interest in the finer things in life, an awareness of the world to which one belonged, and also the world to which one did not belong. One important mark of politeness was to take an interest in the world outside one's own social grouping, that of 'women, children, foreigners, slaves, distant peoples, animals, and every other living creature not blessed with the inestimable divine gift of birth as a freeborn propertied Englishman' (op. cit., p. 7). These were also the very individuals who populate fancy pictures.

It was not an accident, as John Brewer has observed, that the rise of the consumer coincided with the decline of the royal court in Britain, which in turn opened up a large 'cultural vacuum' (Brewer, 1997, p. 343). As the court declined so others stepped in to take over the reins of patronage, 'impresarios who engineered new cultural commodities – novels, essays, the conversation piece, and, of course, the fancy picture, which was merely one aspect of this new culture of free enterprise. One casualty was morality, and those arts – like history painting – which purported to support established codes of ethics. Instead, the satisfaction of whims, fads, caprices, the provision of 'pleasure', an appeal to the senses, became the order of the day. Culture, says Brewer, 'as a commodity, was an end not a means' (op. cit., p. 346). It was no coincidence therefore that the marketplace was quite literally a key site for the fancy picture in the eighteenth century.

Among the most abiding images thrown up by the fancy picture are the numerous portrayals of street vendors, selling fruit, flowers, vegetables, ballads, matches and a whole range of consumable goods. The tradition of depicting these characters belongs to a graphic tradition which can be traced back to the Middle Ages. For our purposes, however, the most influential precursors of the eighteenth-century fancy picture were the images contained in Marcellus Laroon's *Cryes of the City of London Drawn after the Life*, published in 1687, in which over seventy engravings depicted a range of street vendors and characters, the images often accompanied by the cry associated with the particular trade (Fig. 33). In the eighteenth century it was William Hogarth who most successfully captured the spirit of Laroon's world, in series such as *Four Times of the Day* and in characters such

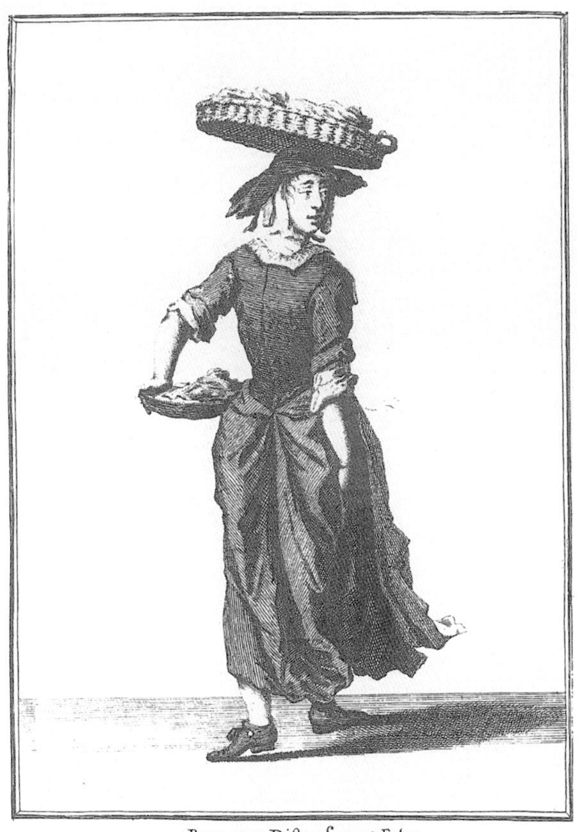

33 '*Buy my Dish of great Eeles*' by Marcellus Laroon (1653-1702). Line engraving from *The Cryes of the City of London*

as the long-suffering Sarah Young, heroine of *A Rake's Progress*, who takes up the honest trade of selling trinkets (Fig. 34), while her erstwhile lover whores and gambles himself into the madhouse and the grave. For the most part, Hogarth preferred to incorporate these characters into a complex narrative structures; the *Shrimp Girl* (cat. 54) is a notable exception.

Hogarth's art, however, represented only one aspect of the fascination with street characters. Less well known were cheap prints featuring a whole range of characters, often based on particular individuals: Betty Monro, fruit-girl at the Exchange in the Strand; 'Old Coe', the oyster seller of Cambridge, Dunstan, the crier of old wigs; James Moss, the dog-seller; or John Woolderidge, of East Clandon, Surrey, ballad-maker and singer. Many of these images came in the form of cheap prints, although occasionally, as in Nathaniel Hone's *Brickdust Man* (cat. 58) (who was probably based on a well known character), or Zoffany's *Watercress Girl ('Jane Wallis')* (cat. 57), they were produced at the highest artistic and technical level. Yet, while old dog-sellers and dustmen were of anthropological interest to the curious consumer, the most popular and best-selling images were those of young, nubile oyster-sellers, ballad-singers, and fruit- and vegetable-vendors. The attraction of these figures was not simply based on their superior physical charms, when compared to small children or wizened old men, but the deeper way in which they were made to enact a fantasy (a male fantasy) about the role of women in the market place: in other words, the enduring fantasy of sex and shopping.

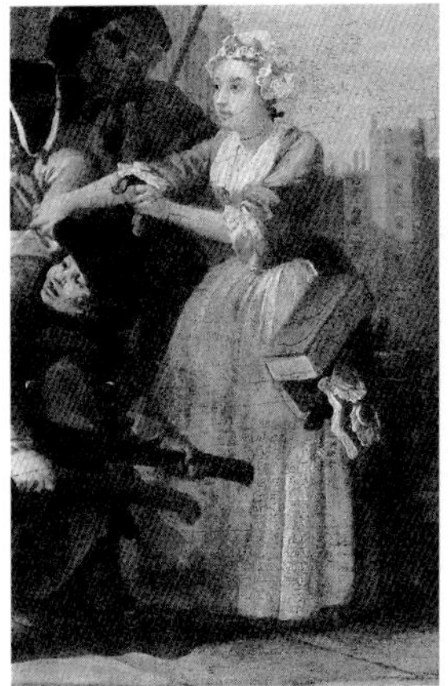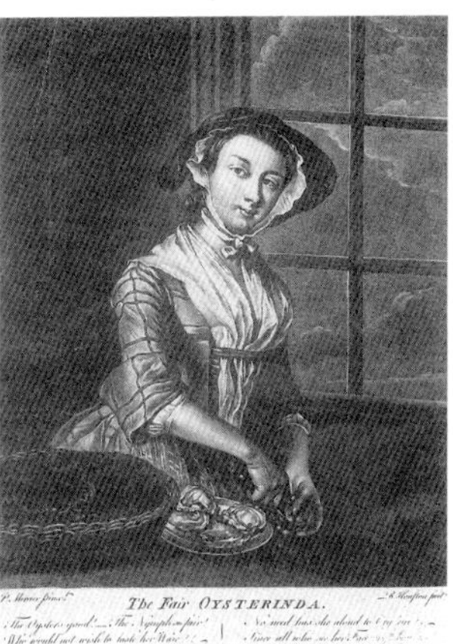

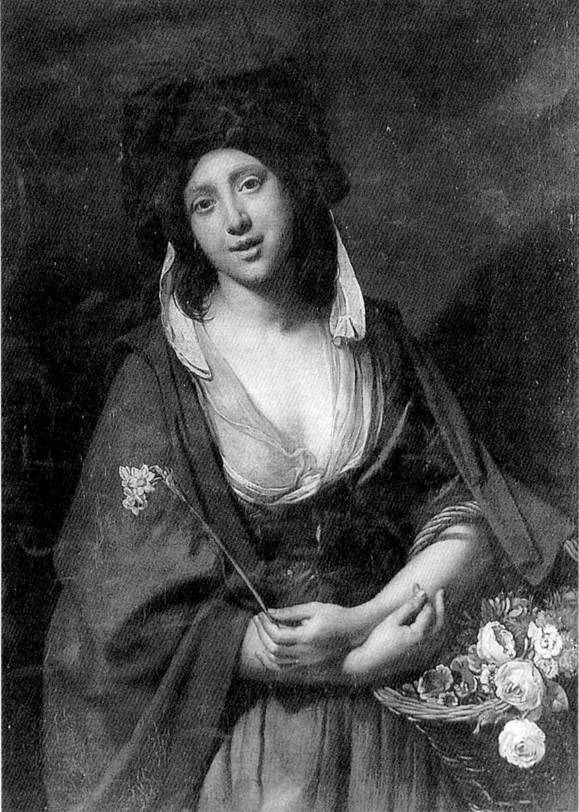

34 'Arrested for Debt', *A Rake's Progress* (detail) by William Hogarth (1697-1764). Oil on canvas, 62.2 x 74.9 cm. Sir John Soane's Museum, London

35 *The Fair Oysterinda* by Richard Houston, after Philip Mercier (?1689-1760). Mezzotint engraving. Courtesy of the Paul Mellon Centre, London

36 The Flower Girl by Johan Zoffany (1733-1810). Oil on canvas, 91.5 x 71.2 cm. Private Collection

In the late seventeenth century the presence of women in the marketplace became increasingly evident in major British cities. Moreover their appearance was increasingly as independent trades people in their own right, making their own goods, and their own livings independent of existing male dominated market. One manifestation of this phenomenon was the appearance of a slew of obscene populist poems, songs, ballads and pamphlets, designed to portray women's industry as a form of prostitution (in Brewer and Bermingham, 1997, pp. 419ff). Collectively, as James Turner has recently observed, such literature connived to give the impression that all the businesses in which women engaged 'must be covers for prostitution, and the only "commodity" a woman can sell is herself' (ibid., p. 420). The language of these pamphlets was brimming with innuendo. The word 'commodity', for example, in popular common parlance referred to the vagina, as in William William Wycherley's poetic description of the 'Juicy, Salt Commodity', offered by an oyster girl (op. cit., p. 421). It was precisely this kind of metaphor, well established in literature by the early eighteenth century, which wormed its way into the fancy picture, exemplified by Mercier's *Oyster Girl*, 'The Fair Oysterinda' (Fig. 35), who beguilingly cracks open a tasty bivalve, while at the same time purveying a fantasy on the sexual availability street girls. Similarly, when the stipple engraver Francesco Bartolozzi took the liberty of adding an exposed nipple to Hogarth's *Shrimp Girl*, and retitled the image '*Shrimps!*' (cat. 55), we can be sure that he was not preoccupied with the sales appeal of small crustaceans. Yet, as Turner points out, 'As consumers and as traders, women whose sexual "credit" was broken could not obtain financial credit or employment' (op. cit., p. 427). Besides, although there can be no doubt that some women did supplement their income by working as part-time prostitutes, the back-breaking labour of selling perishable goods on the streets of London left little time for the average street-trader to indulge in sex with her customers. Nor were street-vendors as alluring as fancy pictures suggest. Tobias Smollett's Humphry Clinker remarks graphically upon the 'dirty barrow bunter… cleansing her dusty fruit with her own spittle; and who knows but some fine lady of St James's parish might admit into her delicate mouth those very cherrries which had been rolled and moistened between the filthy and perhaps ulcerated chops of a St Giles huckster' (quoted in Hill, 1994, pp. 168-9).

As well as the general appearance and demeanour of female street-vendors, their street cries too were interpreted as sexual invitations and linked to the coarse banter of prostitutes. At their most basic level the comparisons were vulgar puns linking the properties of curiously shaped vegetables and cuts of meat with the delights of the sexual act. Yet even at the more refined level of the fancy picture, the impression that these woman are engaged in 'cunning' dialogue is quite evident, not least in Zoffany's *Flower Girl* (Fig. 36), whose pouting open lips form a crucial aspect of her intended allure. In 1709 Edward Ward's *London Spy* even 'respectable' women traders in London's new Exchange, by their very dress and deportment are portrayed as latter-day sirens, vying to tempt passers-by, 'begging of Custom, with such Amorous Looks, and after so Affable a manner, that I could not but fancy they had as much mind to dispose of themselves, as the Commodities they deal in' (quoted in Kubek, 1997, p. 444). Compared to these shop girls, the lowly market trader bawling 'six pence a pound fair Cherryes' was positively soliciting. Yet, unlike the women portrayed in cheap salacious pamphlets and earthy ballads, the cosmeticised street vendor who featured in the fancy picture – whether in original painted form or in print reproduction – could hold a respectable, if mildly flirtatious, presence in any broadminded cosmopolitan household.

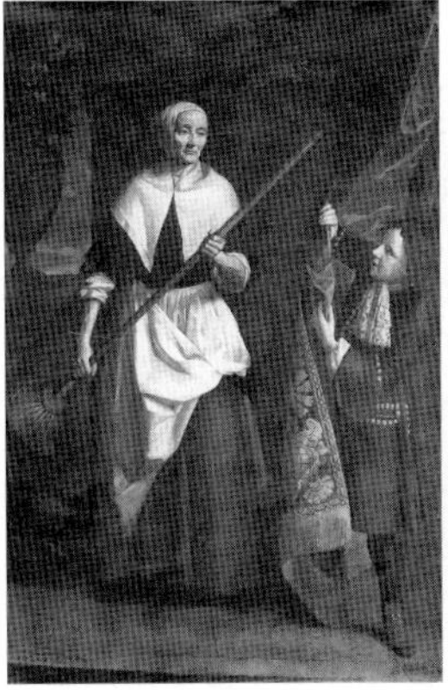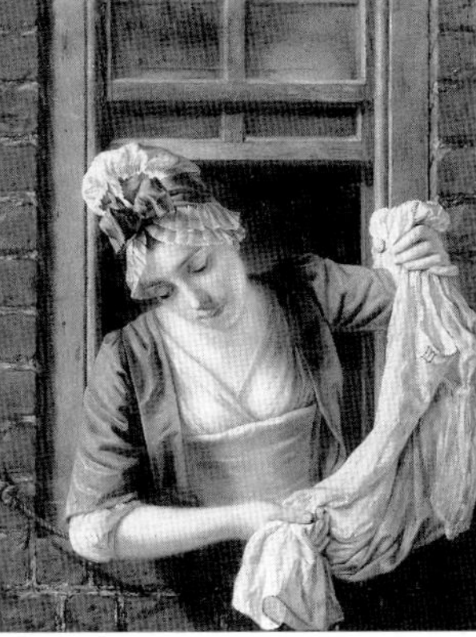

37 *Bridget Holmes* by John Riley (1646-91). Oil on canvas, 225.4 x 148.6 cm. Her Majesty The Queen

38 *The Laundry Maid* by Henry Robert Morland (?1719-1797). Pastel, 76.2 x 64.4 cm. Private Collection

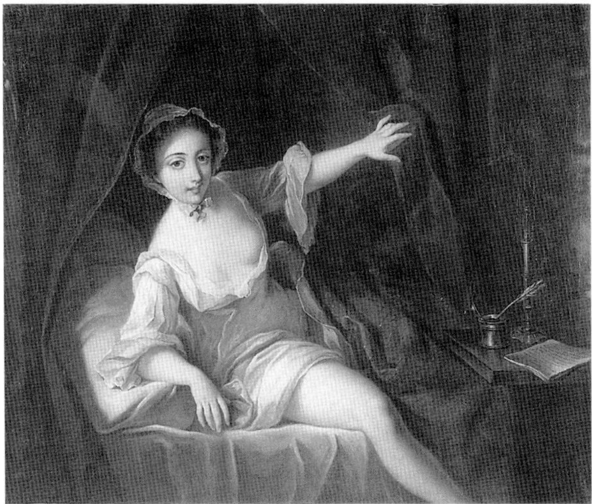

39 *Pamela Getting Out of Bed* by Philip Mercier (?1689-1760). Oil on canvas, 58.3 x 76.1 cm. Private Collection

There was, of course, as in any fantasy of this kind, a fetishistic hierarchy of availability. Hence, just as today male fantasies inevitably revolve around nurses and chambermaids, so in the eighteenth century they concentrated not only upon those who provided services outside the home, but under one's own roof. Before the eighteenth century there was no established tradition of portraying domestic servants in their own right, a notable exception being John Riley's portrayal of the aged 'Necessary Woman', Bridget Holmes, a servant in the Royal household (Fig. 37). And in any event, the image of the wizened old servant wielding a broom could not compete with the comely domestic servants of Henry Morland (Fig. 38), lovingly washing, ironing and hanging out their master's shirts (cats. 69 and 70).

The cult of the maid-servant was fuelled by the trials and tribulations of Pamela, the virtuous lady's maid, heroine of Richardson's eponymous novel, who tirelessly fends off the amorous advances of her hot-blooded master, 'Mr. B'. The popularity of images of ladies' maids was no doubt also boosted by the increased presence of servants within bourgeois menages, although it is quite clear, from the sales of the pictures, that the images themselves appealed equally to the middle classes and to the aristocracy. By the mid-eighteenth century London households were filled with young women from countryside, lured by the expectation of decent wages and the bright lights. It was estimated in 1775 that one in eight people in the metropolis was a domestic servant (Hecht, 1956, p. 33). While there were far more servants in the average English household than in France, however, 'More than half of them,' according to one French commentator, 'are never seen – kitchen-maids, stable-men, maidservants in large numbers' (op. cit., p. 67). Unlike winsome girls in Morland's fancy pictures, laundry maids were actually among the least visible in the home; they were hired by upper servants and often unknown by their masters.

Finally, the fantasy element in these images was also fuelled by the popularity of the maid as a masquerade character, whereby women of bourgeois and aristocratic pretensions would ape the dress of their own servants and various social inferiors. Of course, the ritual of down-dressing and even cross-dressing was by no means limited to maid servants, extending to milk maids, shepherdesses and their male equivalents. According to Samuel Johnson, the well off 'live in a perpetual masquerade, in which all about them wear borrowed characters' (*Rambler*, No. 75). As Terry Castle has noted, eighteenth-century English society was in general a world of 'masqueraders and artificers, self-alienation and phantasmagoria' (quoted in Rousseau and Porter, 1987, p. 156). Masquerades and fancy pictures both traded on fantasy. But while the fancy picture merely identified and gave a visual form to the 'other', the masquerade allowed one to be the 'other', at least for the evening. In this context it is not surprising that in the nineteenth century it was rumoured that the models for Morland's laundry maids were not mere models but prominent female members of the aristocracy.

The image of the prostitute was, according to Brewer's analysis of culture as a commodity, a cause of immense anxiety. She was, he concludes, 'the figure that exemplified the immoderate passions, desires, and pleasures that were integral to the most polite age but whose suppression could acquit it of the charge of being the most vicious' (Brewer, 1997, p. 358). In the fancy picture, the image of the prostitute was largely suppressed, emerging as we have seen through women onto which male fantasy could be more safely and obliquely projected, as, for example, the chaste (and chased) lady's maid Pamela Andrews, captured by Mercier 'innocently' sitting on her bed in supposed solitude (Fig. 39). That is not to say that images of prostitutes did not exist within the canon of the fancy picture, merely that they took on allegorical or mythical forms, as in Reynolds's quasi-erotic nymphs and Venuses of the 1780s (see cat. 19). Even when prostitutes did appear in fancy pictures they were removed from the immediate sphere of reality.

In 1739 for example John Faber engraved an image of a 'Venetian' Courtesan, after Mercier (Fig. 40). Not only did the adjective 'Venetian' allow a safe distance between the viewer and object of his presumed desire, but the verses appended to the print ('... For Affectation shocks, not tempts, the Sight; /And checks Desire, where most it would invite') indicate that her exaggerated come-on is actually a turn-off. Later, when Reynolds painted the notorious prostitute Kitty Fisher, her trade was alluded to, as we have seen, through a visual comparison with Cleopatra. And even

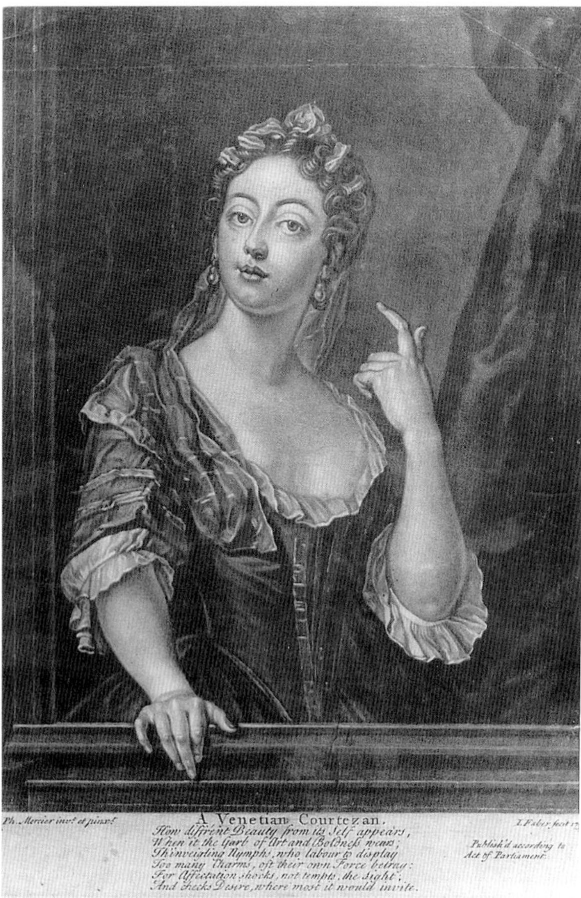

40 *A Venetian Courtesan* by John Faber II, after Philip Mercier (?1689-1760). Mezzotint engraving. Private Collection

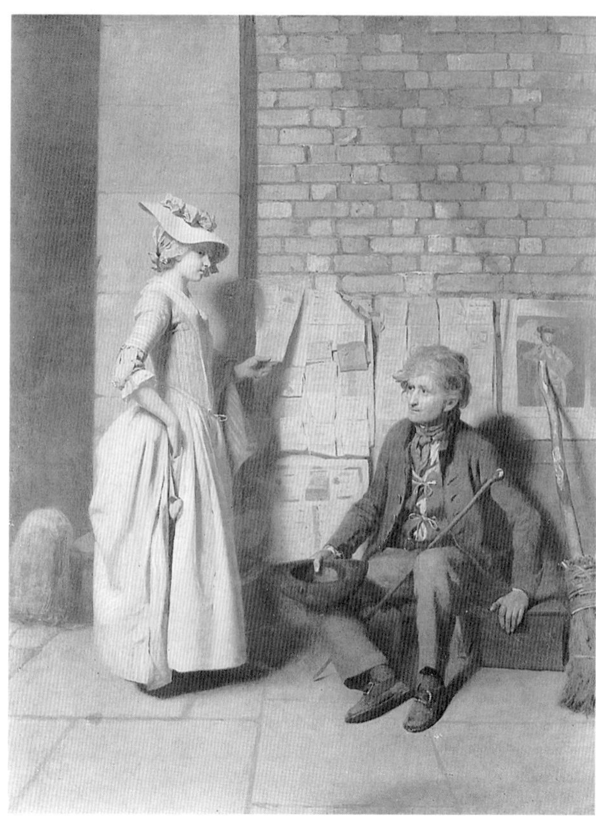

41 *A Girl Buying a Ballad* by Henry Walton (*c* 1746-1813). Oil on canvas, 94 x 73.6 cm. Private Collection

Nathaniel Hone, who was more irreverent than most, did no more than picture her suggestively in the boudoir, a diaphanous shift covering any potential embarrassment. Among 'serious' artists only Matthew Peters dared to defy convention by producing fancy pictures of prostitutes which left no room for ambiguity (see cats. 74 and 75). It is significant that Peters produced these images immediately upon his return from the continent, and he made them for a clique of 'gallant' aristocrats fresh from their exertions on the Grand Tour. When Peters actually had the temerity to exhibit *A Woman in Bed* in public at the Royal Academy, he was roundly criticized, to the point that he stopped producing them altogether (and this was before he had any serious intention of entering the Church, which he subsequently did).

While sex continued to play a significant role in selling the fancy picture, there was a discernible move towards a more sober interpretation of the wheels of everyday commerce later in the century. It is to be found in the handful of pictures produced by Henry Walton during the 1770s, occasional works like Zoffany's *Porter with a Hare* (cat. 59), of the same period, and most notably in the *Cries of London* series made by Francis Wheatley in the mid 1790s (cats. 62 and 63). While it is hard to evaluate contribution of Walton, there can be no doubt that he conveyed, in pictures such as *Girl Plucking a Turkey* and *Girl buying a Ballad* (Fig. 41), a more sympathetic image of labour and commerce. Stylistically these most impressive paintings appear to owe something to the example of Chardin, whose work Walton

may have known in France. More significantly, while they resist any narrative interpretation, they have certain affinities with the moralising household dramas of Greuze, the so called 'genre sérieux'.

Morality, which had rarely figured in earlier fancy pictures, maintained a hovering presence in the *Cries of London* and in Wheatley's other fancy and genre pictures where virtuous labour is inevitably rewarded, vice thwarted, and love is contained within the chaste bonds of formal courtship and matrimony. Nor was it coincidental that at this very time the miscellaneous ranks of philanthropists, suppressers of vice and general do-gooders were turning their collective attention to cleaning up the culture of the streets. Common prostitutes were suppressed, and the purveyors of obscene books and pamphlets hounded. In the wake of the French revolution casual attitudes towards sex were frowned upon, and even equated with disloyalty. At the same time ballad sellers were encouraged to distribute religious tracts, and even turn into agent provocateurs, in order to give 'a better turn to the minds of the lowest classes of people' (Bristow, 1977, p. 44). By the 1820s it was observed proudly that there were no longer 'groups of servant girls standing in the streets to hear songs which the prostitutes themselves would pelt those who attempted to sing them' (ibid.). Sex did not, however, desert the marketplace. It simply moved on to other popular sites of entertainment and commerce; to taverns, 'free and easies' and, later in the nineteenth century, to the Gin Palace and the Music Hall.

The Deserving Poor

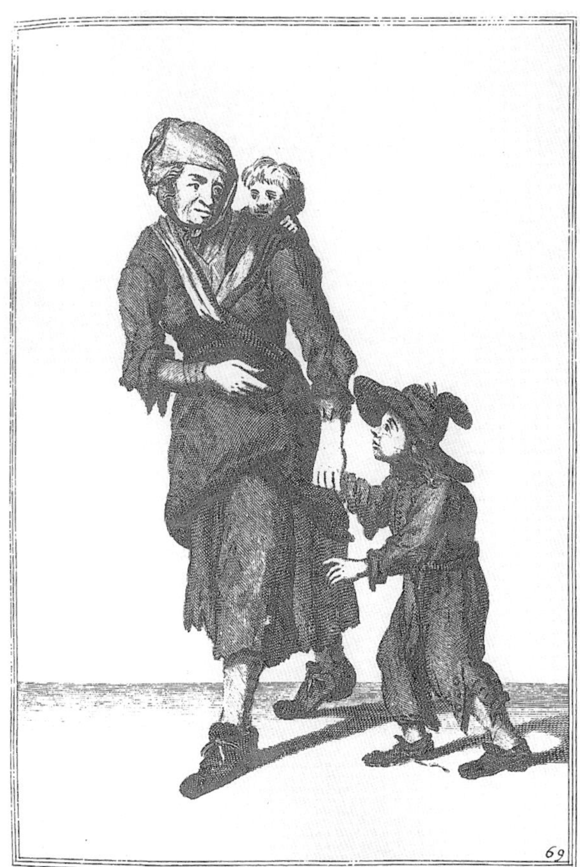

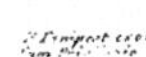

Marcellus Laroon's *Cryes of the City of London* includes a print of the 'The London Begger' [*sic*] (Fig. 42). Within the boundaries of their own parish, and provided they were parochial pensioners, such beggars could legitimately earn a living by seeking alms. While begging continued to be a means of support for the poor, during the eighteenth century attitudes towards beggars, vagrants and the amorphous mass of the poor changed radically as they increasingly became recognized as a 'problem' rather than an abiding presence. Awareness of the plight of the poor surfaced in the works of poets and painters who, as John Barrell has shown, couched their responses in very similar ways. In art, the poor featured in landscape and genre painting, and in the fancy picture. But while in landscape and genre painting they remained remain distant figures, part of the scenery, the fancy picture brought the poor into close and immediate focus, allowing polite society to witness indigence and old age face to face (Fig. 43).

The English Poor Law, enacted in statutes of 1598 and 1601, settled the responsibility for the administration of poor relief, the curbing of vagrancy, and of finding work for the able-bodied upon the 9,000 or so parishes of England and Wales. Over the next hundred years beleaguered attempts were made to improve and refine the system with the Act of Settlement of 1662, which attempted to restrict vagrancy, and the Workhouse Test Act of 1723, which provided some sort of institutionalized labour for the poor. Throughout this period expenditure on the poor increased, and costs doubled during the first fifty years of the eighteenth century alone (Slack, 1990, pp. 22ff.). Whether or not the Poor Law helped to relieve poverty, it certainly increased the visibility of the poor, and shaped the attitudes of contemporaries towards them as an identifiable 'other'. As Keith Thomas states, people disliked the burden imposed on them by the poor and the threat they constituted to law and order, but 'they also recognised that it was their Christian duty to give them charity when no public relief was forthcoming' (Thomas, 1971, p. 673). As the eighteenth century wore on, the screw was turned increasingly on the givers as well as the recipients of charity.

By the mid-eighteenth century a more 'caring' attitude towards the poor was evident, if by that we mean that the establishment of private philanthropic endeavours such as Thomas Coram's Foundling Hospital, Jonas Hanway's Marine Society, or the Magdalen Hospital, the last set up to cater for 'poor, young, thoughtless females'. Yet philanthropy, however caring, often had an element of purgative self-interest. As the Bishop of Lowth sermonised in 1757, 'The Miseries of our Fellow-Creatures affect us so sensibly, that to relieve them is really relieving ourselves, and refreshing our own Bowels' (Rodgers, 1949, p 8). The communal concern over the concept and practice of administering charitable relief ensured its presence in visual images of the poor, including Gainsborough's *Charity Relieving Distress* (Fig. 44 and cat. 90), Wheatley's *Benevolent Cottager* (Fig. 45), and William Beechey's portrait of the children of Sir Francis Ford giving money to a beggar boy

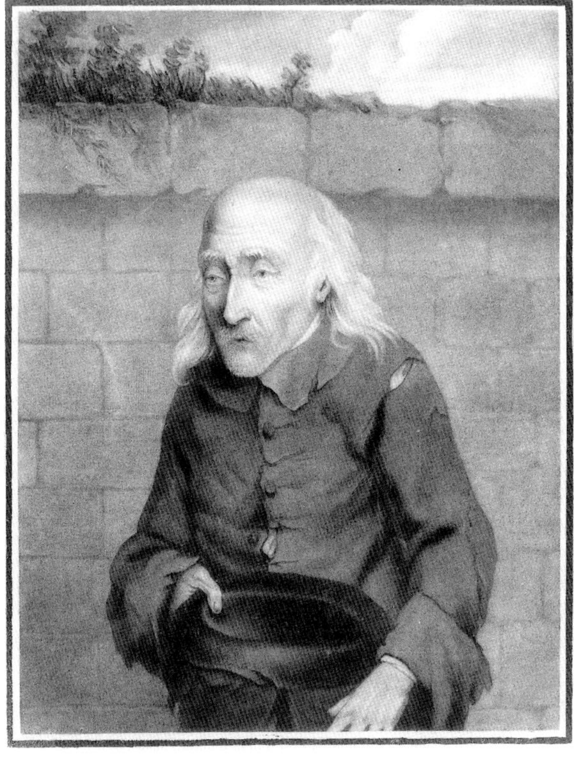

42 '*The London Begger* [sic]', by Marcellus Laroon (1653-1702). Line engraving from *The Cryes of the City of London*

43 '*Pity the Sorrows of a poor old man*' by John Dean (175556-1796). Mezzotint, 1789, The Trustees of the British Museum

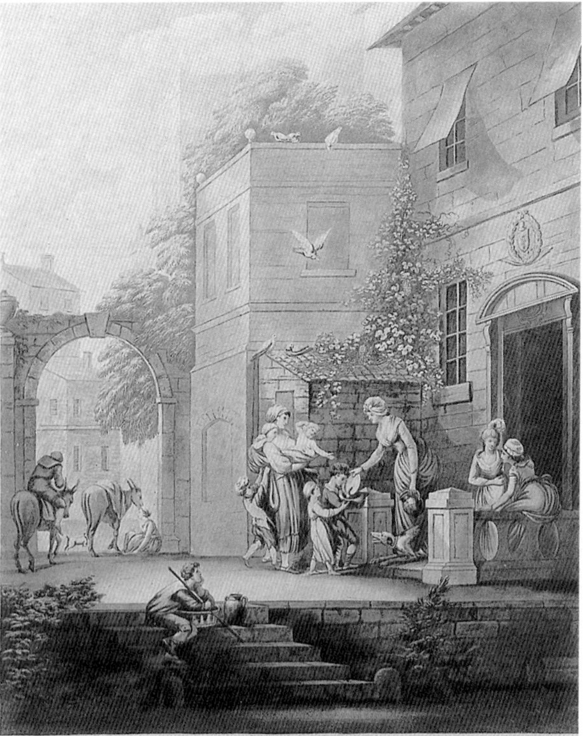

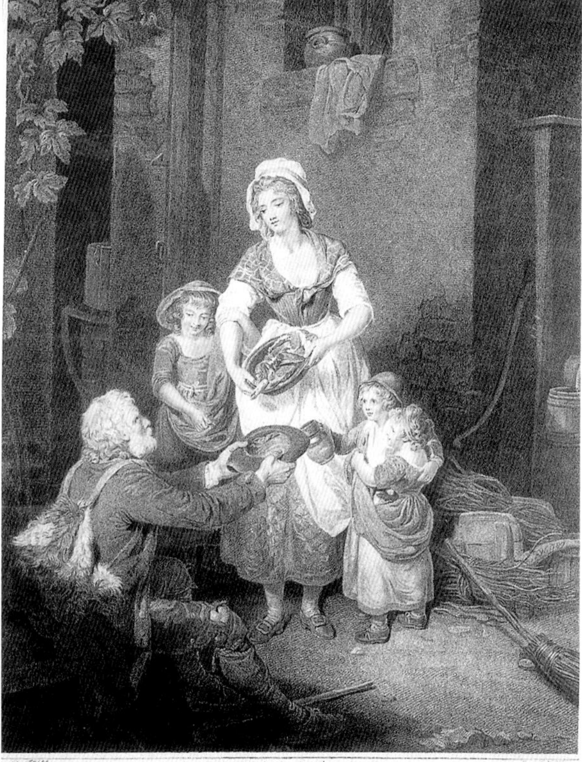

44 *Charity Sympathizing with Distress* by Richard Harraden, after Thomas Gainsborough (1727-88). Mezzotint Engraving. By kind permission of the Trustees of Gainsborough's House, Suffolk

45 *The Benevolent Cottager* by W. Nutter, after Francis Wheatley (1747-1801). Stipple engraving. The Trustees of the British Museum, London

46 *A Scottish Fortune Teller* by Thomas Barker (1769-1847). Oil on canvas, 83.1 x 62 cm. Private Collection

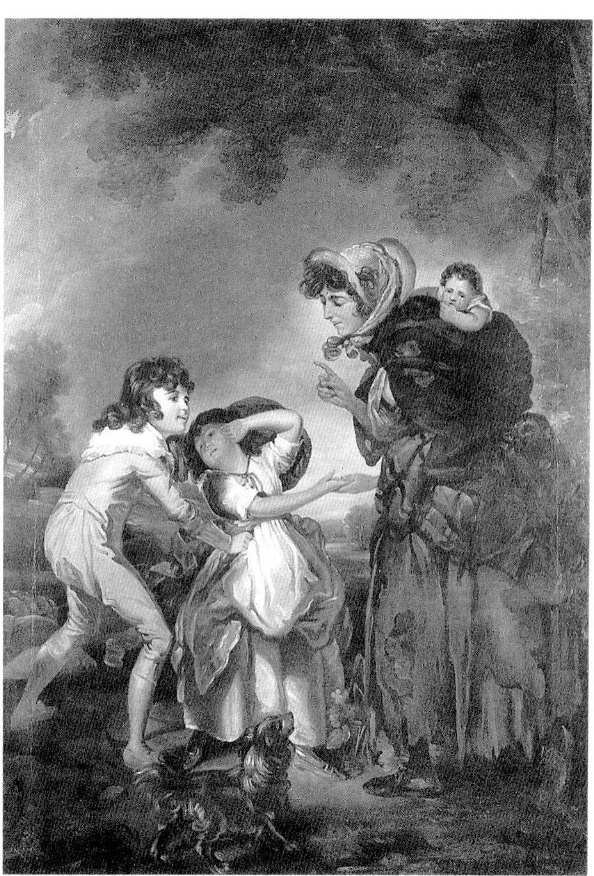

(cat. 91). Beechey's painting is fascinating in that it unites two genres, child portraiture and the fancy picture. The conjunction is telling because, without the mollifying presence of the 'charitable' young Ford children, the image of the starving beggar boy would have been too stark an image to thrust upon the sensibilities of the exhibition-going public. After all, Beechey's painting was shown at the Royal Academy in 1794, during a period of deep political anxiety consequent upon the anarchic state of events in France, bread shortages on the home front, and the disruptive activities of radical writers and pamphleteers who promoted, albeit from a marginal position, egalitarian ideas on land ownership and the advocacy of revolutionary programs for redistributing rent on land. In the circumstances, it is revealing that Beechey's picture prompted at least one art critic to suggest that the image might prick the public conscience into further review of the Poor Law, a process which, as it happens, was already very much on the political agenda.

Despite the appearance of Beechey's starving beggar boy, visual representations of the poor – at least within the orbit of the fancy picture – were more often encapsulated within images drawn from the popular folklore tradition. Traditionally, the archetypal beggar evoked an air of mystique and even fear, and as Keith Thomas notes, the legend of the Beggar's curse 'enjoyed a continuous currency from the Dark Ages to the nineteenth century' (Thomas, 1971, p. 604). The poet William Shenstone observed in the mid-eighteenth century: 'If anyone's curse can effect damnation it is not that of the Pope but that of the poor' (ibid., p. 605). Not surprisingly, however, artists preferred to dwell on the more pleasant aspects of the beggar's magical powers – the ability to read palms, and tell fortunes. Popular myths included the story that forms the subject of *The Blind Beggar of Bethnal Green* (cat. 94), dating from the reign of

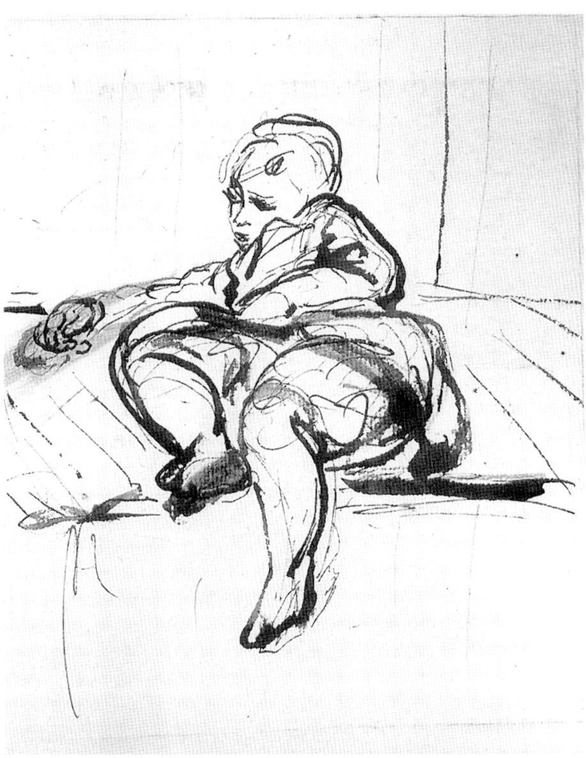

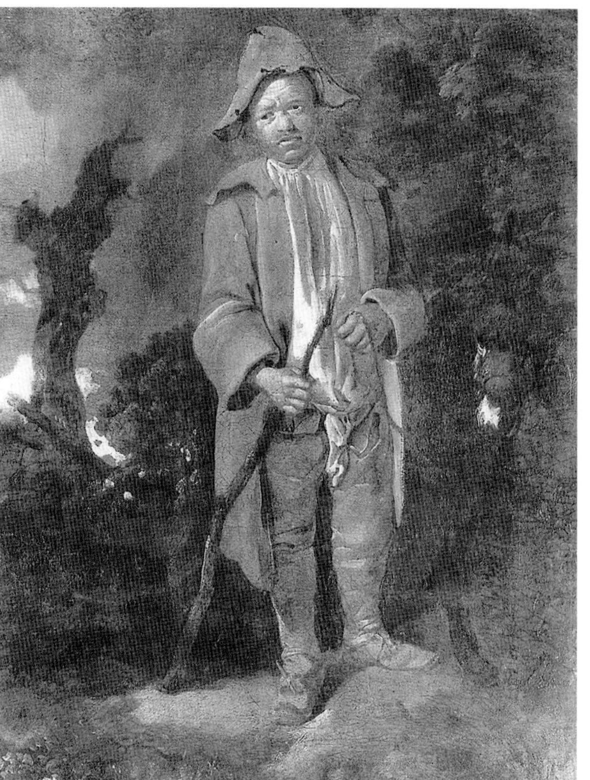

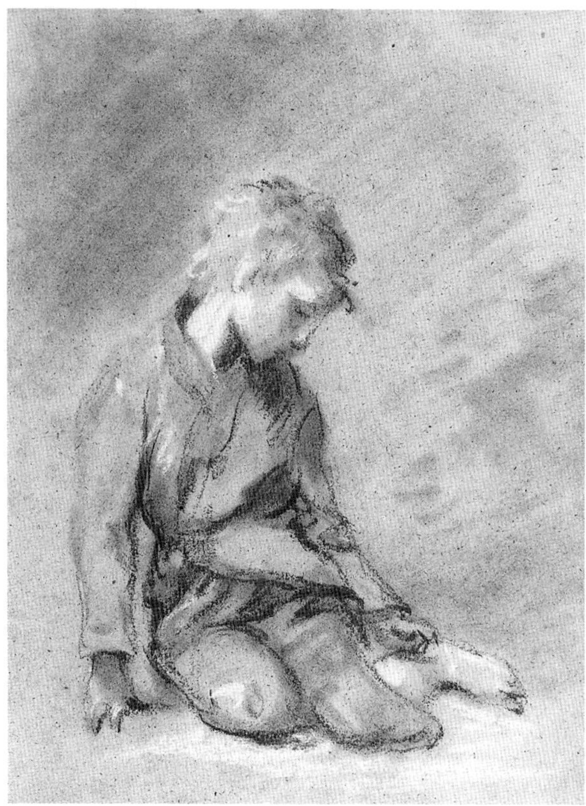

47 *Study of a Seated Girl* by Sir Joshua Reynolds (1723-92). Pen-and-ink drawing on paper. Mrs R.A. Lucas, on loan to the Royal Academy of Arts, London

48 *An Old Peasant with a Donkey* by Thomas Gainsborough (1727-88). Oil on canvas, 48 x 38 cm. Private Collection

49 *Beggar Boy Seated* by Thomas Gainsborough (1727-88). Chalks on buff paper, 24.9 x 19 cm. The Ashmolean Museum, Oxford

Henry VI and later revived in Thomas Percy's *Reliques of English Poetry*. Contemporary quarry included Henry Mackenzie's best-selling novel, *The Man of Feeling*, which involved a friendly encounter between Harley, the book's hero, and a friendly beggar (cat. 93), who recounts how he turned to fortune-telling, and instead of telling his own misfortunes, 'began to prophesy happiness to others'. Although fortune-tellers by this time were regarded as little more than a part of the entertainment industry by the middle classes, they would have still been familiar figures among the homes of the poor. Robert Southey noted in 1807 that a 'cunning-man, or a cunning-woman, as they are termed, is to be found near every town' (Thomas, p. 295). They were also featured in fancy pictures by Reynolds, John Russell, Matthew Peters (cats. 78-80), and Thomas Barker (Fig. 46). Here, old grey-bearded men and dark-skinned gypsy women titillate giggling young girls with tales of tall, dark handsome strangers. In Nathaniel Hone's celebrated painting *The Conjuror* (National Gallery of Ireland), Reynolds's old beggar-model, George White, is himself transformed into a wizard.

Reynolds frequently employed impoverished old men, women and children to model for his fancy pictures, 'dependant people', who were 'quiet and gave no trouble' (quoted in Postle, 1995, p. 62). His *Iphigenia* was modelled upon the form of a 'battered courtesan', his patriarchs were taken from the faces of old beggar men, and his infant saints from street urchins, whom he painted and sketched incessantly (Fig. 47) during the summer months, when his portrait practice was slow. Rarely, if ever, however, did he allow their own personae to disturb his flights of fancy. The same cannot be said, for example, of Zoffany or Gainsborough. Zoffany's beggars (cat. 89) are remarkable for the graphic manner in which they are portrayed, but also for the way in which they represent, by implication, not only the recipients of charity but also the benefactors who granted them relief.

Zoffany's picture is compelling but it stands almost alone in his oeuvre. For a more thoroughgoing and extended treatment of the rural poor we must turn to Gainsborough, who painted the rural poor repeatedly for over forty years,

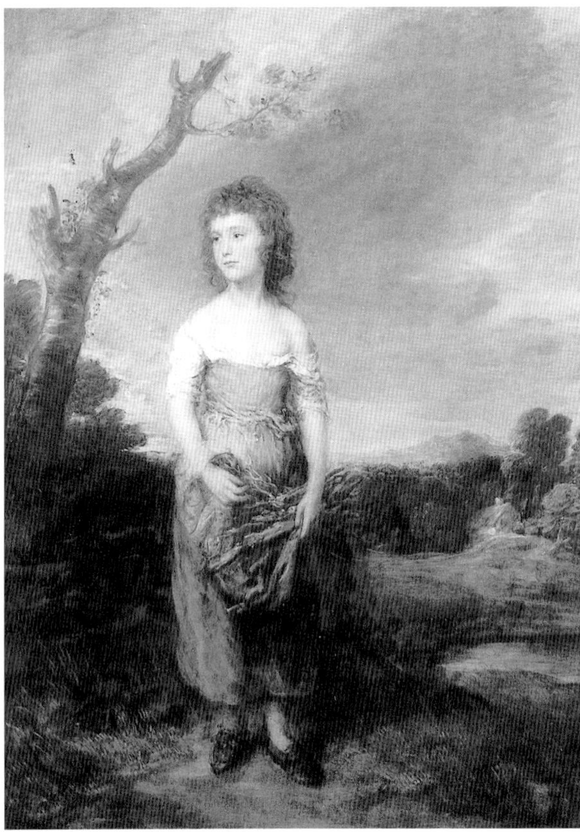

50 *A Peasant Girl Gathering Faggots* by Thomas Gainsborough (1727-88). Oil on canvas, 123 x 169 cm. Manchester City Art Gallery

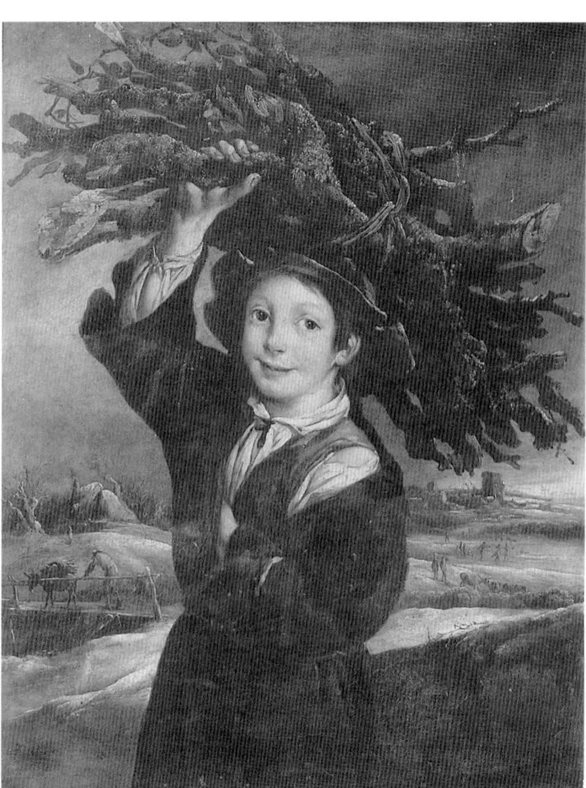

51 *The Young Faggot Gatherer* by Thomas Barker (1769-1847). Oil on canvas, 91.5 x 71.2 cm. Private Collection

from his little studies of shepherd boys and old peasants of the 1740s and '50s (Fig. 48) to the rapid sketches of beggar boys (Fig. 49), and the heroic *Woodman* (see cat. 86) of the mid-1780s. Among the most important stimuli for Gainsborough were the paintings of artists he admired, including Berchem and Van Goyen, Rubens and Murillo. None of Gainsborough's paintings was produced in an artistic vacuum. He was aware of the poor as an entity in their own right, to the point that he was willing to take in a beggar child to live in his own home. Yet, while his fancy pictures are poignant reminders of the burden of the labouring poor they remain strangely ambivalent. Moreover, personal sympathy for the situation of the poor does not explain in itself the function or form of such images.

In a penetrating analysis of the depiction of the rural poor in eighteenth-century art and literature, John Barrell has argued that the demise of what might be termed the pastoral image of the poor, cheerful, peasantry in bucolic settings, was supplanted later in the century by more subdued, sober images evoking pity and pathos. In a thesis which draws upon poetic, economic and political factors, Barrell notes the paradox later in the eighteenth century, when literature and art appear at once 'more benevolent, and more repressive, in their image of the poor' (Barrell, 1980, p. 77). In literature, he sees the change epitomised in poetry of Crabbe, whose attitude towards the labouring poor was that 'we may pity them, but should not suggest that they are capable of being anything else' (op. cit., p. 82). Poverty, though it could be alleviated by benevolence, was abiding. One could be sensitive to it, chronicle it, respond charitably, but not eradicate it. It was at once an apparent and unsettling mixture of 'repression and benevolence'. In a similar vein Patricia Crown, in discussing later fancy pictures by Reynolds and Gainsborough, noted this 'sense

of tension between recognition and suppression, between factual immediacy and poetic distance' (Crown, 1984, p. 163). One aspect of Gainsborough's late fancy pictures underlined by Barrell is the fact that they depict not merely the deserving poor, but the working poor, carrying bunches of faggots (Fig. 50), pitchers or tending pigs (although one can think of exceptions to this rule). These children gain our sympathy because they deserve it by dint of their labour. They are moving, according to Barrell, 'partly because of the evidence they afford of young children early learning the habits of a pious industry' (Barrell, 1980, p. 83). In this context, the link with the art of Murillo becomes more than simply stylistic or art historical. These poor children are in effect secular icons, saintly in their poverty, quite literally 'good shepherds'.

Yet, while we can locate Gainsborough's late fancy picture's within a social and historical framework, the balance in these paintings between fact and fantasy is so finely tuned that their spell as works of art remains unbroken. That cannot be said of those who followed immediately in his footsteps – as one can see in the art of the Bath painter, Thomas Barker (Fig. 51). Barker's paintings, produced from the early 1790s onwards, reveal that images created and perfected by Gainsborough were all too susceptible to commercial exploitation. Barker was aware of the power of these heroic images and set about creating his own highly derivative life-size fancy pictures of the labouring poor. They were exhibited in a specially constructed gallery in Bath, drew huge admiring crowds, and earned Barker a small fortune. Thus paintings of the labouring poor once more found their way into collections in stately homes, while cheap prints and china plates based on these same designs were crafted to furnish cosy middle-class establishments.

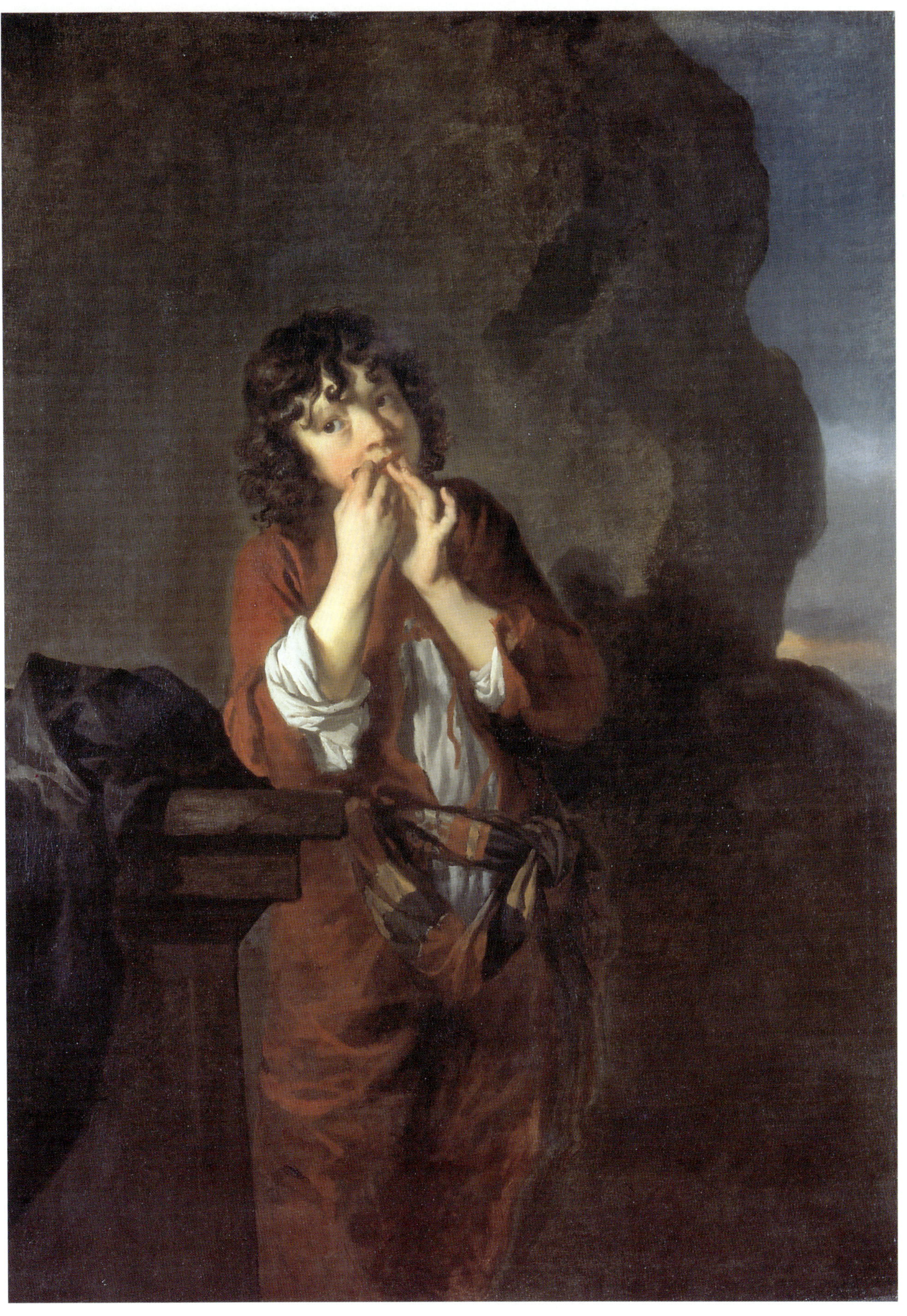

Plate 1
Boy playing a Jew's Harp
Sir Peter Lely

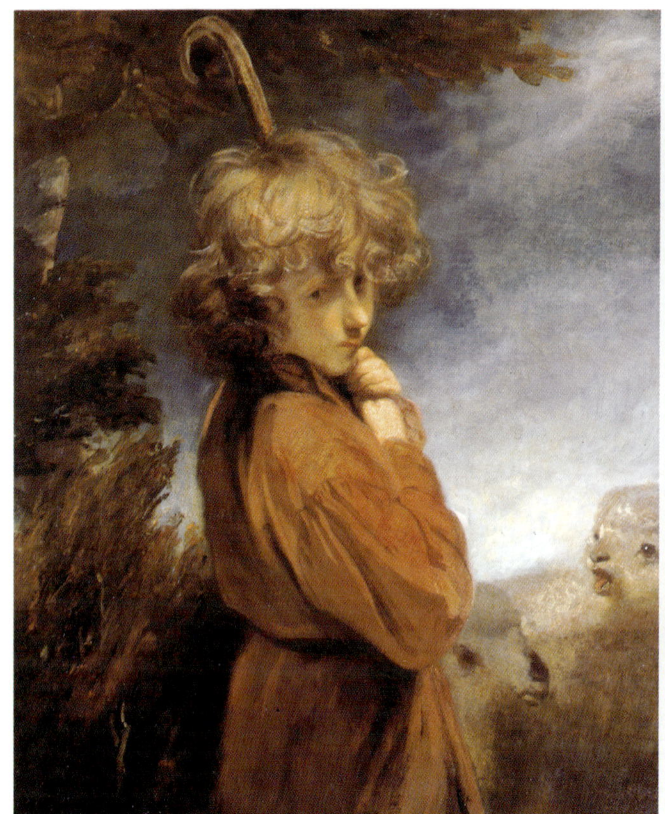

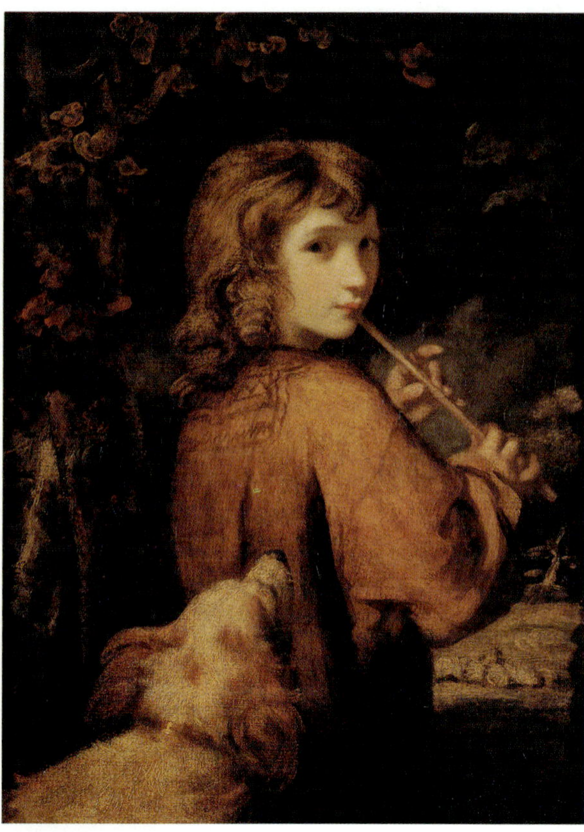

Plate 2
Shepherd Boy (The Young Shepherd)
Sir Joshua Reynolds

Plate 3
Piping Shepherd
Sir Joshua Reynolds

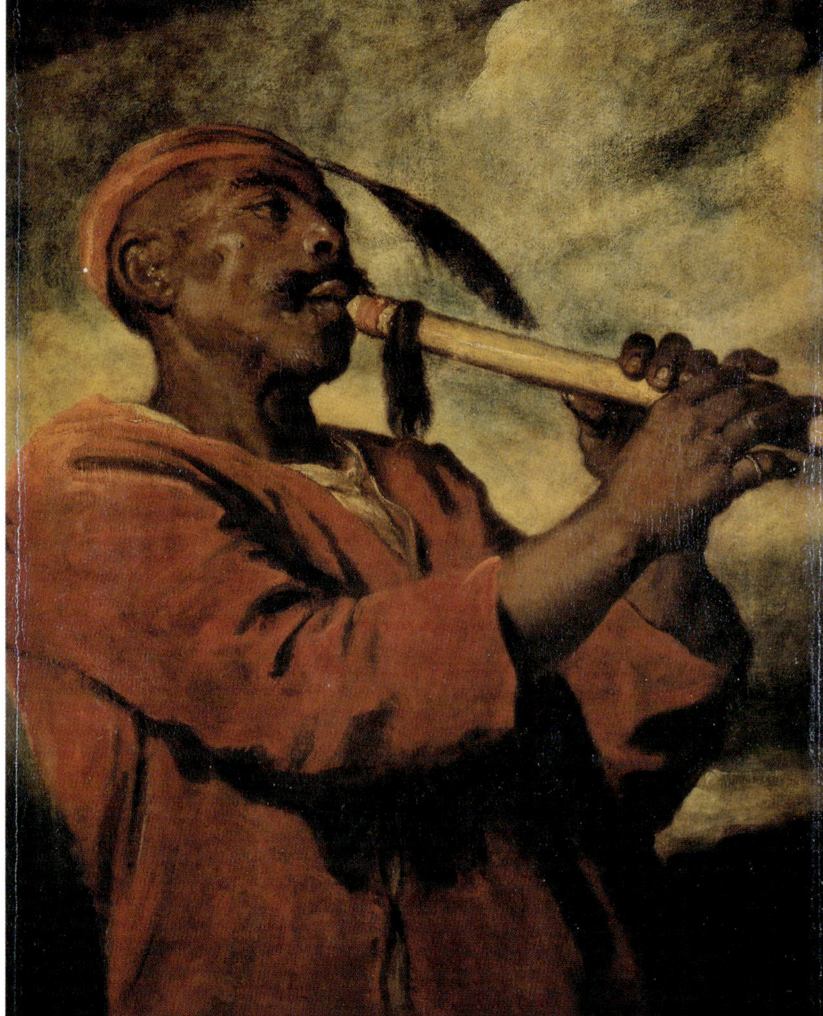

Plate 4
Moor playing a Pipe
Sir Joshua Reynolds

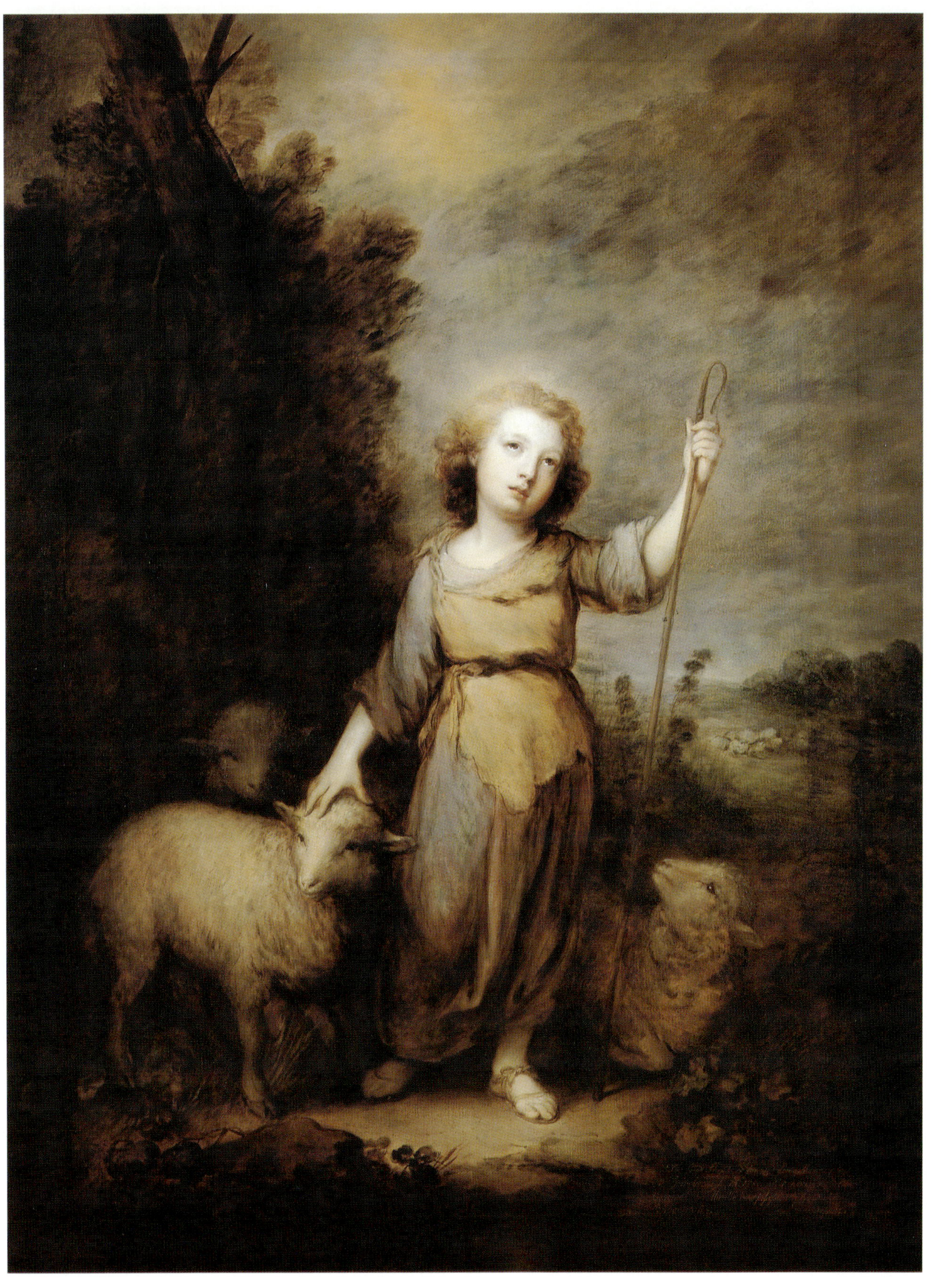

Plate 5
The Good Shepherd
Thomas Gainsborough

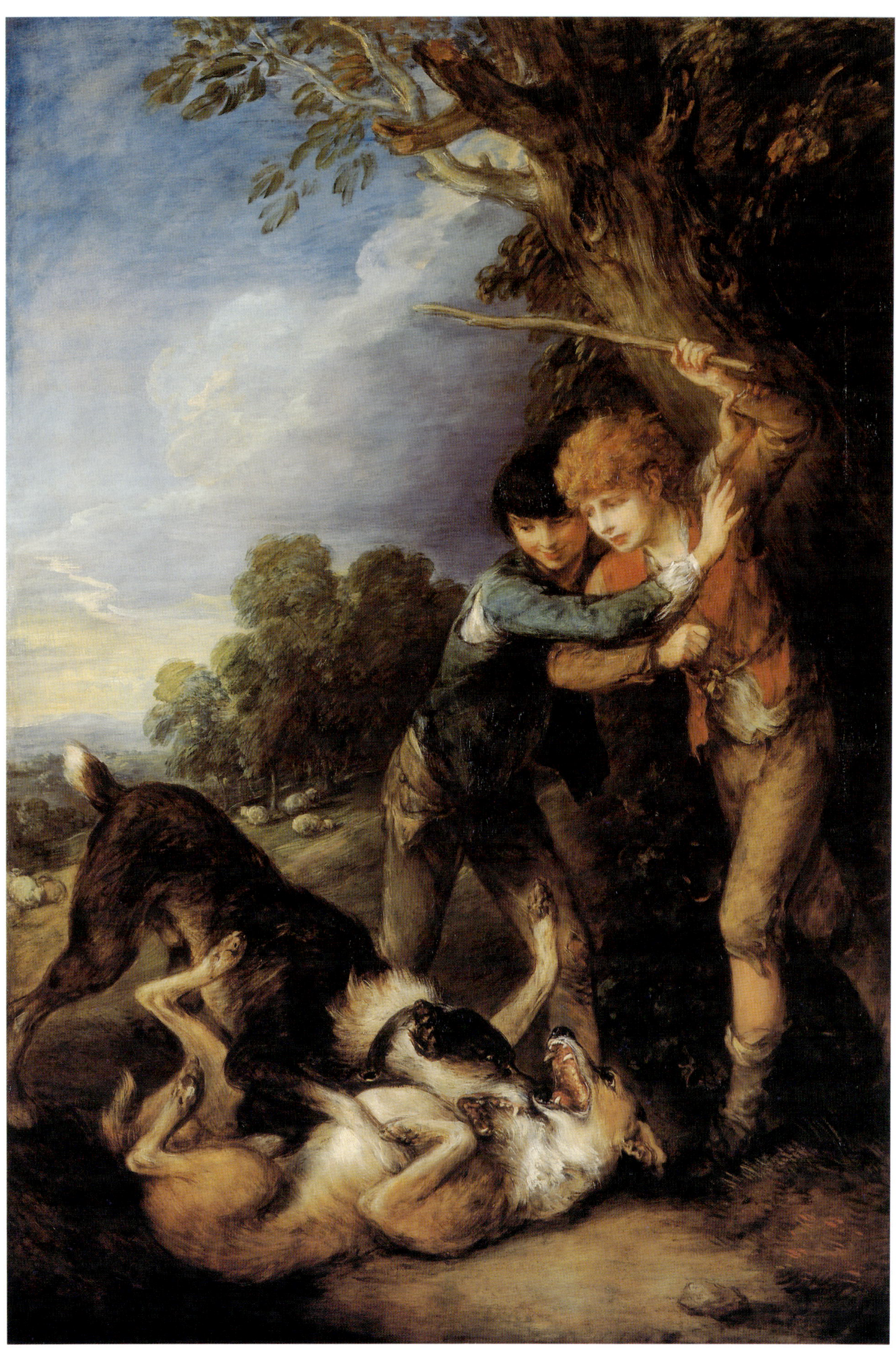

Plate 6   *Two Shepherd Boys with Dogs Fighting*   Thomas Gainsborough

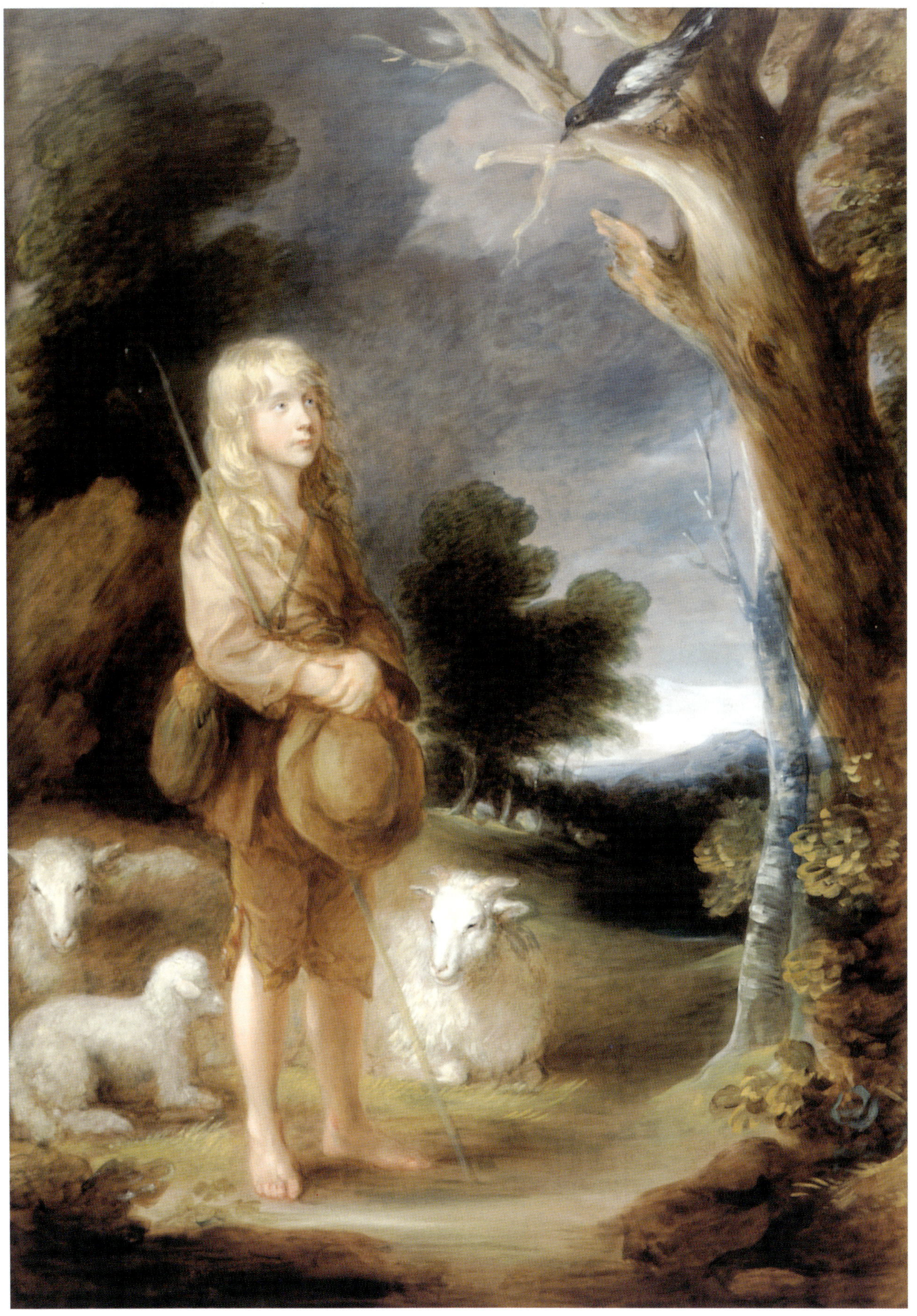

Plate 7
Shepherd Boy Listening to a Magpie
Gainsborough Dupont

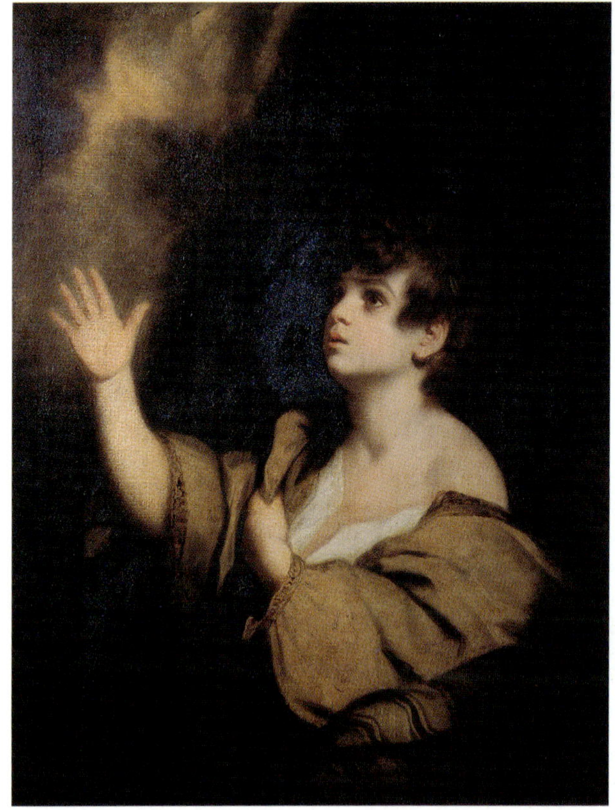

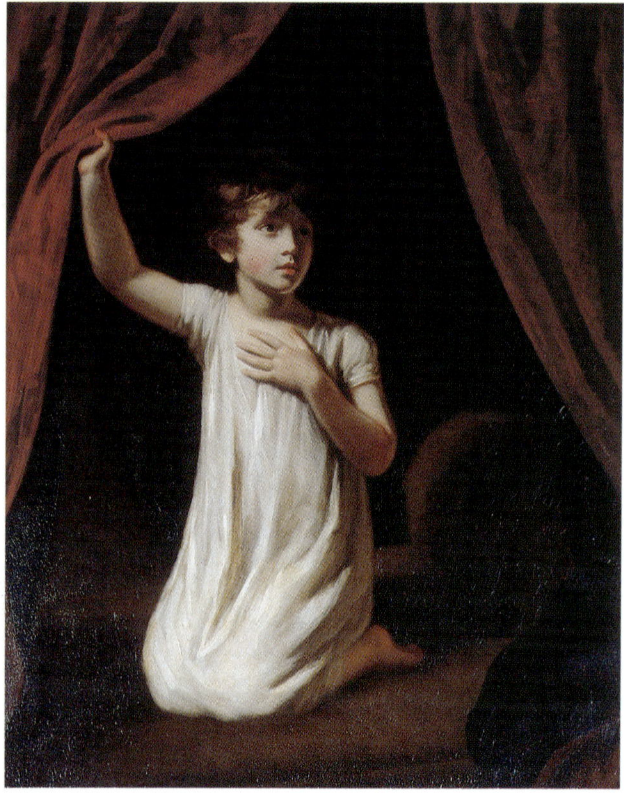

Plate 8
The Calling of Samuel
Sir Joshua Reynolds

Plate 9
The Calling of Samuel
John Opie

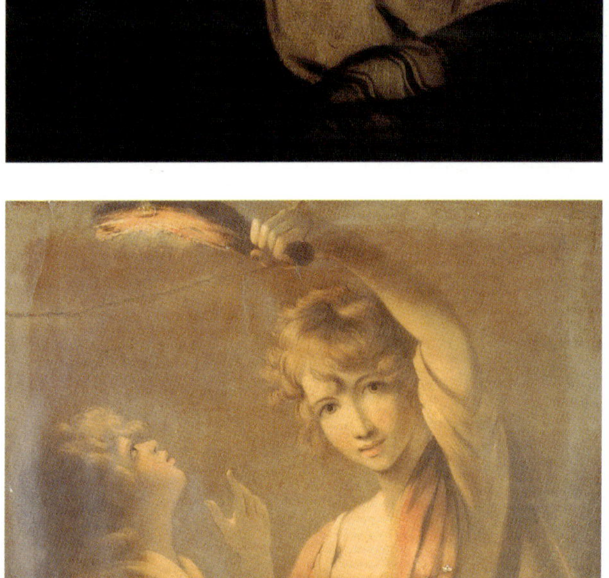

Plate 10
The Mischievous Girl
John Raphael Smith

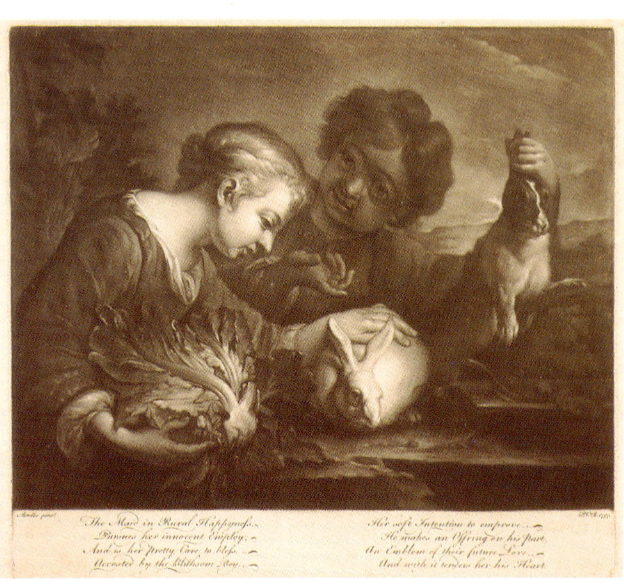

Plate 11
The Maid in Rural Happiness
Peter Van Bleek

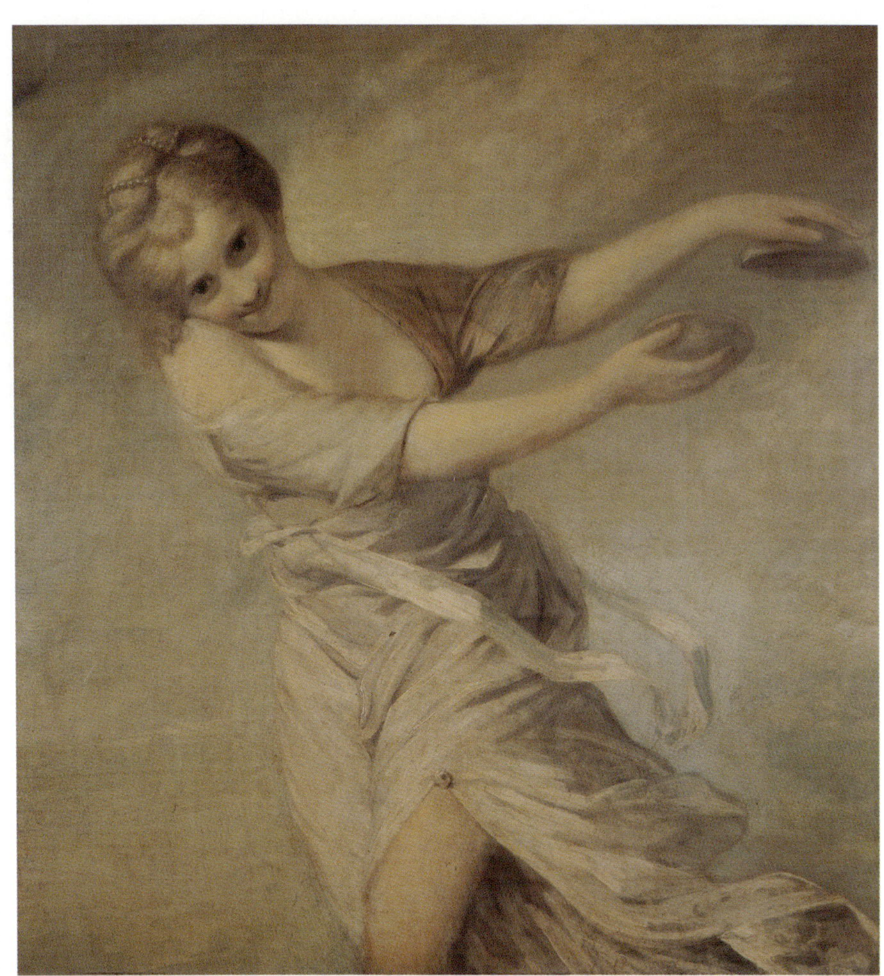

Plate 12
Euphrosyne
(also known as 'Terpsichore' and 'Comedy')
Sir Joshua Reynolds

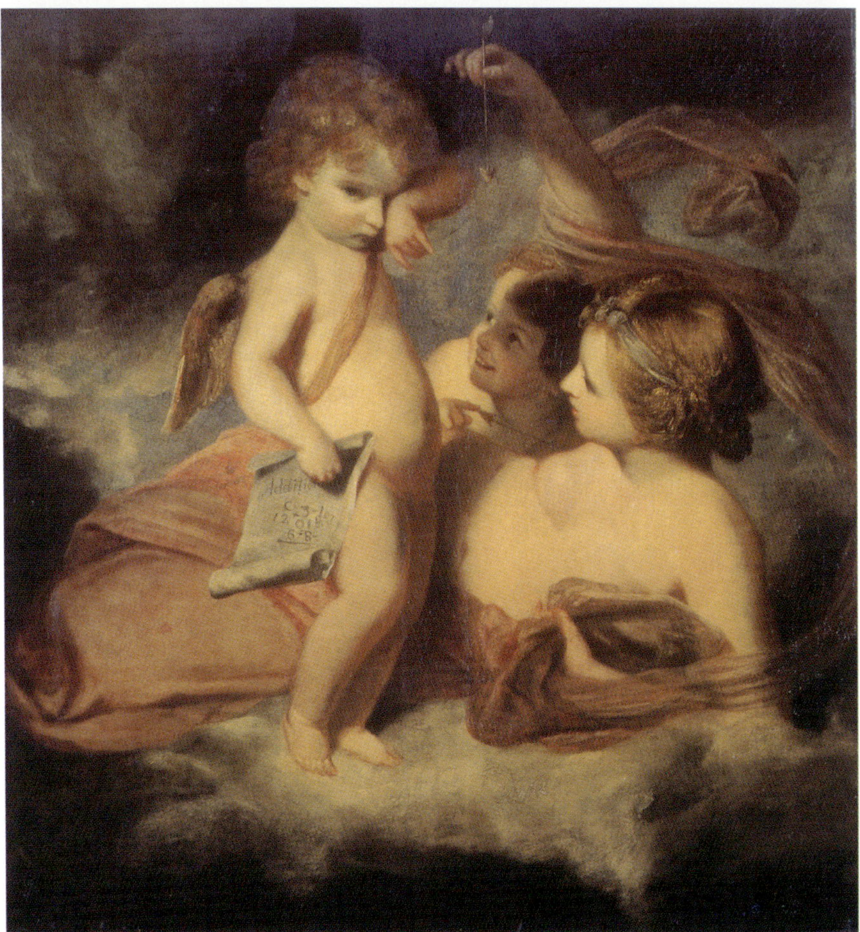

Plate 13
Venus Chiding Cupid for
Learning to Cast Accounts
Sir Joshua Reynolds

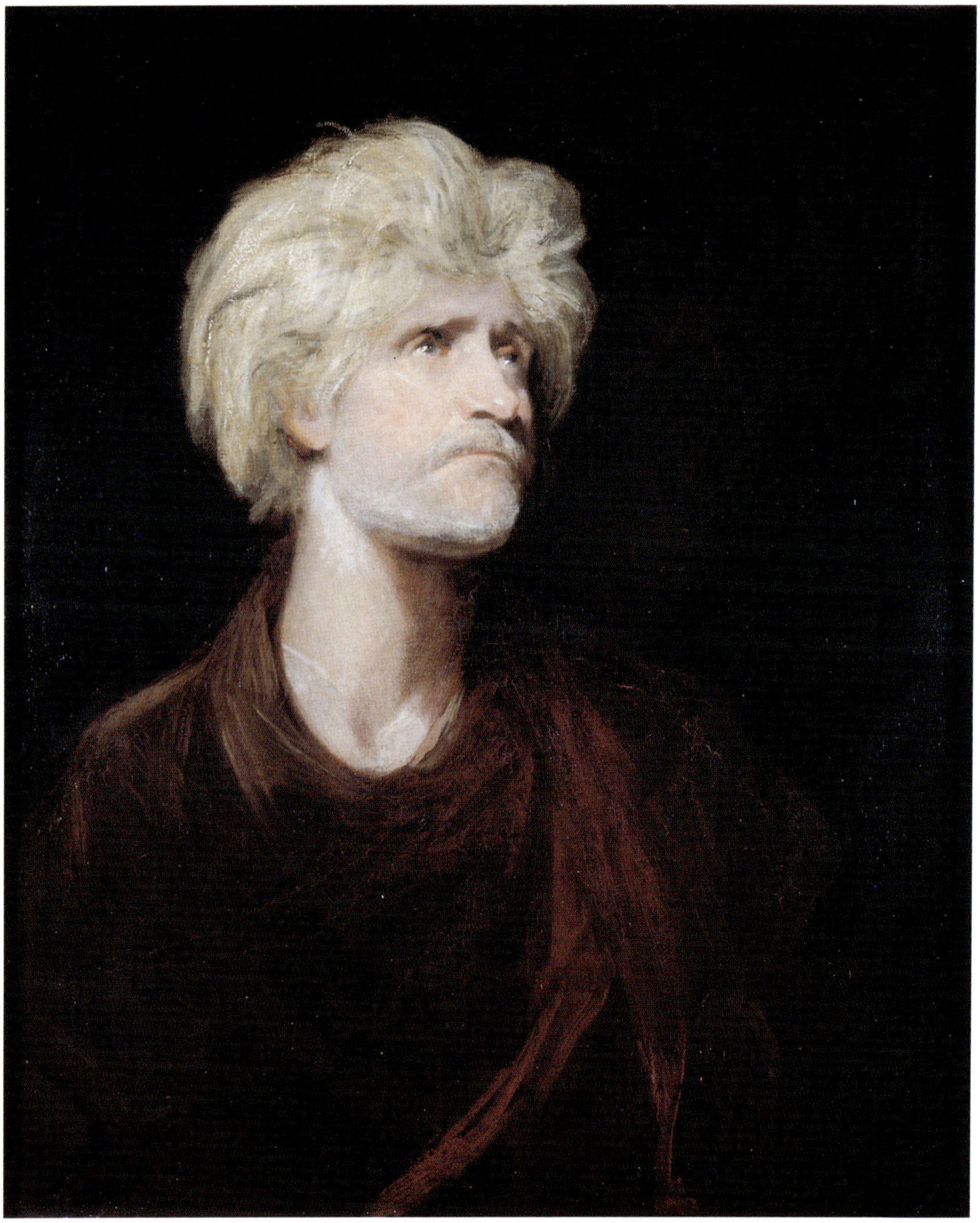

Plate 14
The Captive
Sir Joshua Reynolds

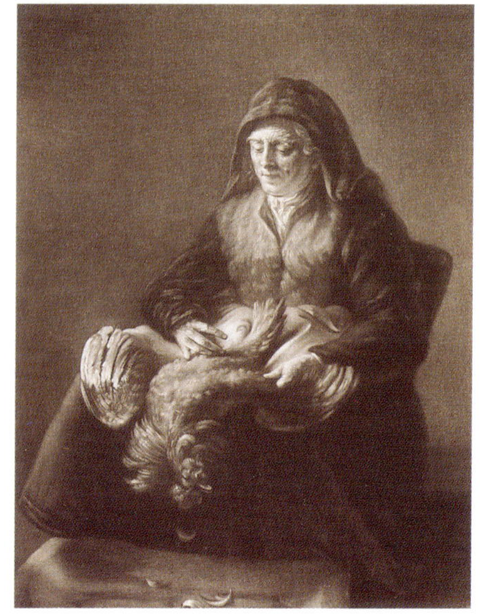

Plate 15
Old Woman Plucking a Fowl
Richard Houston

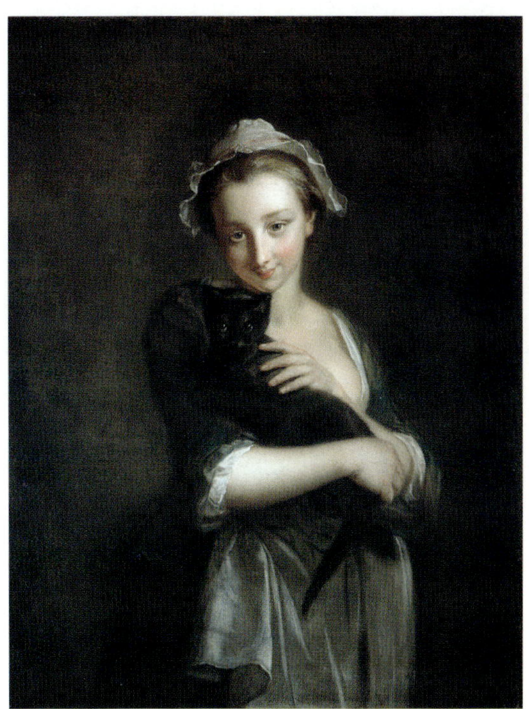

Plate 16
Girl with a cat
Philip Mercier

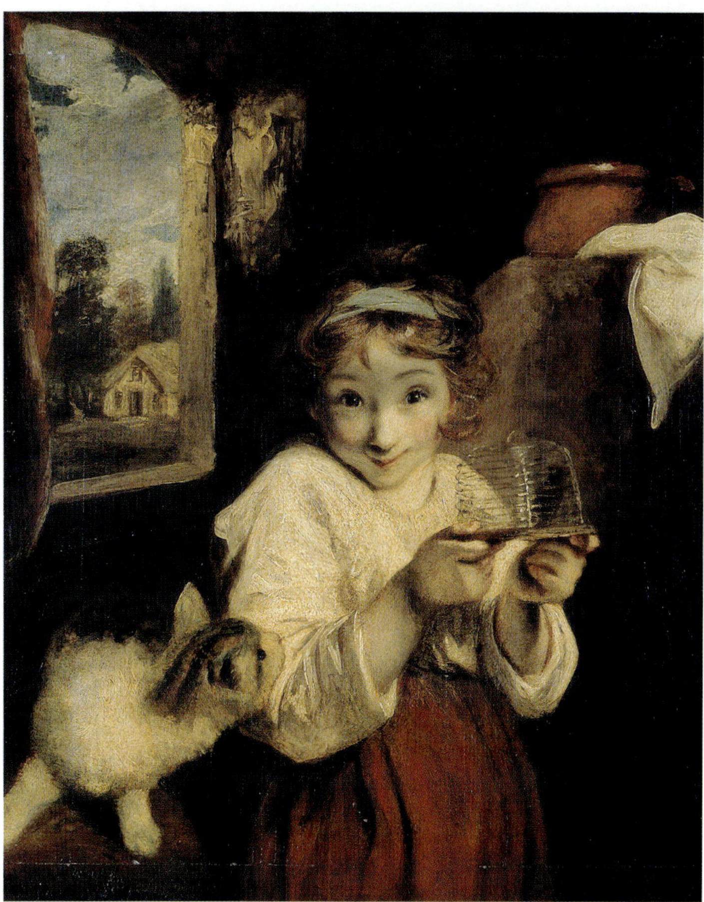

Plate 17
Muscipula
Joshua Reynolds

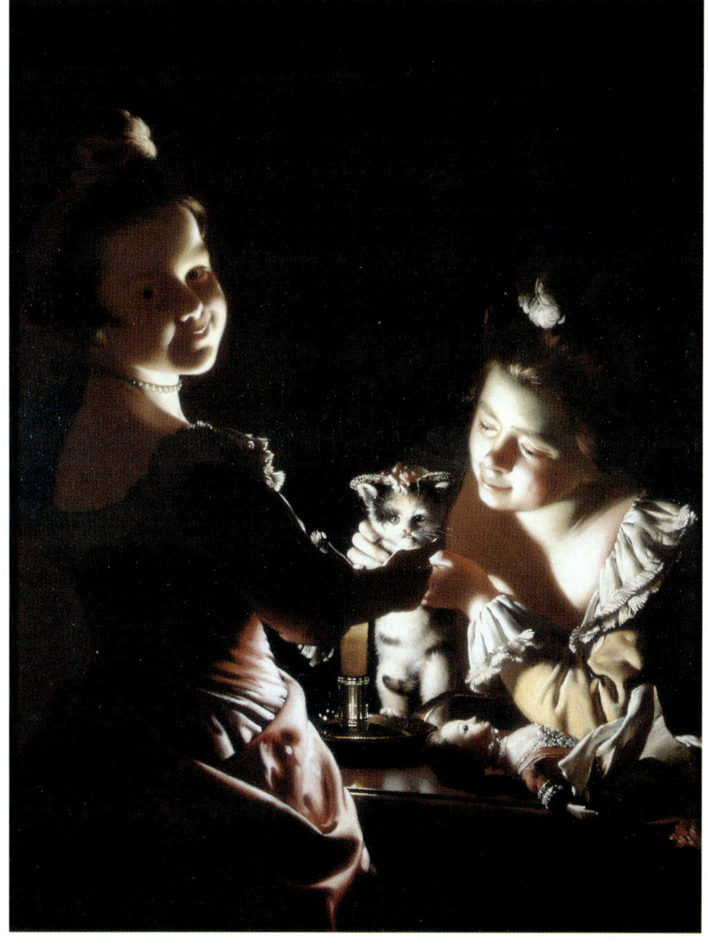

Plate 18
Two Girls Dressing a Kitten by Candlelight
Joseph Wright

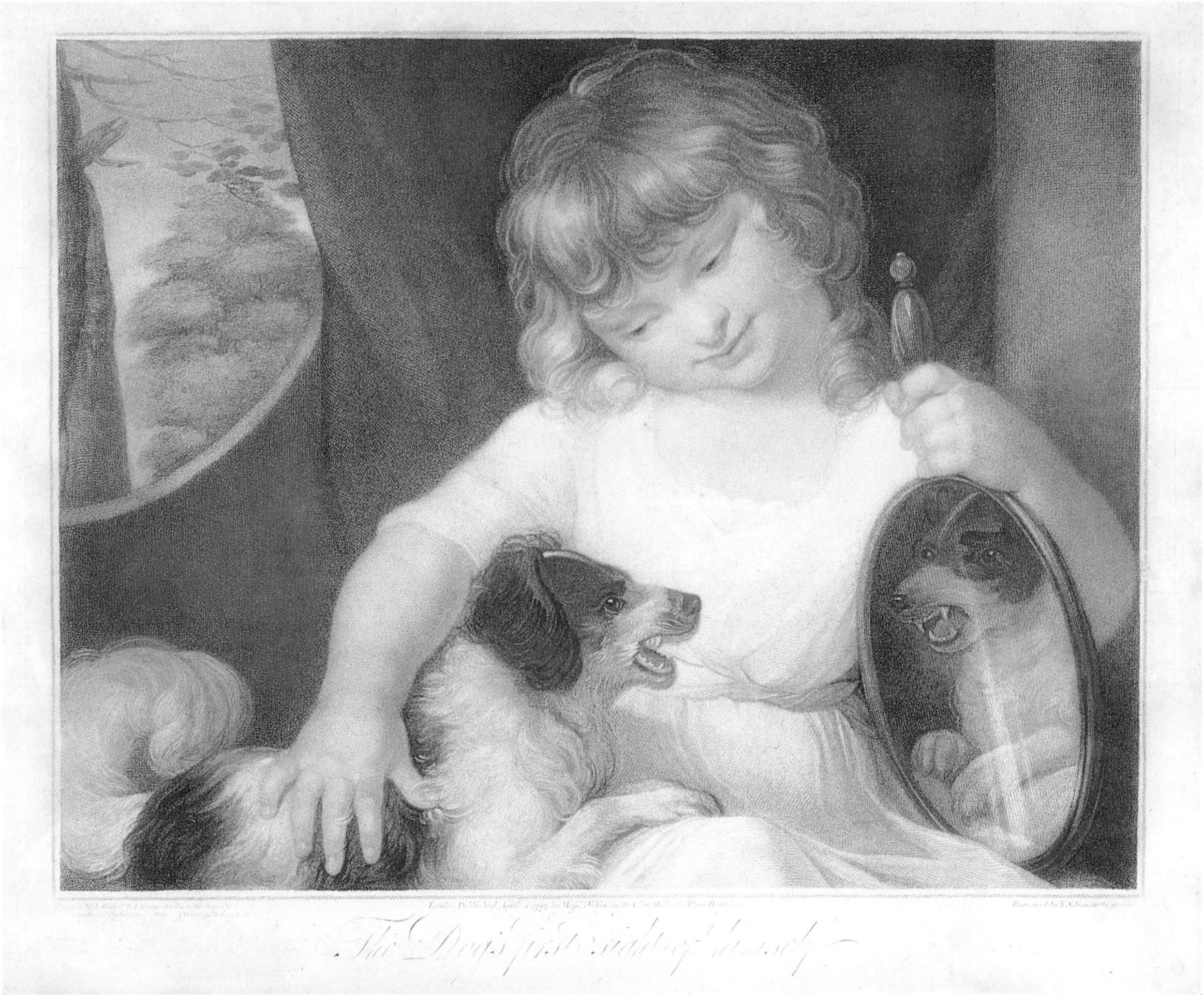

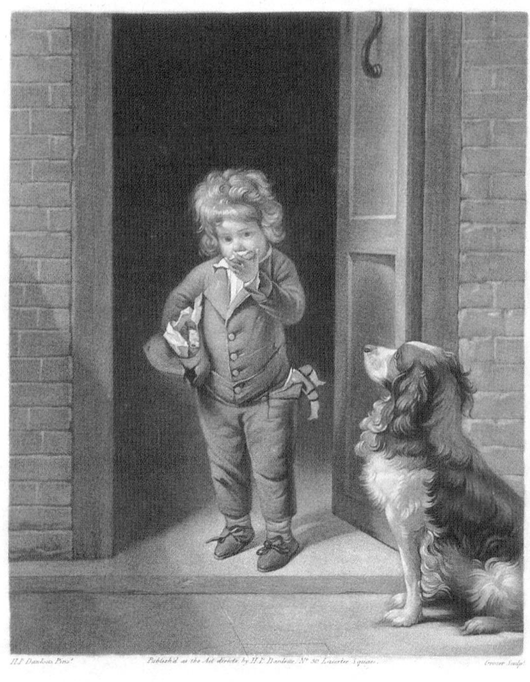

Plate 19   *The Dog's First Sight of himself*   Niccolo Schiavonetti

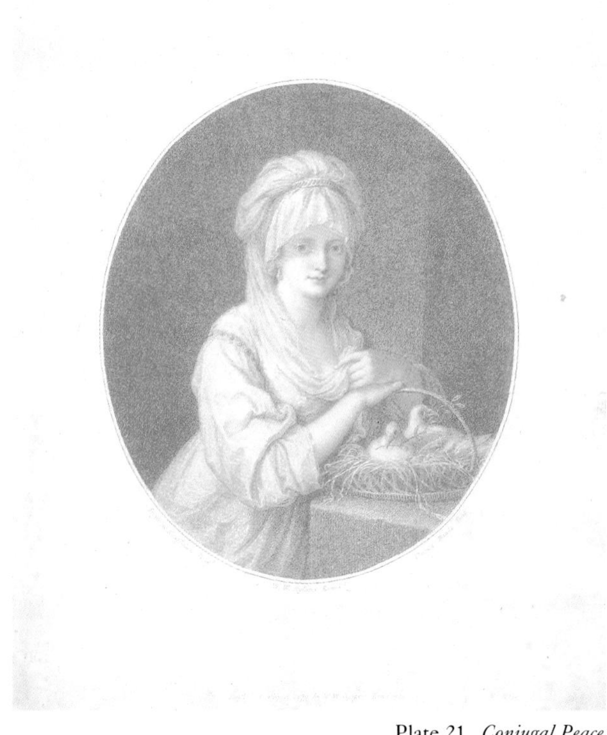

Plate 20 *The Envied Glutton*
Joseph Grozer

Plate 21 *Conjugal Peace*
Thomas Burke

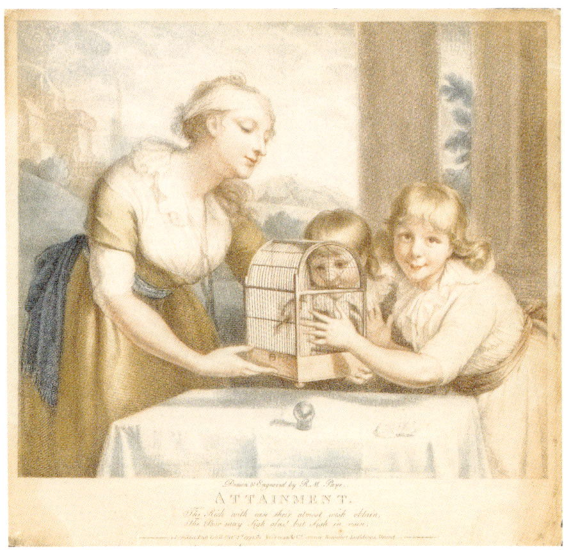

Plate 22
Attainment
Richard Morton Paye

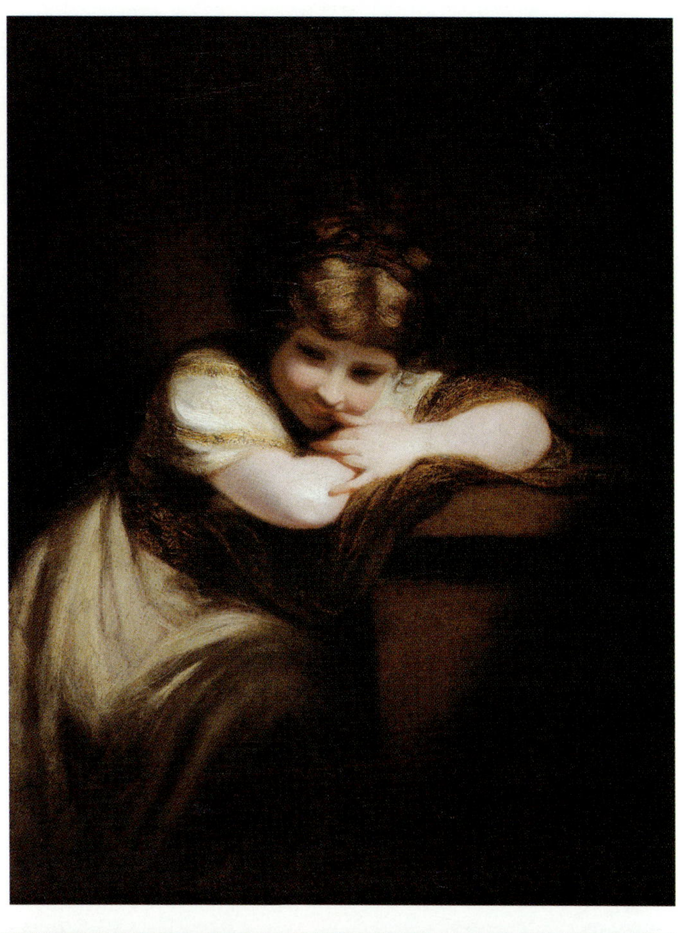

Plate 23
A Girl leaning on a Pedestal ('The Laughing Girl')
Sir Joshua Reynolds

Plate 24
A Piping Boy
Hugh Robinson

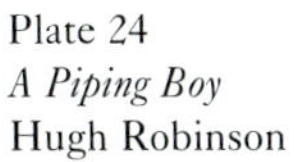

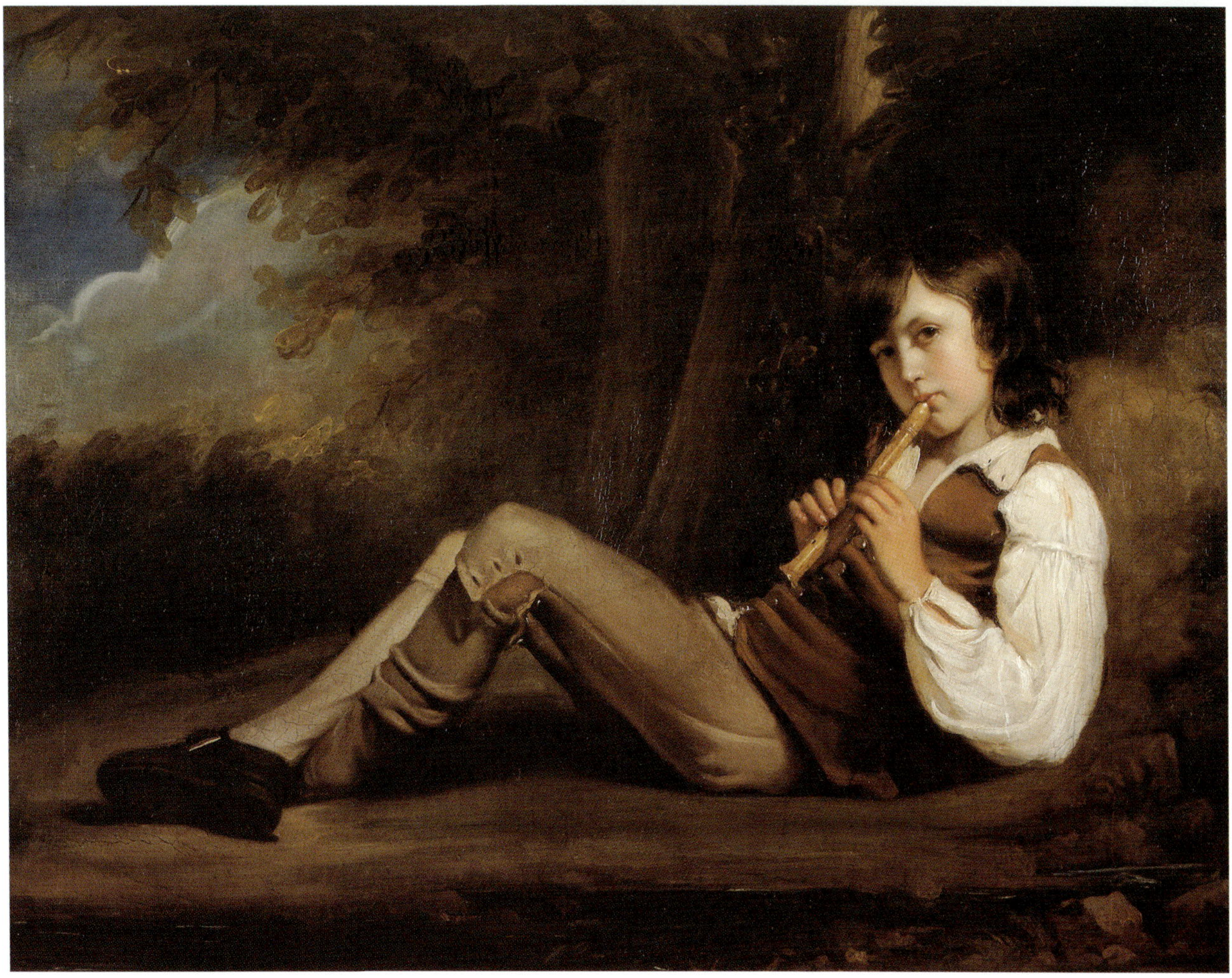

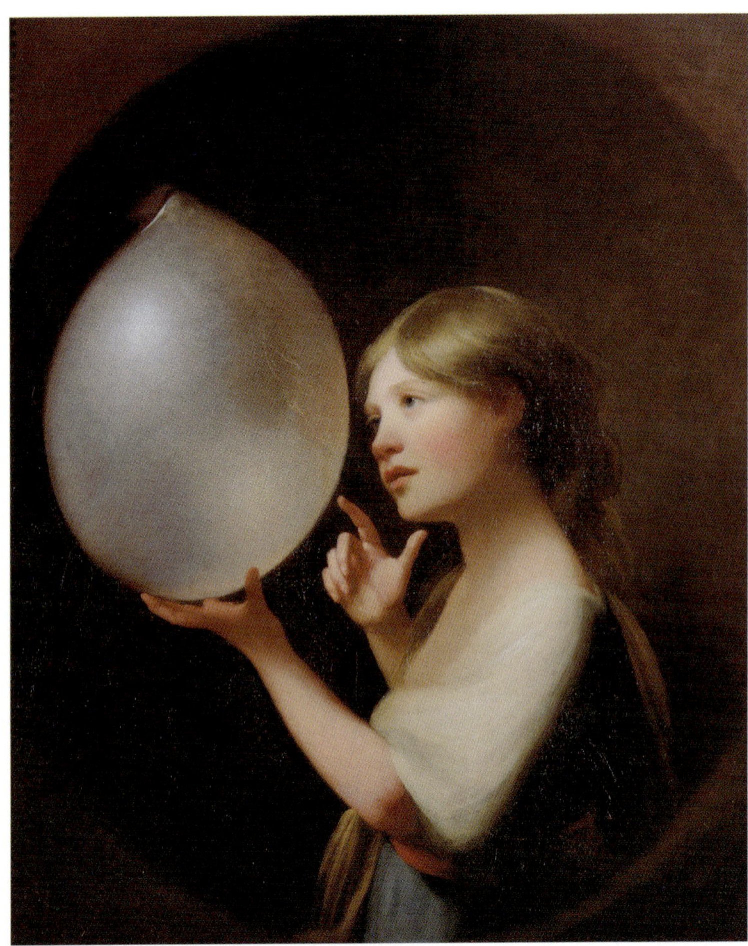

Plate 25 *Girl looking through a Bladder*
Plate 26 *Boy blowing a Bladder*
Joseph Wright 'of Derby'

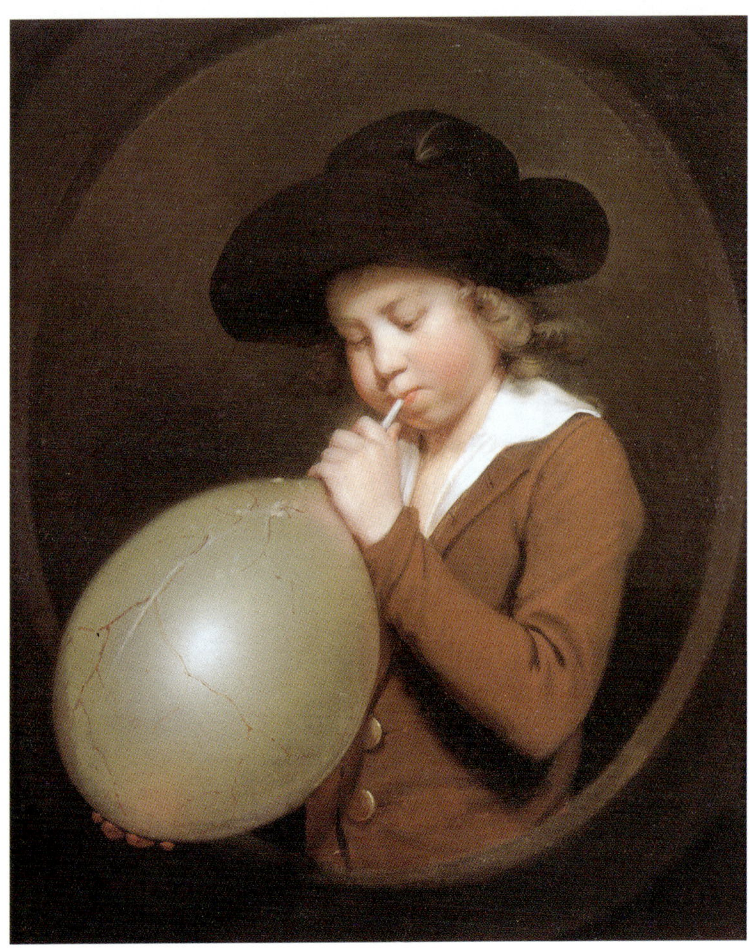

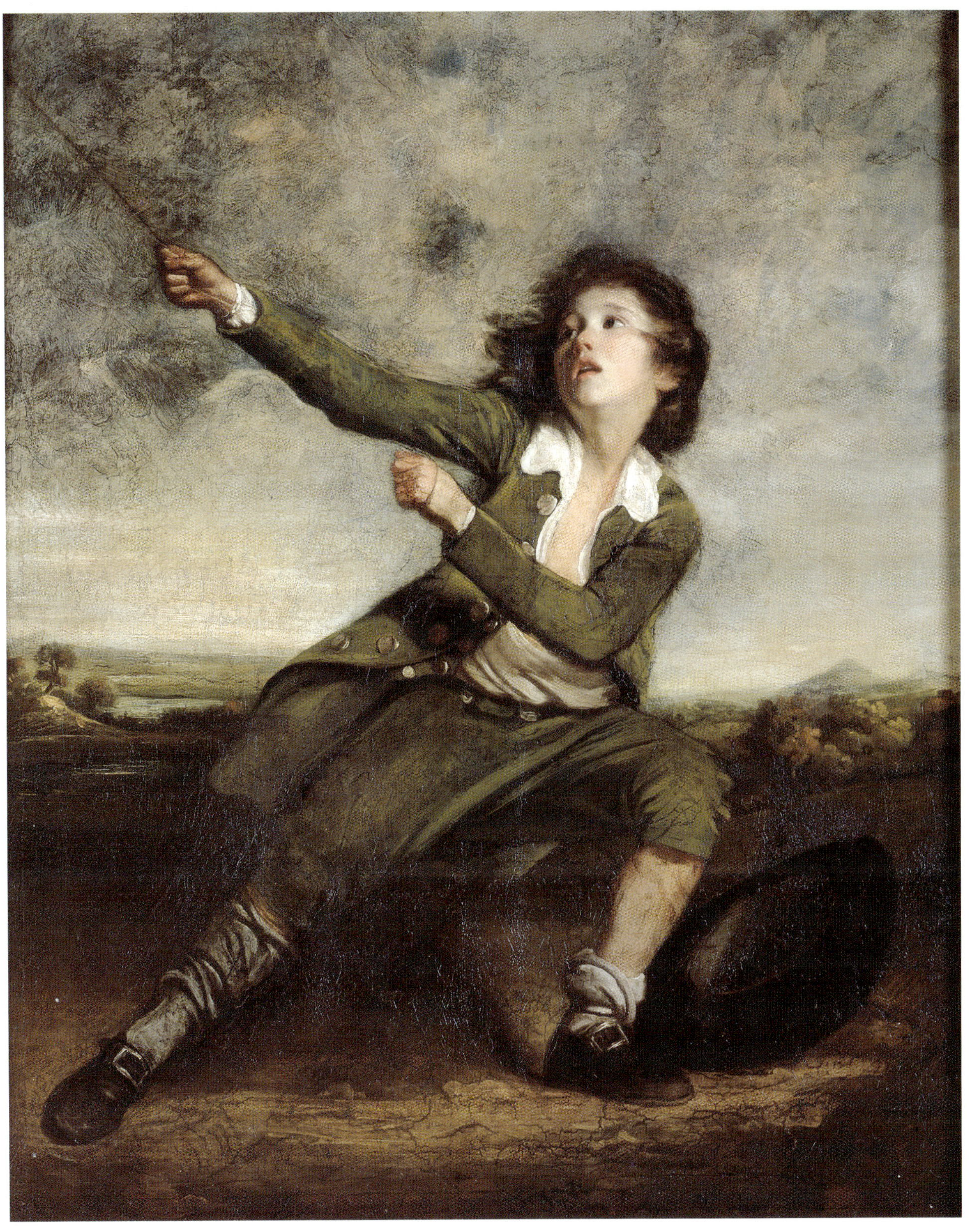

Plate 27
Boy Flying a Kite
Hugh Robinson

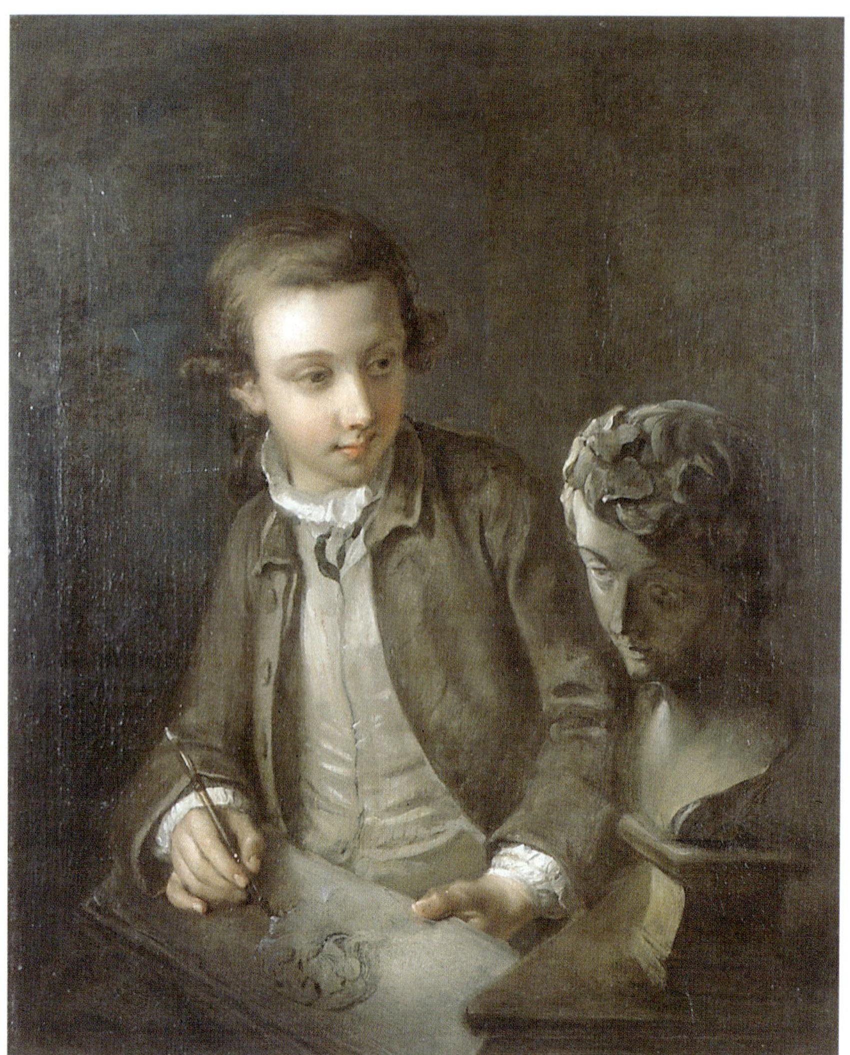

Plate 28
Young Artist
Philip Mercier

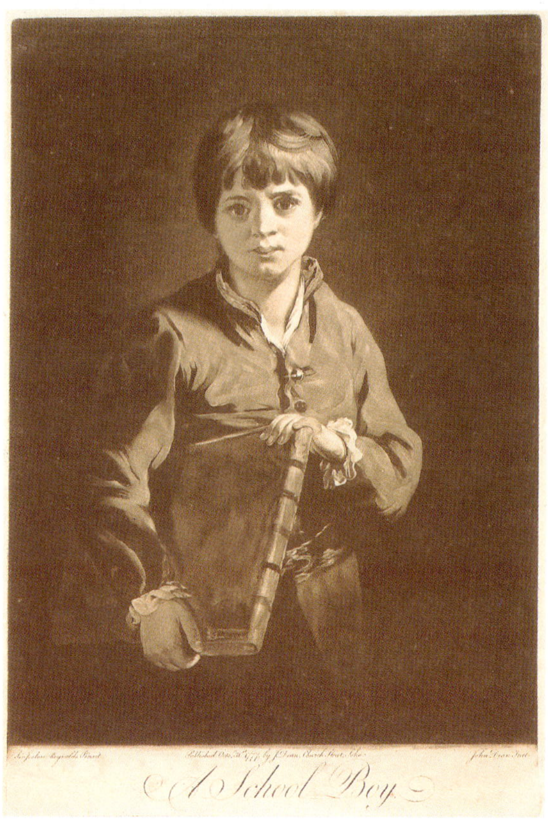

Plate 29   *The School Boy*   John Dean

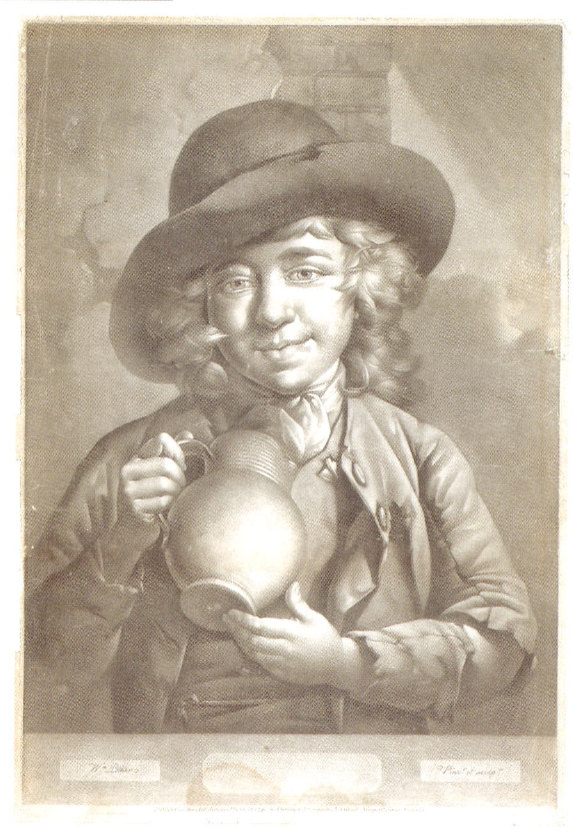

Plate 30   *Felicity*   William Pether

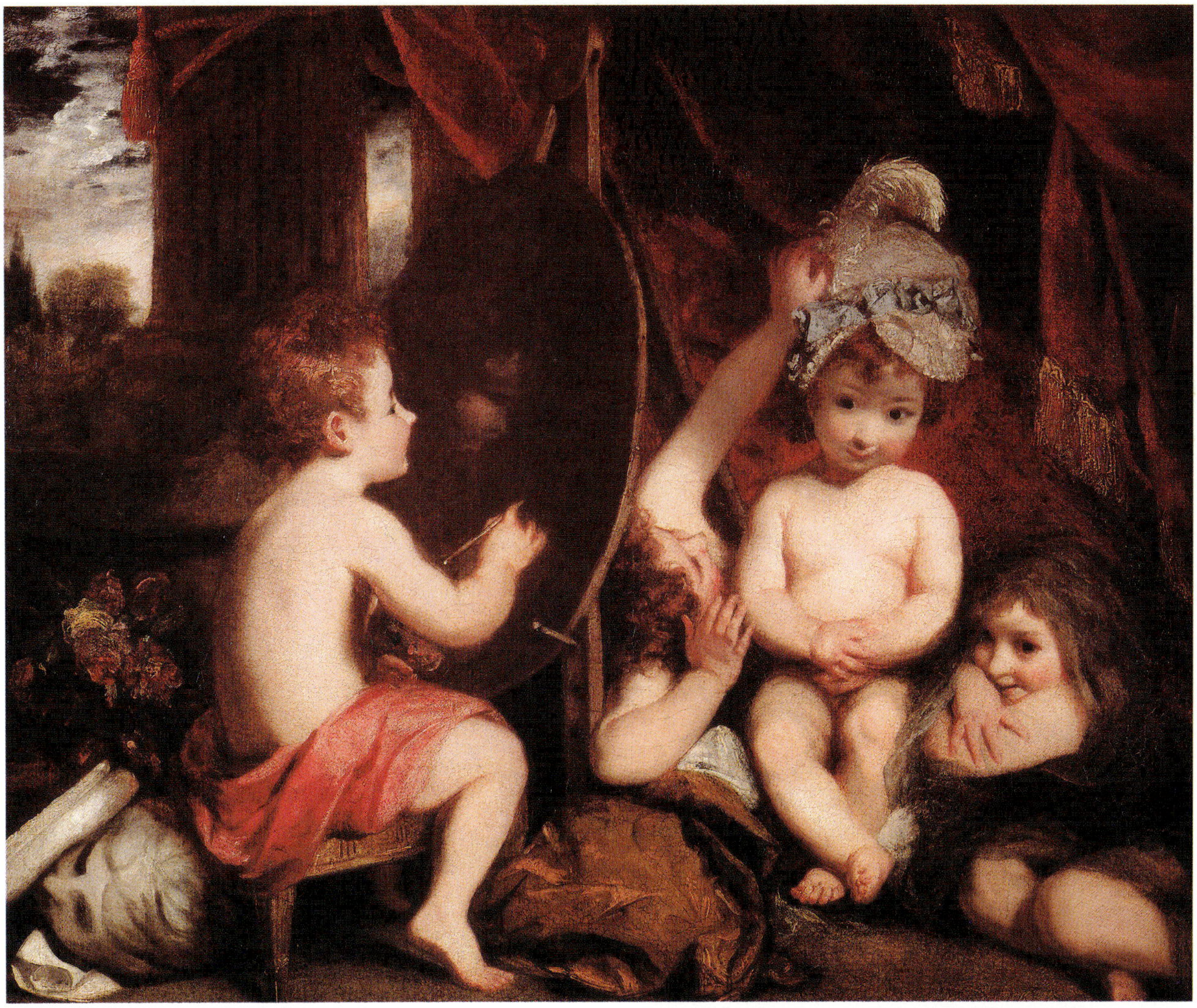

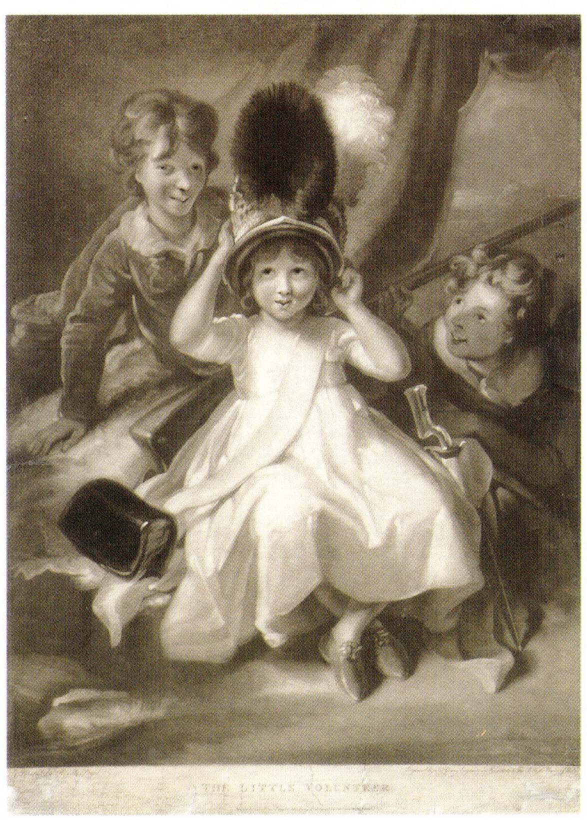

Plate 31
Infant Academy
Sir Joshua Reynolds

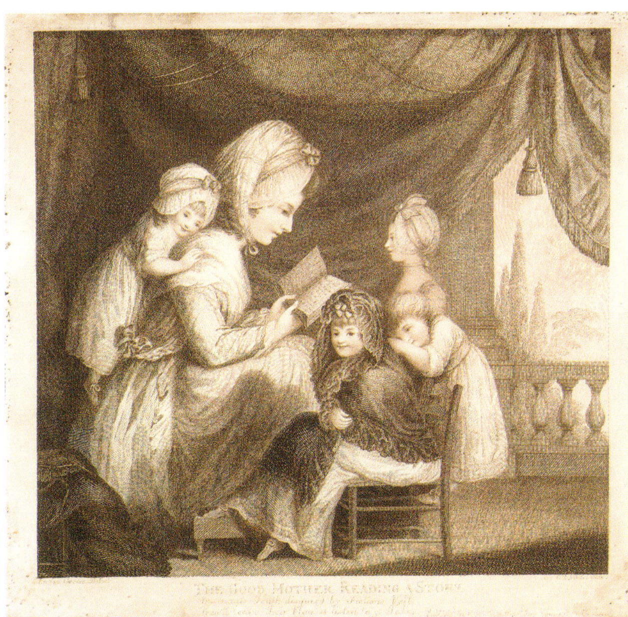

Plate 32   *The Good Mother Reading a Story*   Charles William White

Plate 33   *The Little Volunteer*   John Young

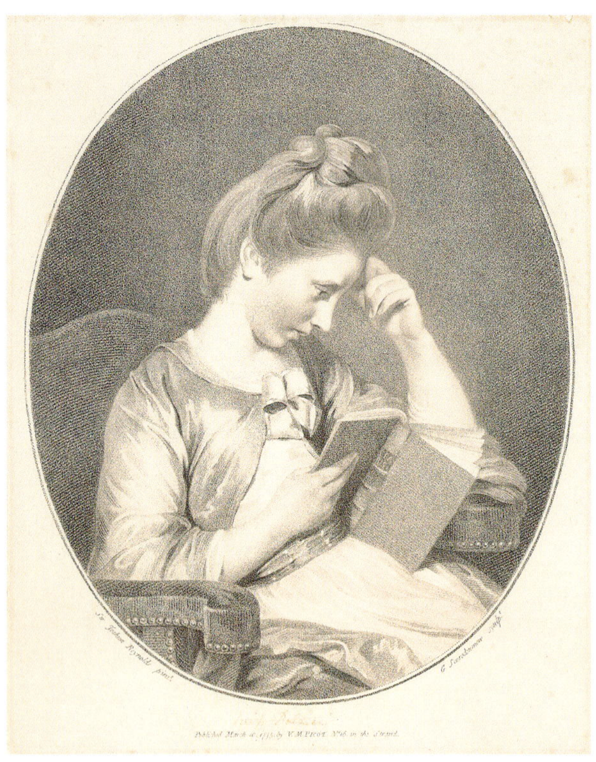

Plate 34
Girl Reading (Reading Clarissa Harlowe)
Garril Scorodumov

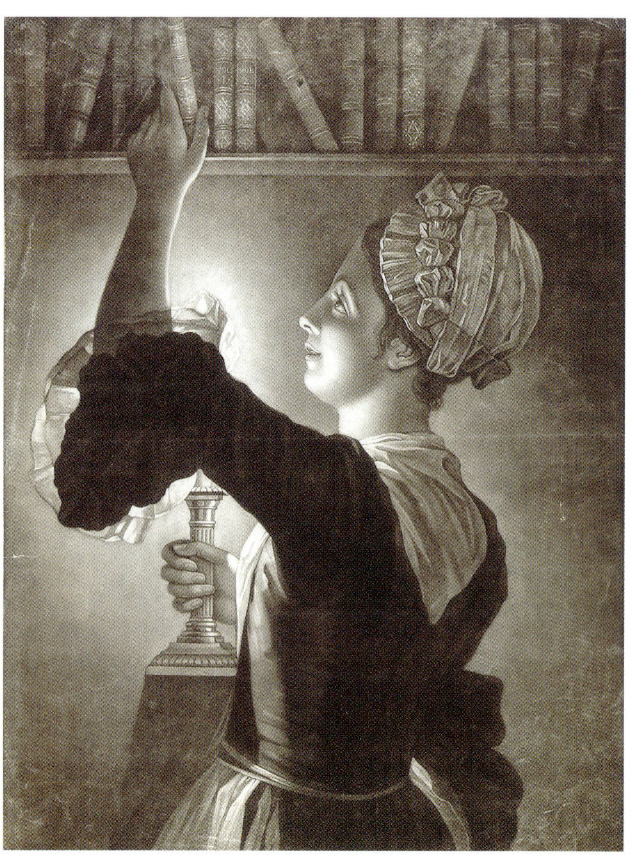

Plate 35
Female Lucubration
Philip Dawe

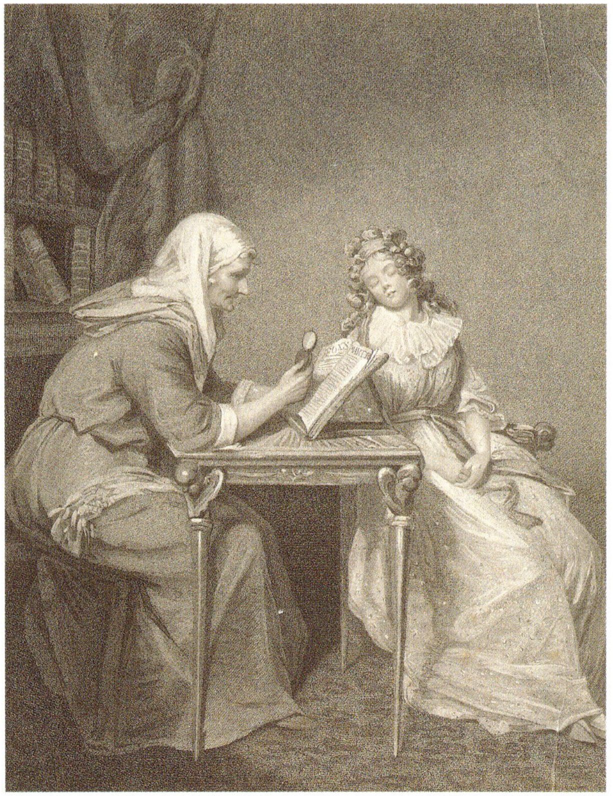

Plate 36   *Inattention*
Robert Meadows

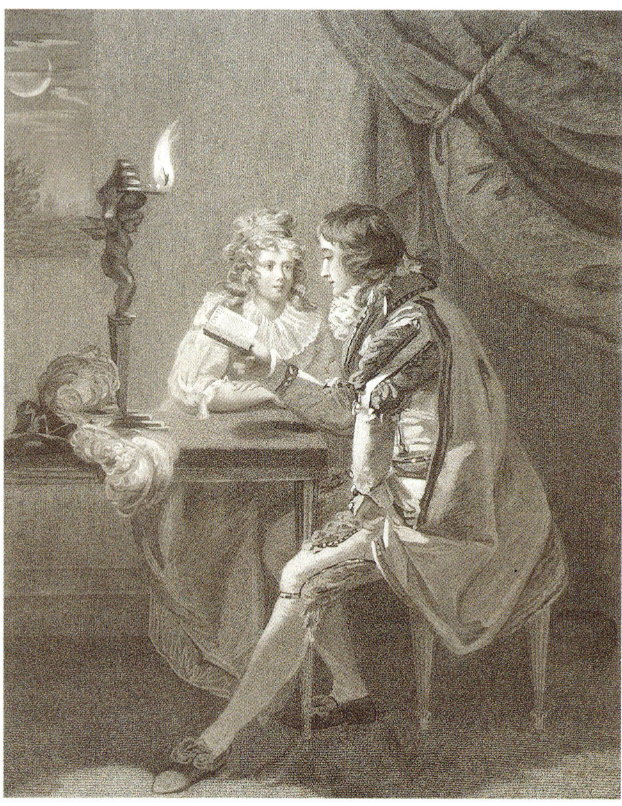

Plate 37   *Attention*
Robert Meadows

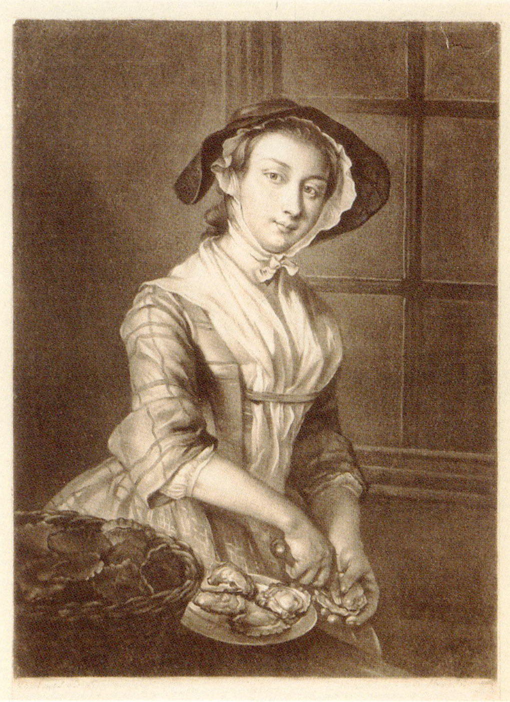

Plate 38
Native Meltons
Richard Houston

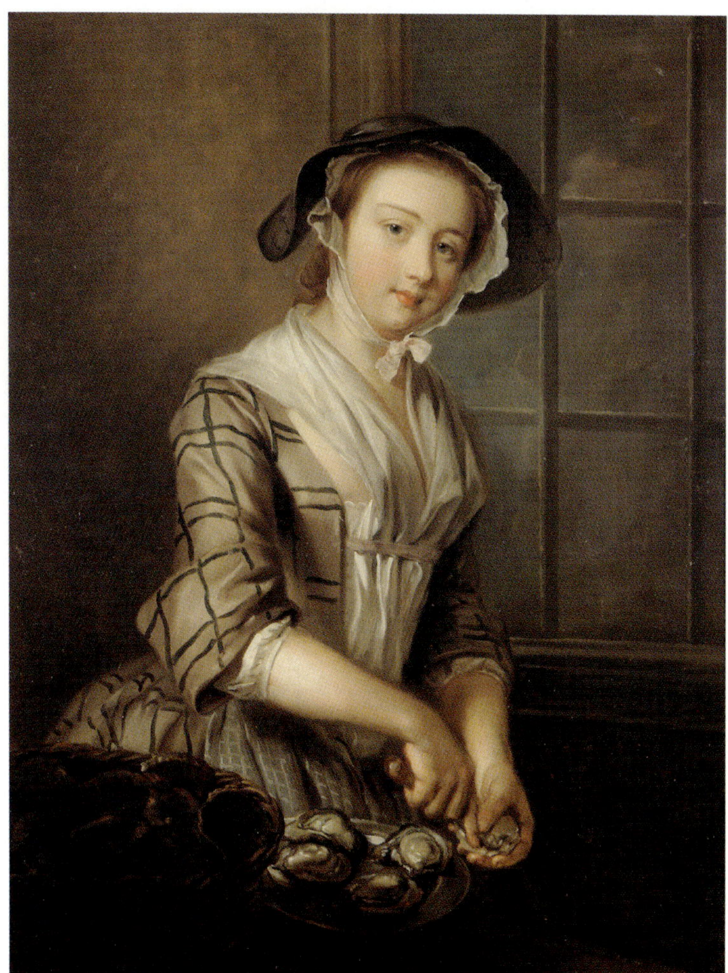

Plate 39
The Oyster Girl
Philip Mercier

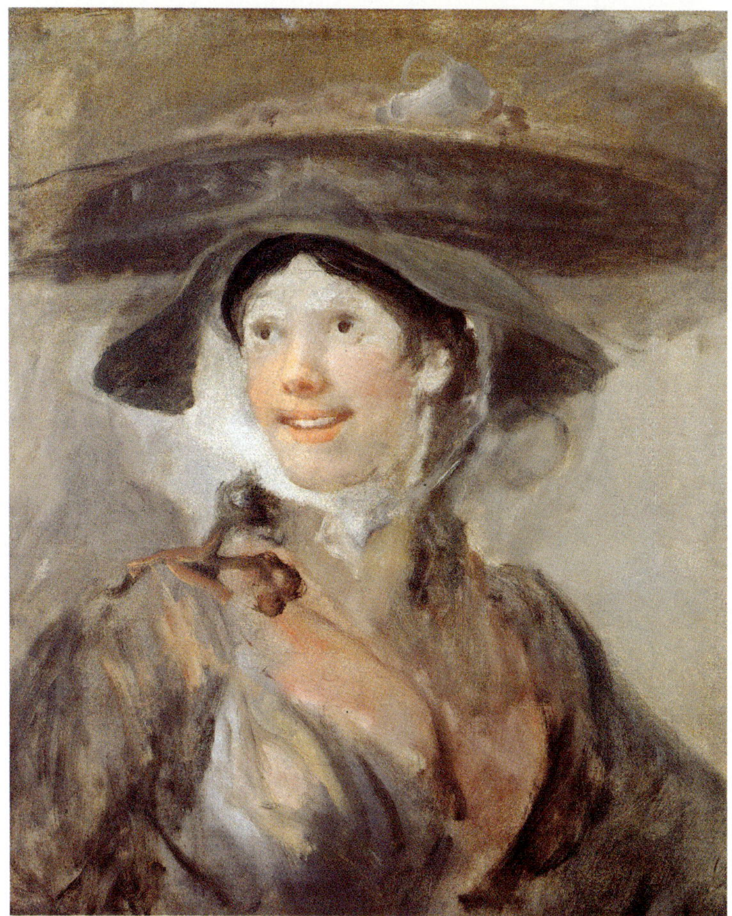

Plate 40
The Shrimp Girl
William Hogarth

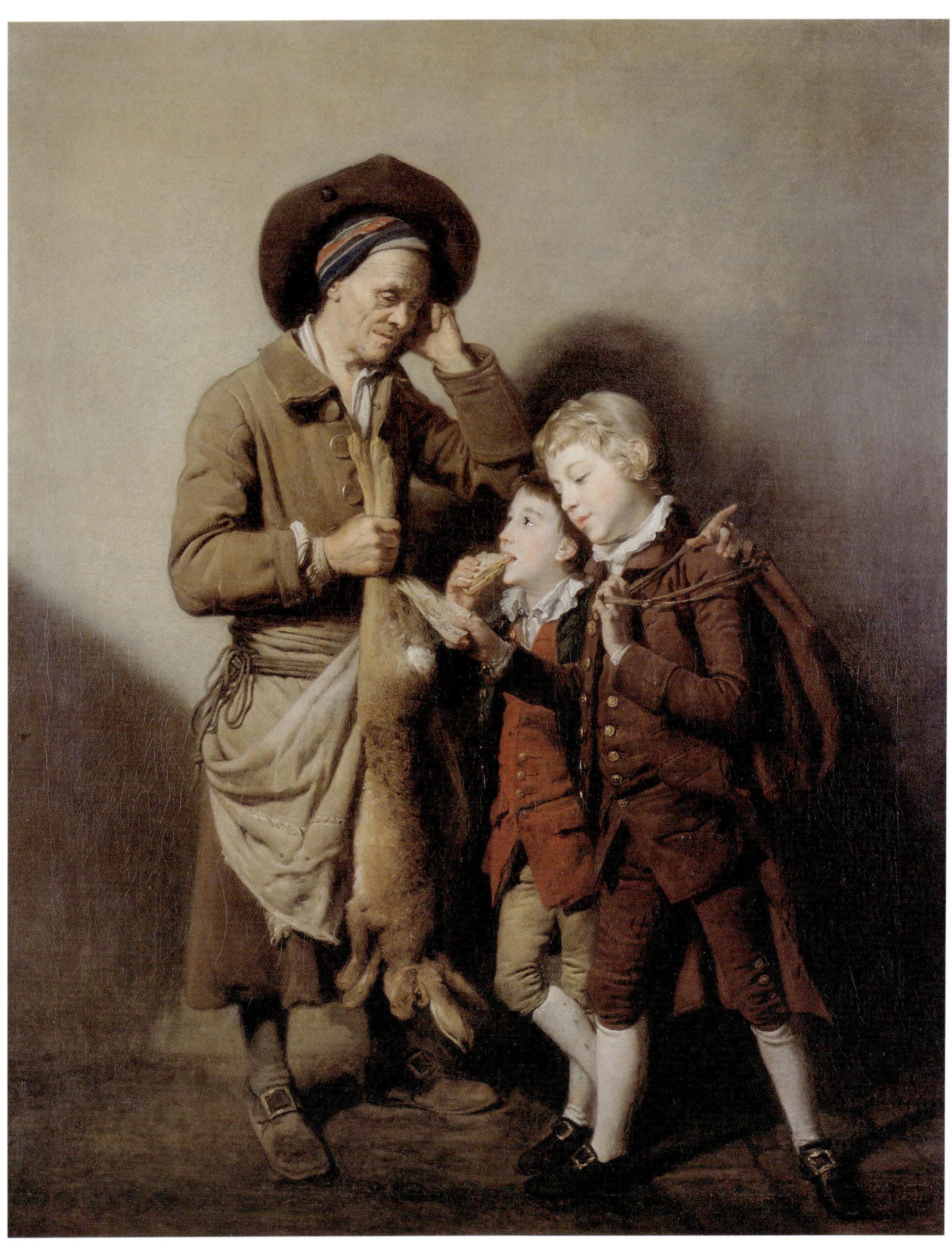

Plate 41
Porter with a Hare
Johan Zoffany

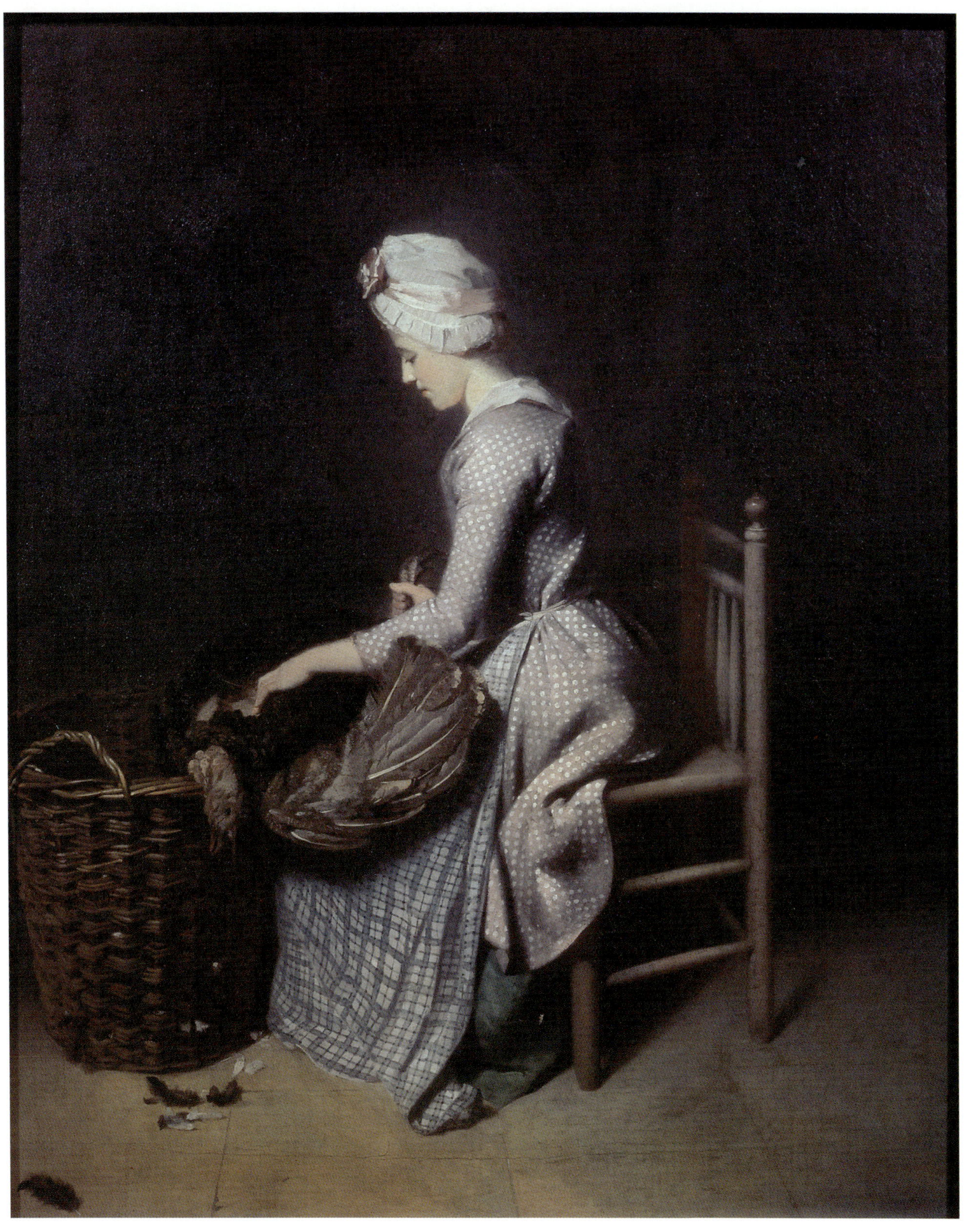

Plate 42
A Girl Plucking a Turkey
Henry Walton

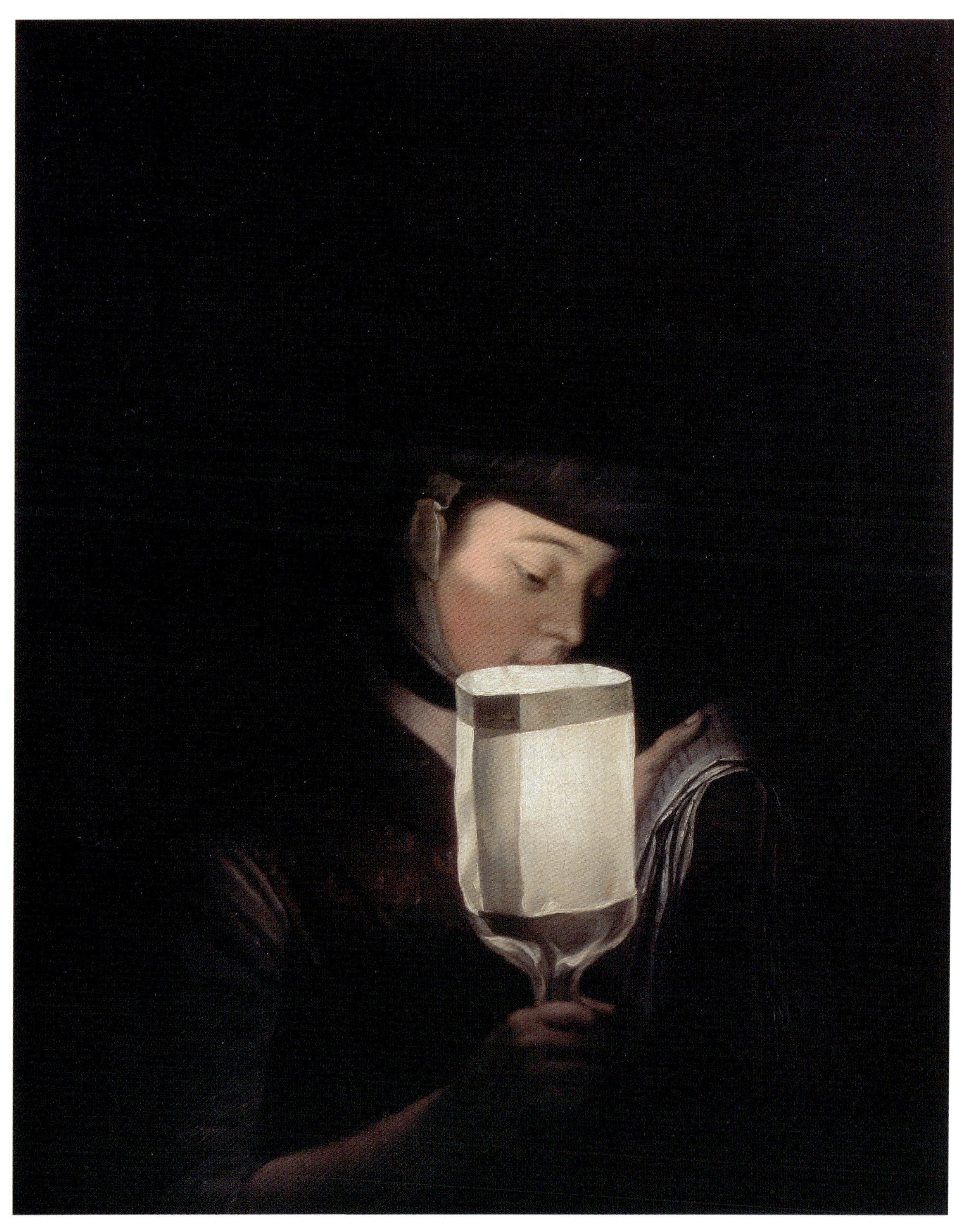

Plate 43
Girl Singing Ballads by a Lanthorn
Henry Robert Morland

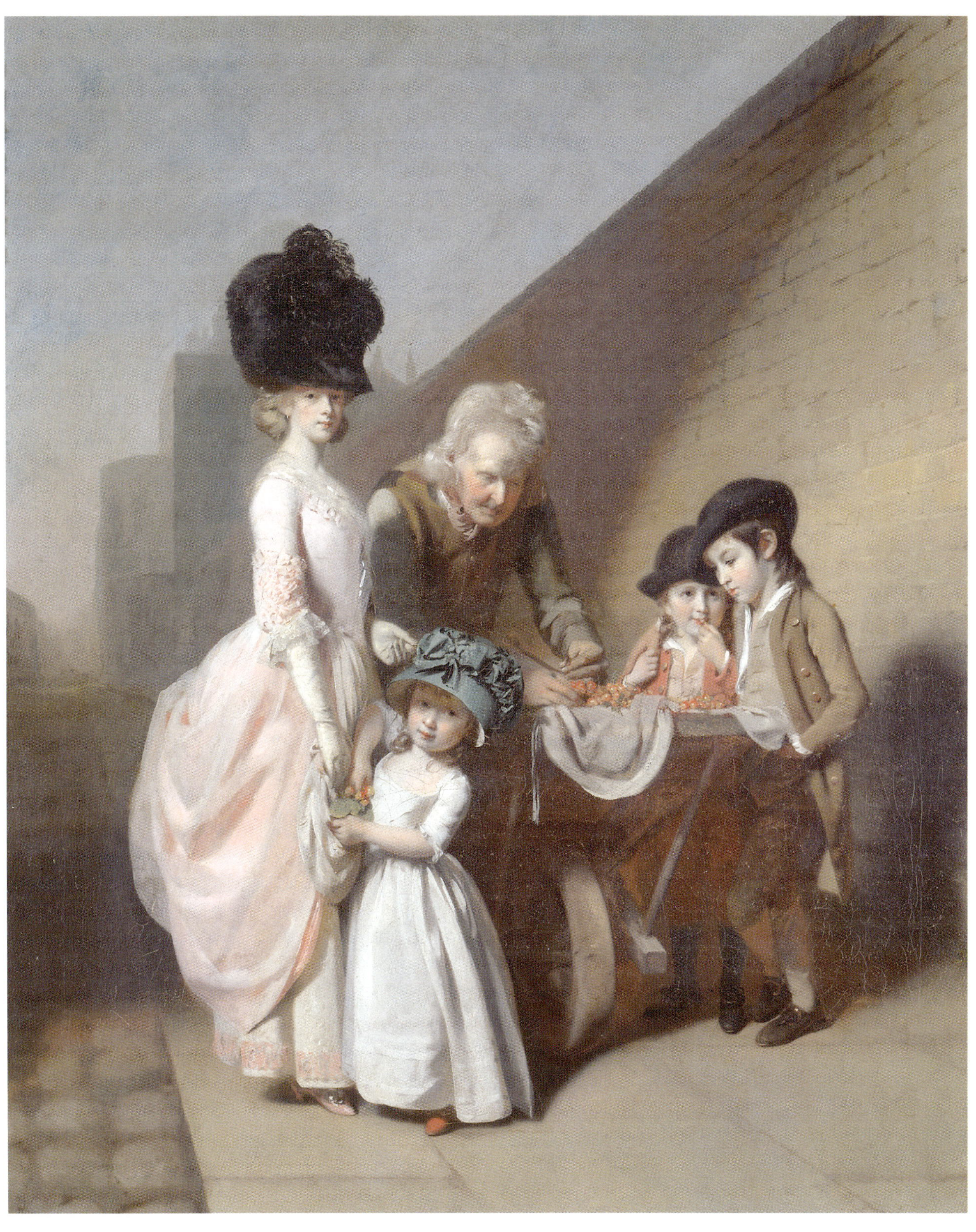

Plate 44
The Cherry Barrow
Henry Walton

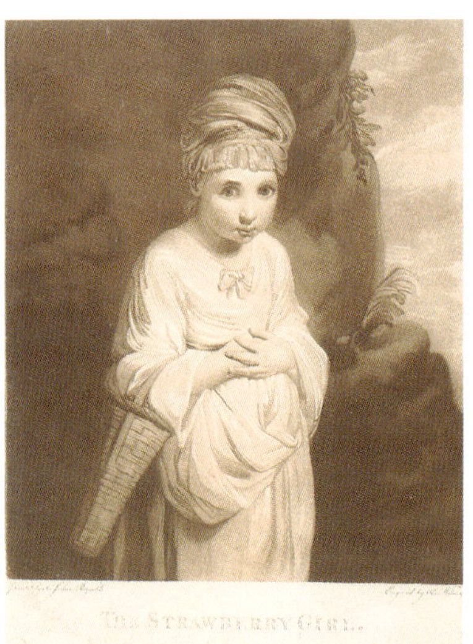

Plate 45
The Strawberry Girl
Thomas Watson

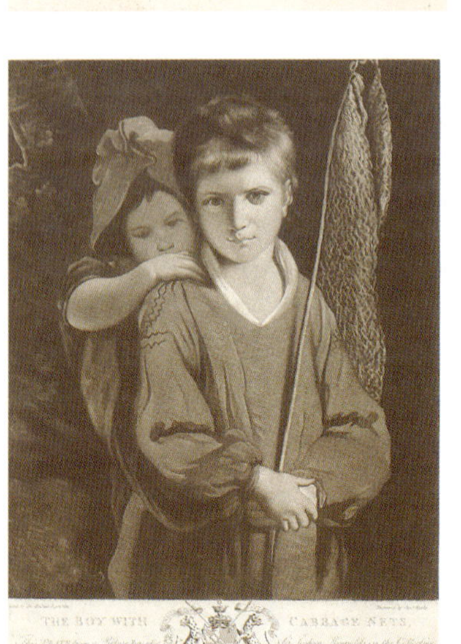

Plate 46
The Boy with Cabbage Nets
Charles Hardy

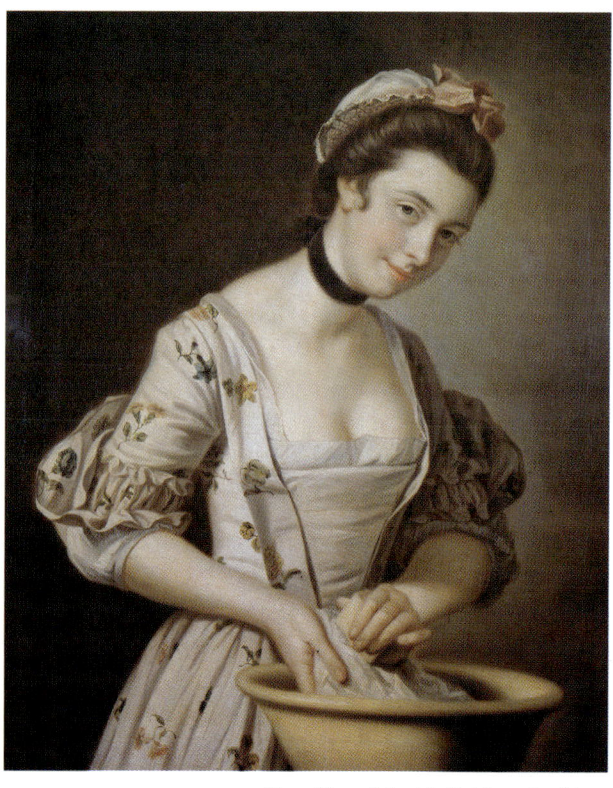

Plate 47
A Girl Sewing (The Sewing Lesson)
Philip Mercier

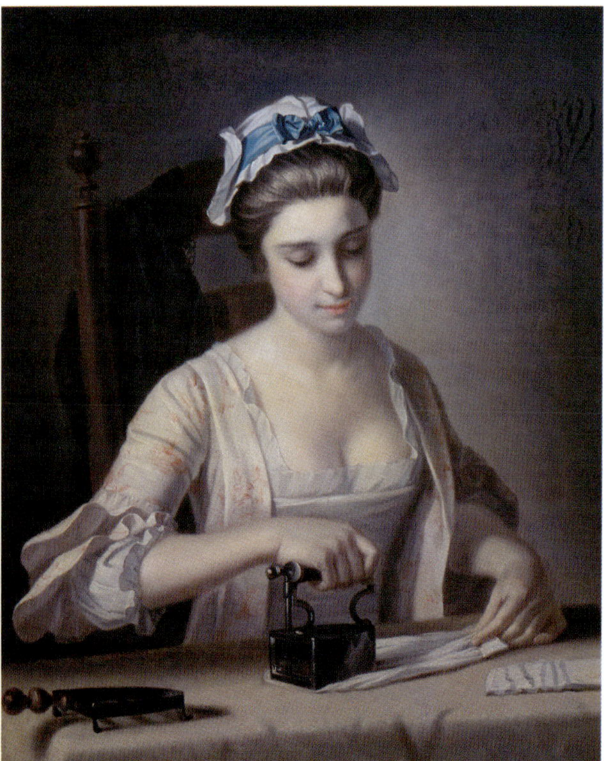

Plate 48   *A Laundry Maid Ironing*
Henry Robert Morland

Plate 49   *A Lady's Maid soaping Linen*
Henry Robert Morland

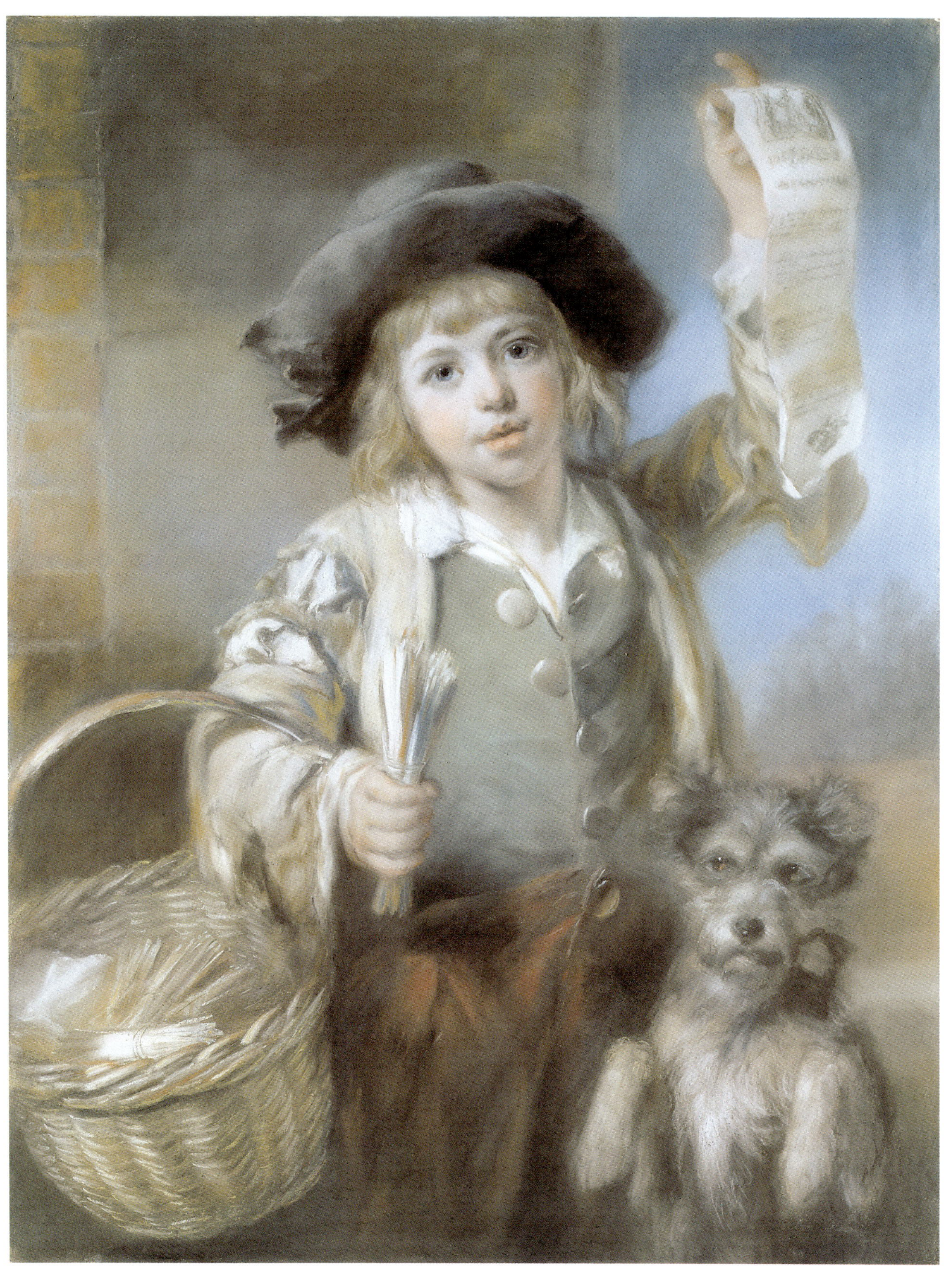

Plate 50
Love Songs and Matches
John Russell

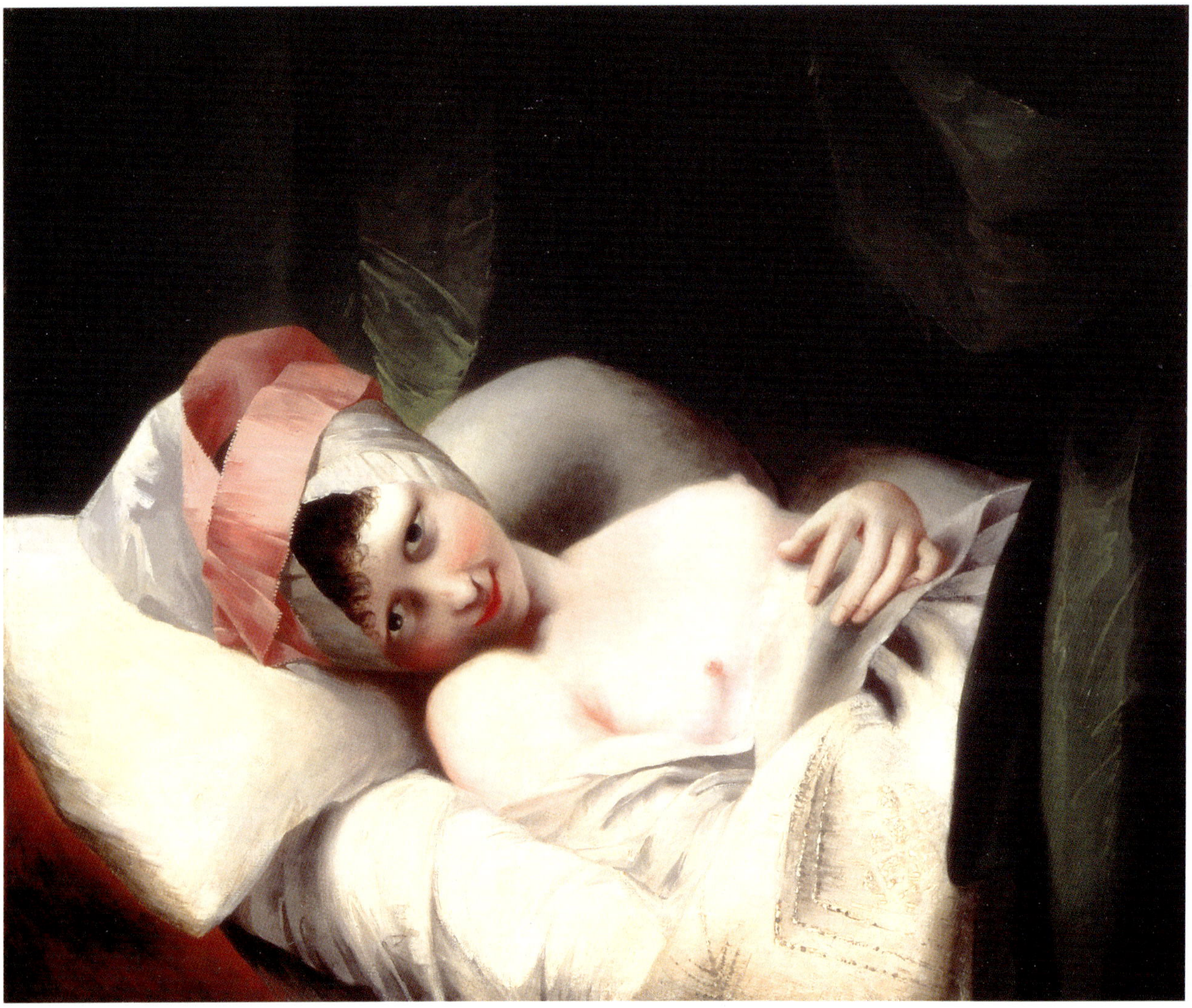

Plate 51
A Woman in Bed (Lydia)
The Revd Matthew William Peters

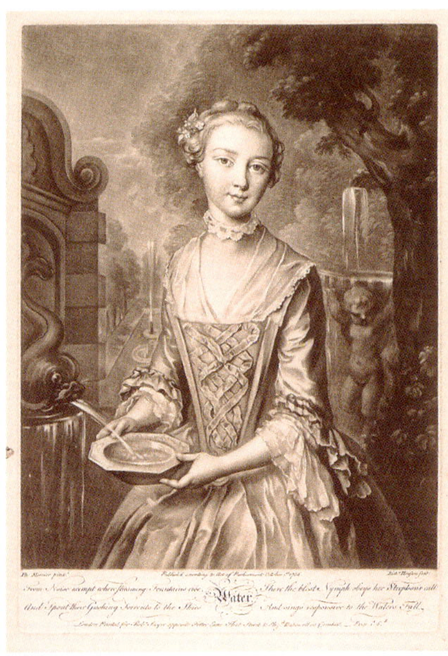

Plate 52
Water
Richard Houston

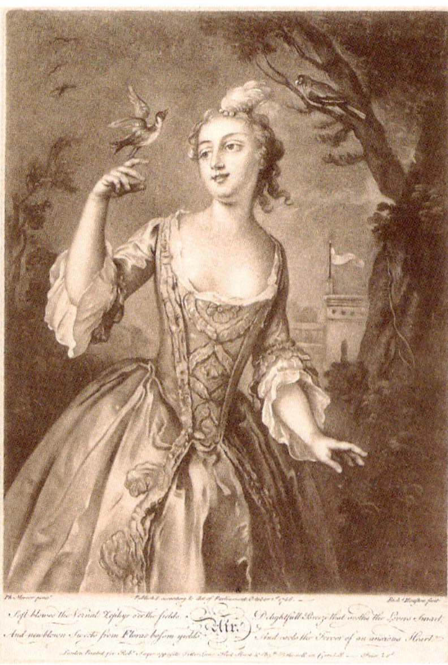

Plate 53
Air
Richard Houston

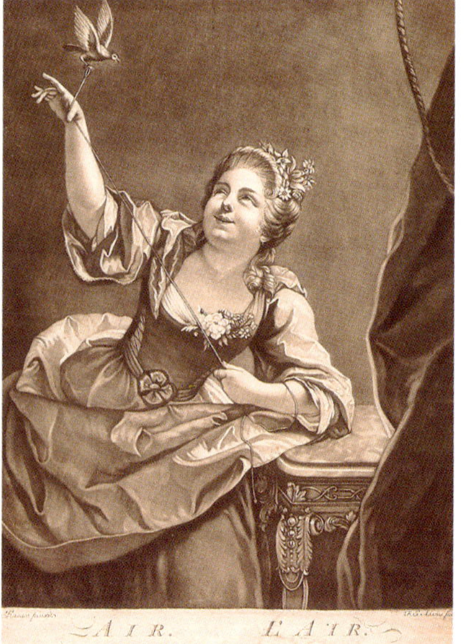

Plate 54
Air
Frederick Edward Adams

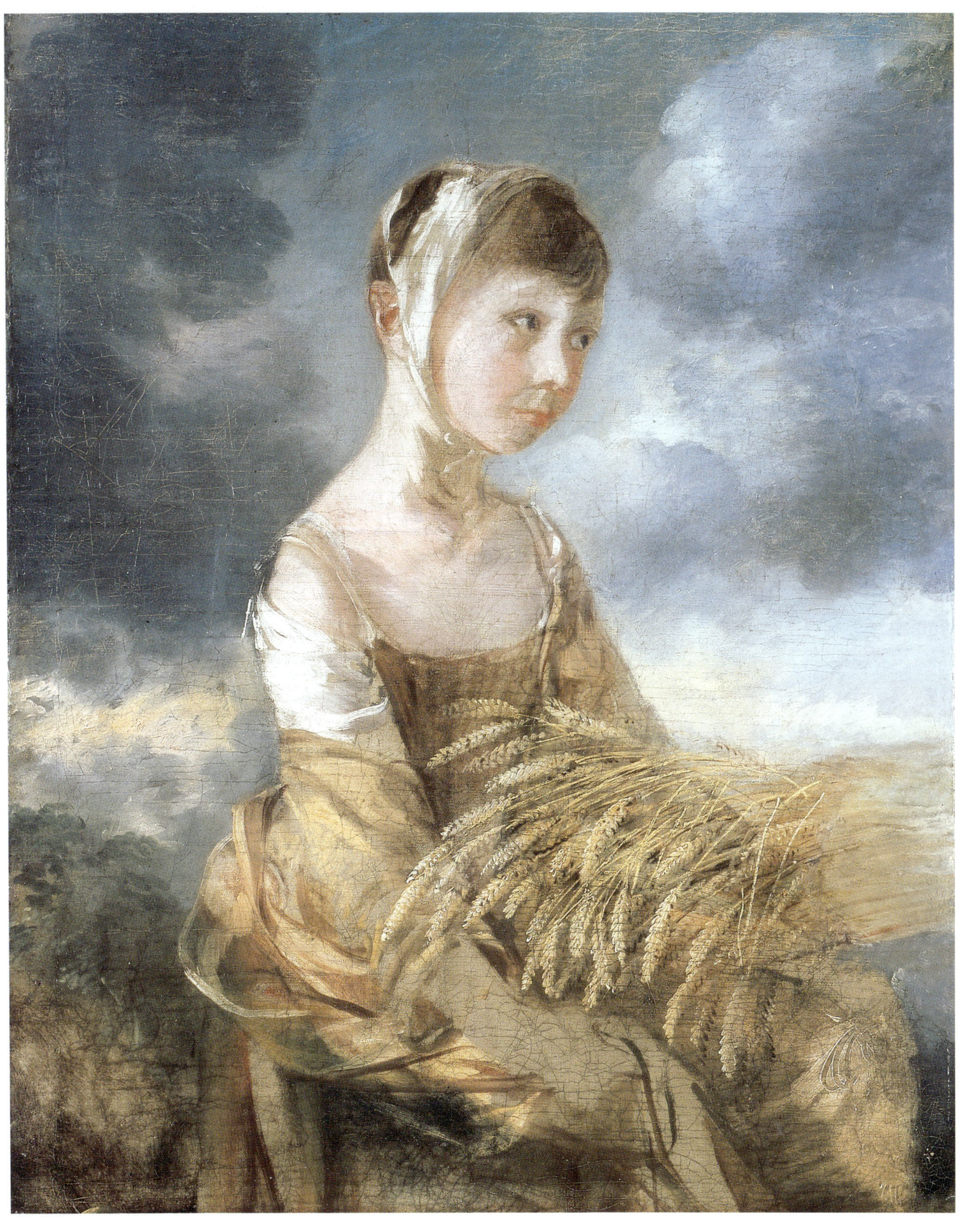

Plate 55
Margaret Gainsborough as a Gleaner
Thomas Gainsborough

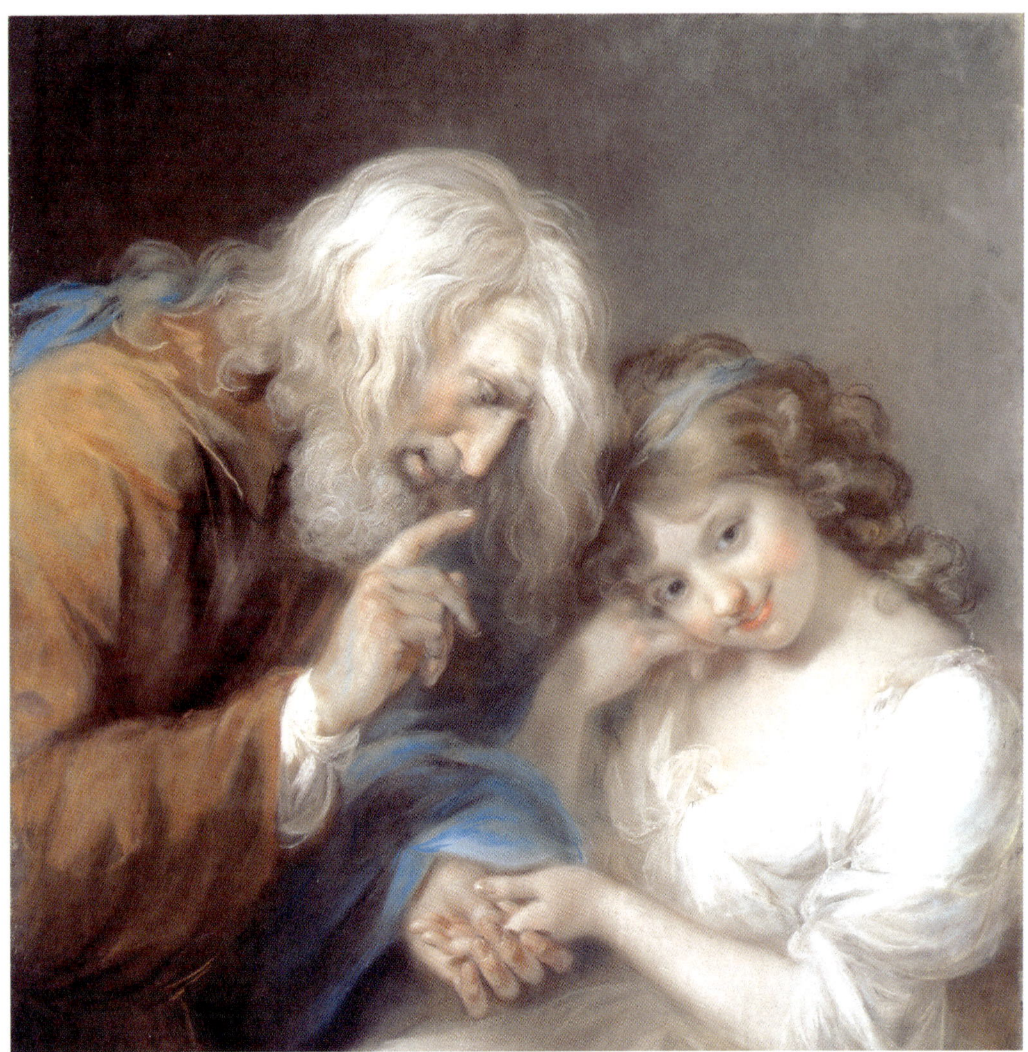

Plate 56
The Fortune-Teller
John Russell

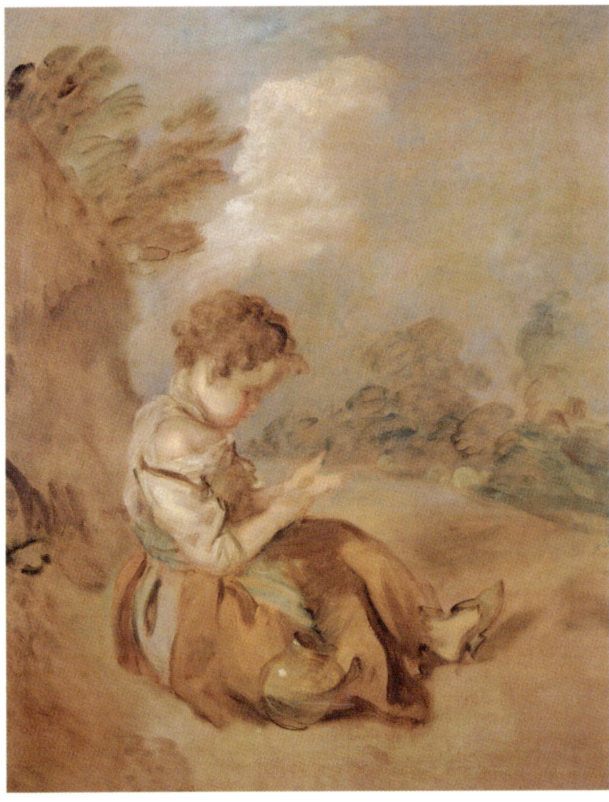

Plate 57 *Girl with a Penny*
Thomas Gainsborough

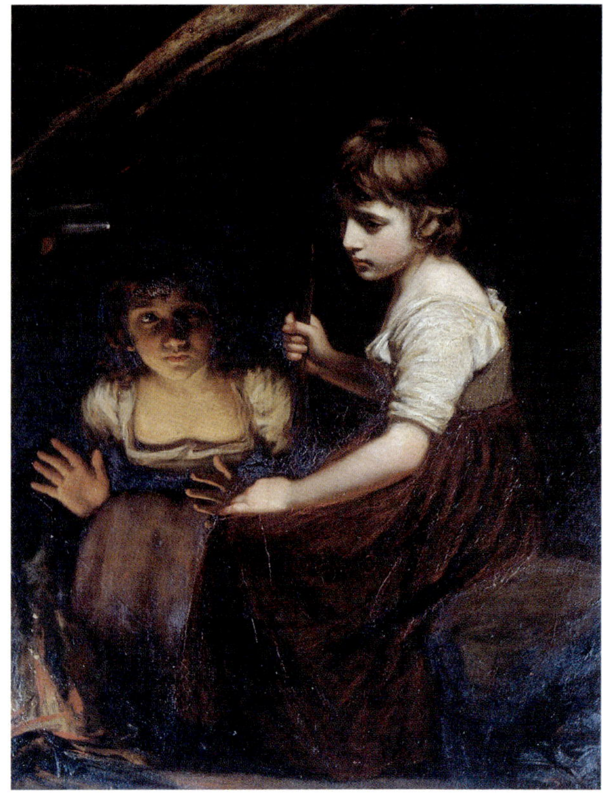

Plate 58 *Children by the Fireside*
John Opie

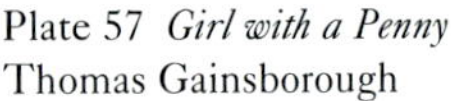

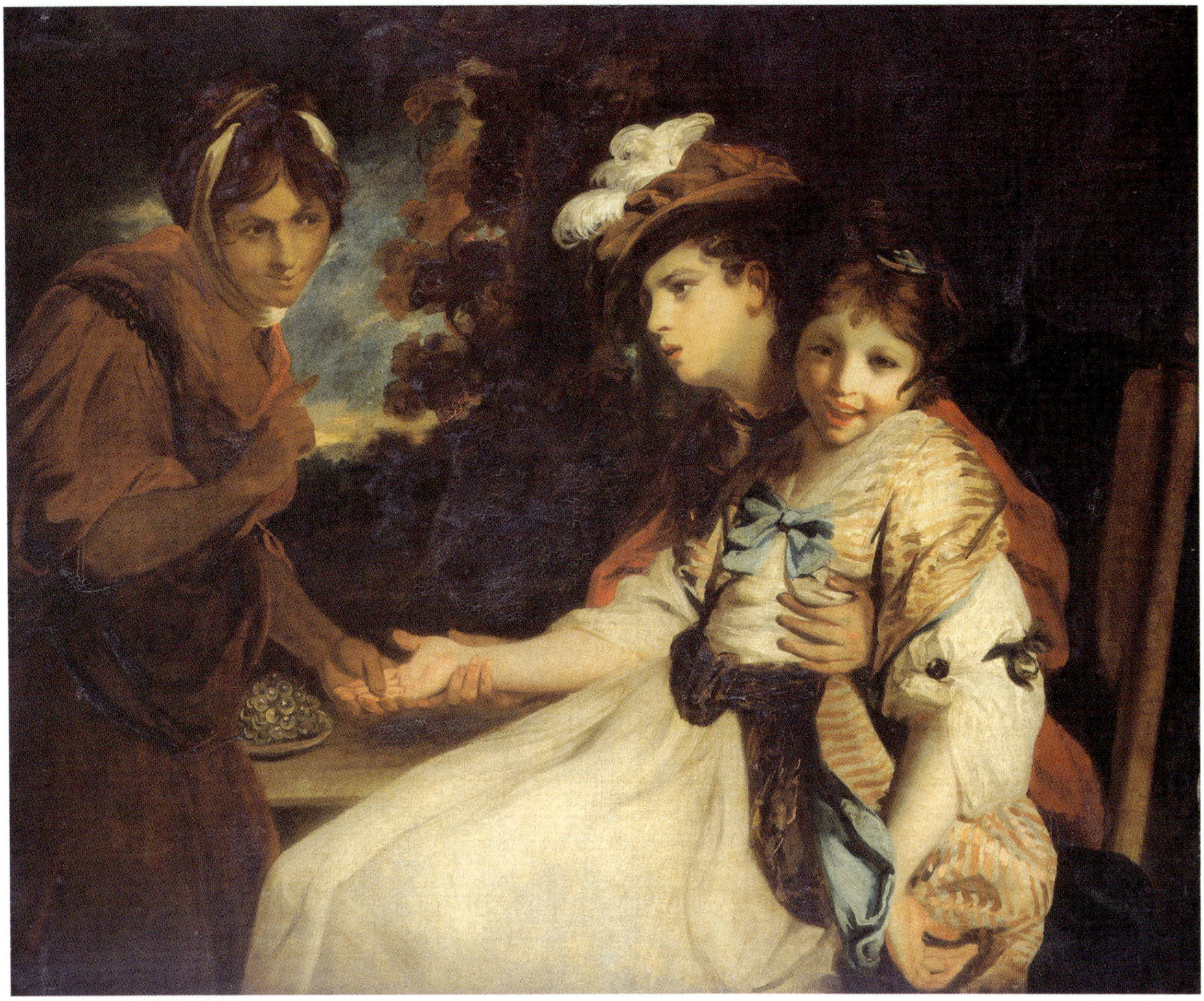

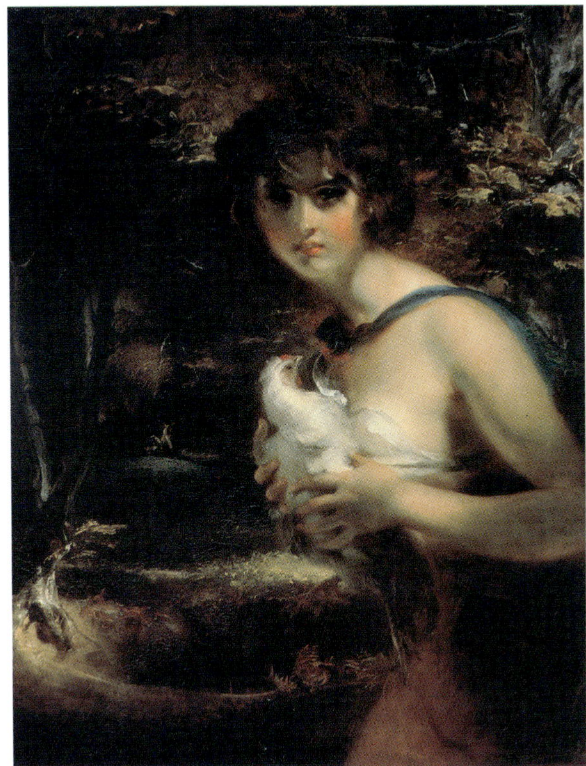

Plate 59   *A Fortune-Teller*   Sir Joshua Reynolds

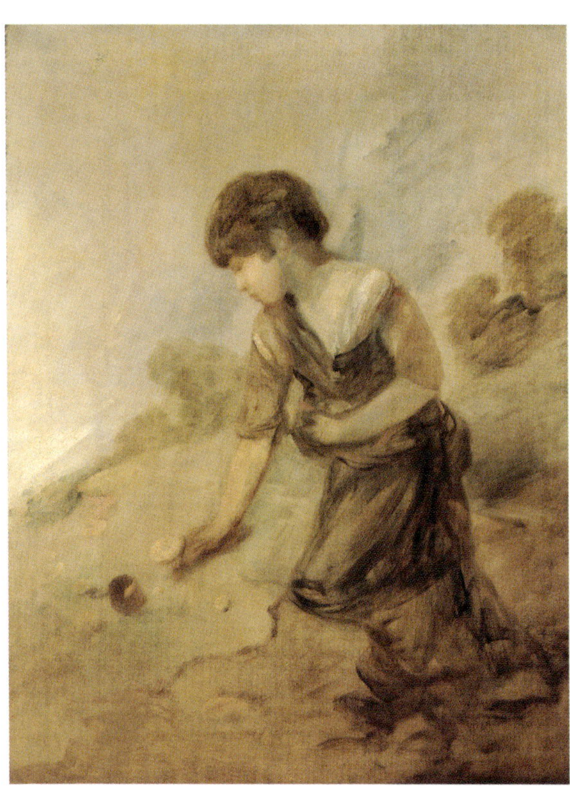

Plate 60 *A Gipsy Girl*
Sir Thomas Lawrence

Plate 61 *Girl Gathering Mushrooms*
Thomas Gainsborough

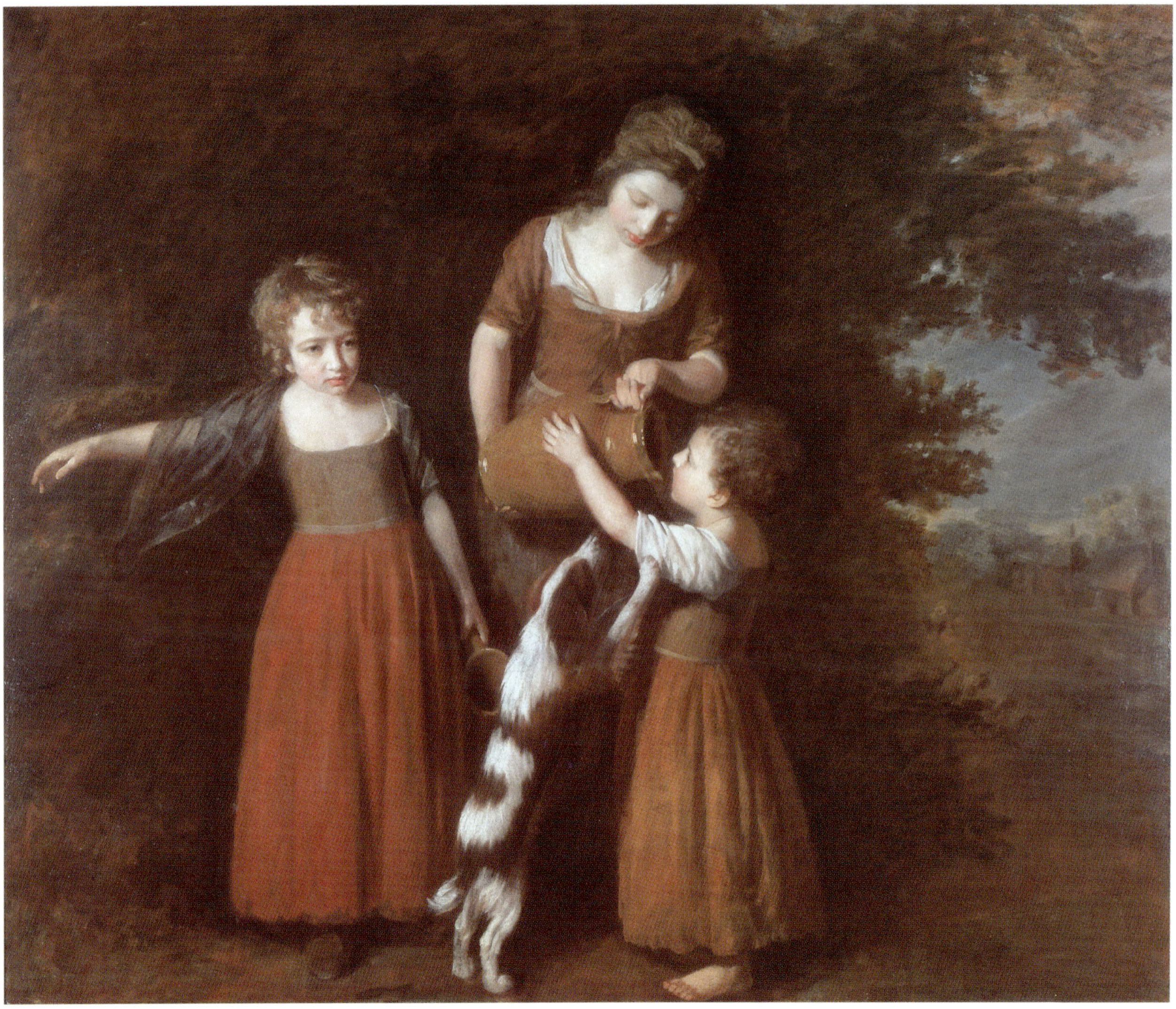

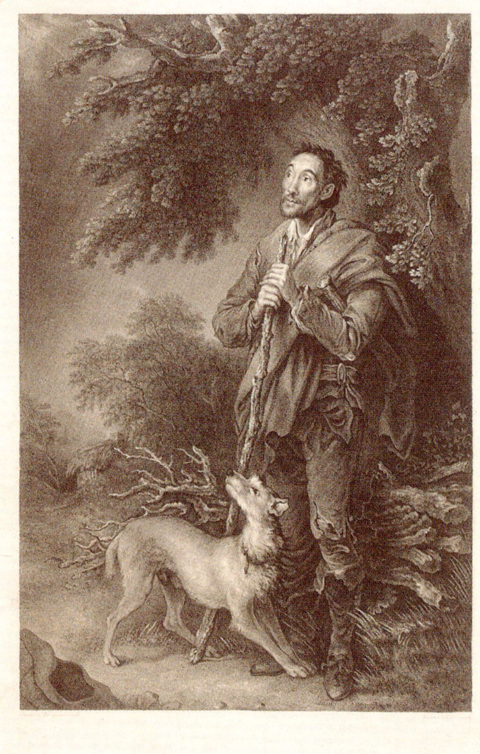

Plate 62   *A Peasant Family*   John Opie

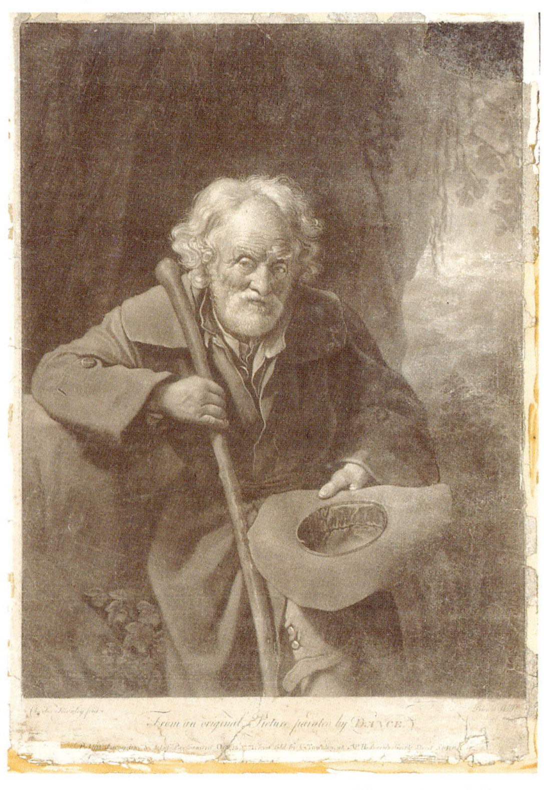

Plate 63   *The Woodman, vide Cowpers Task Book V*
Peter Simon

Plate 64   *A Beggar*
Charles Townley

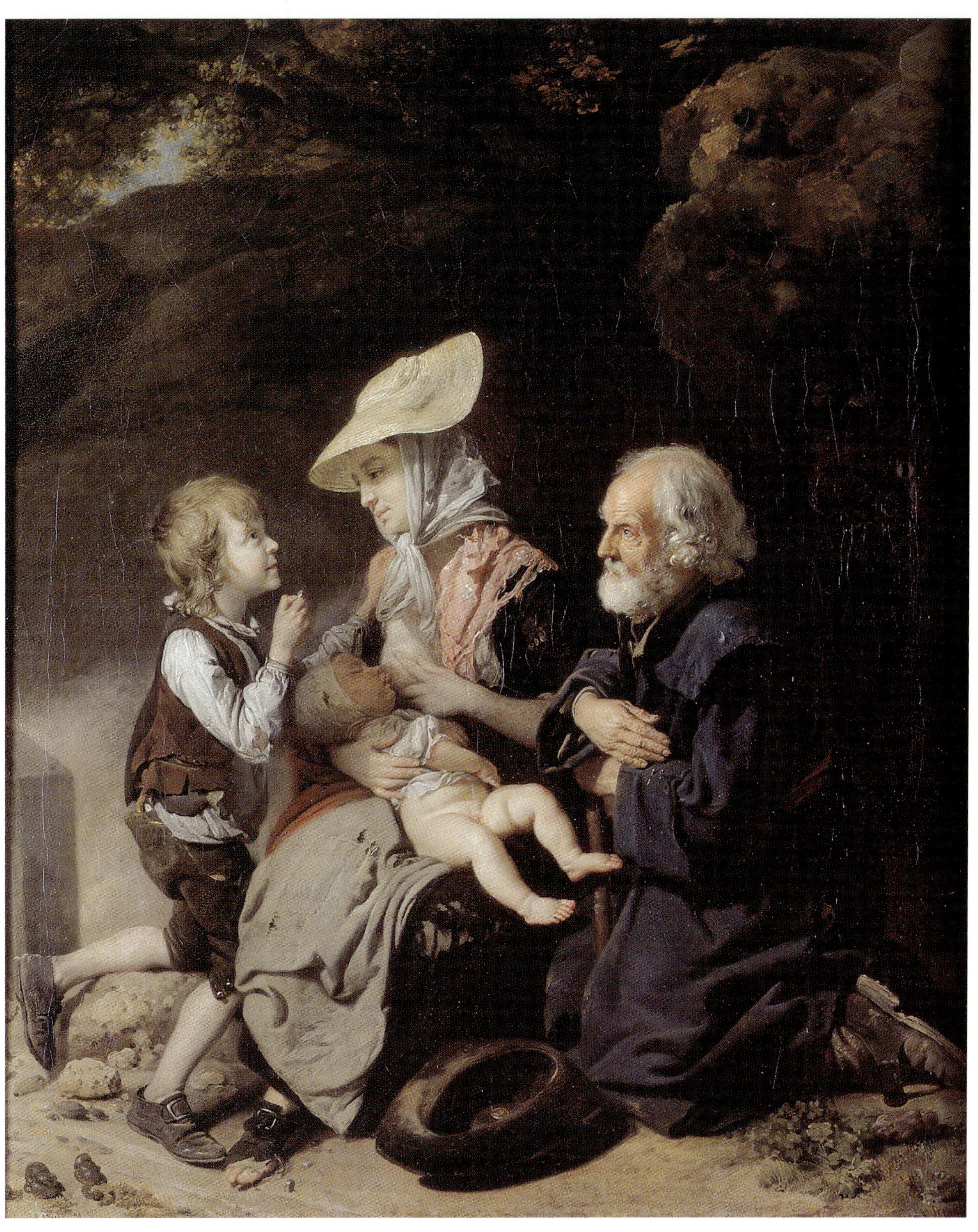

Plate 65
Beggars on the Road to Stanmore
Johan Zoffany

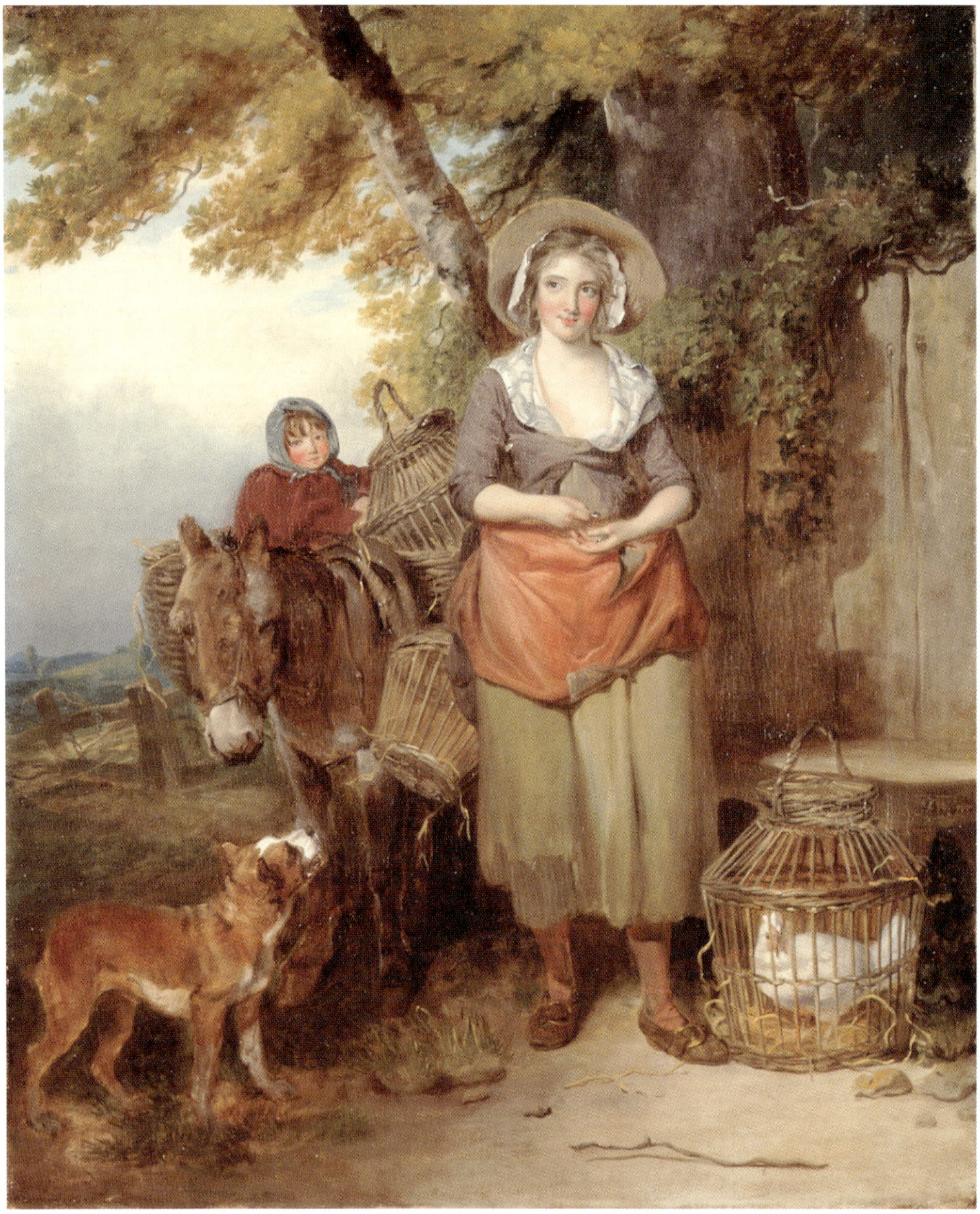

Plate 66
The Return from Market
Francis Wheatley

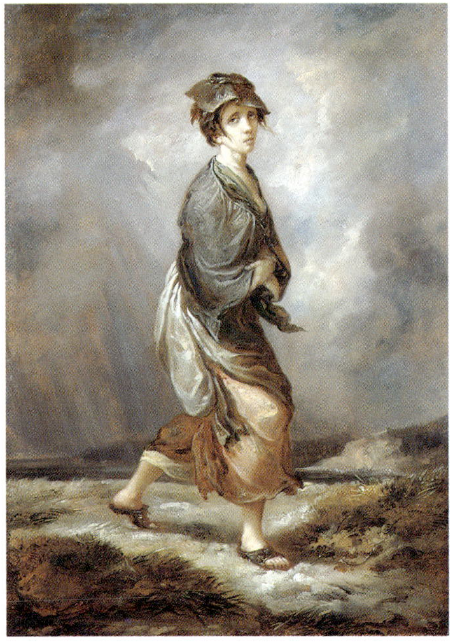
Plate 67
Crazy Kate
Thomas Barker

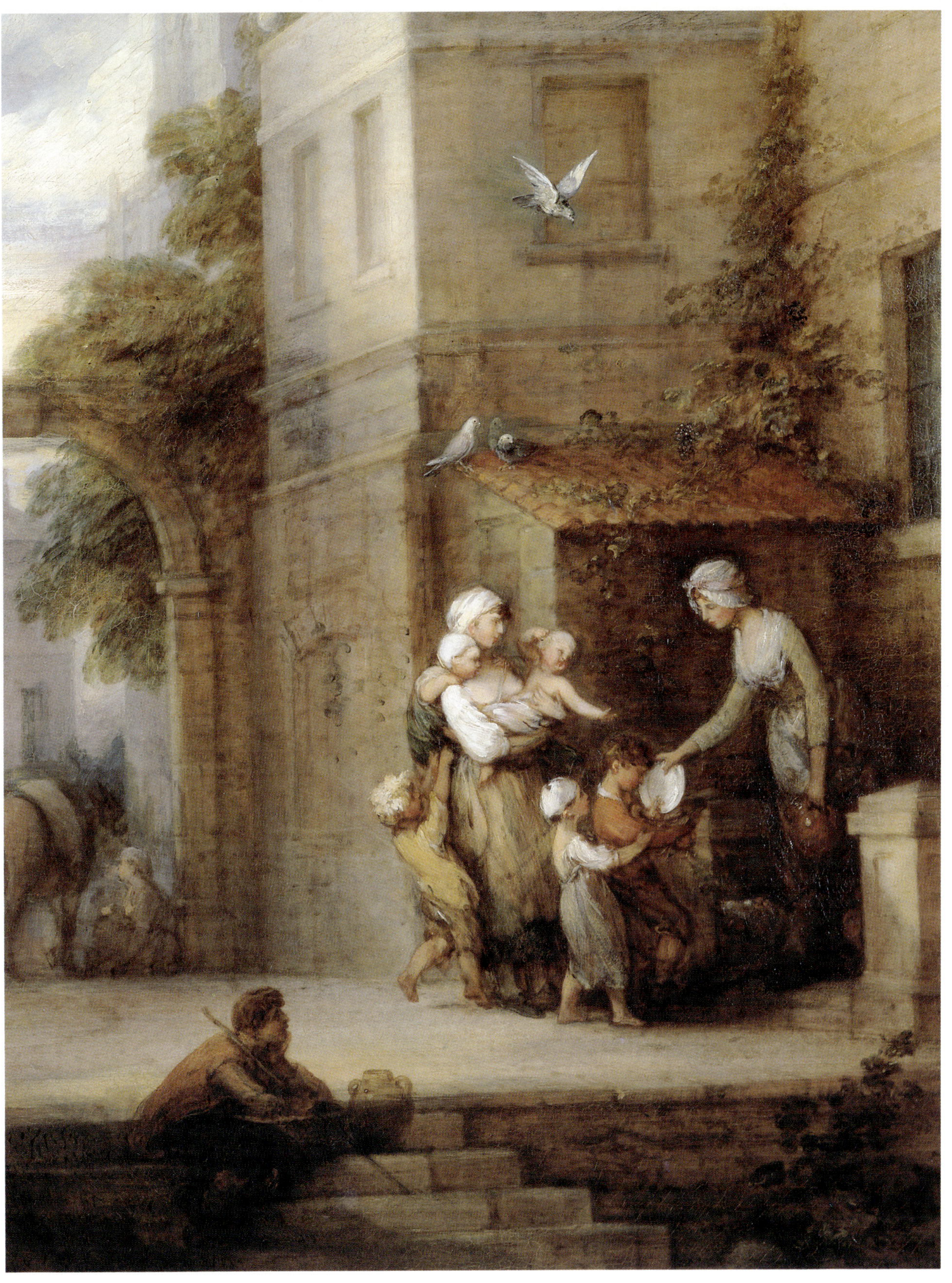

Plate 68
Charity Relieving Distress
Thomas Gainsborough

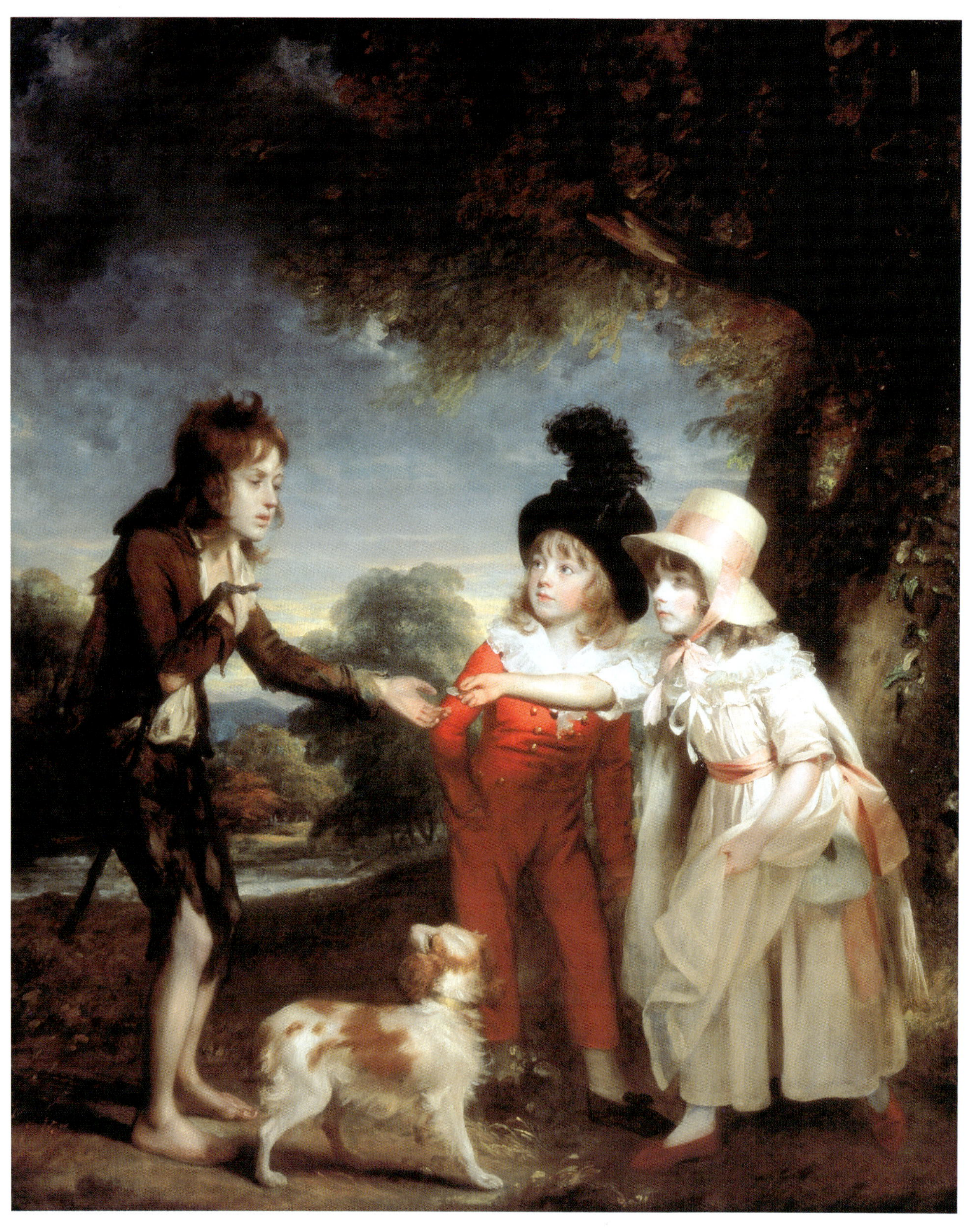

Plate 69
The Children of Sir Francis Ford giving coin to a beggar boy
Sir William Beechey

ANGELS & URCHINS

CATALOGUE*

I: The Old Master Tradition

1 *Boy playing a Jew's Harp*   (Plate 1)
SIR PETER LELY (1618-80)

Oil on canvas, 141 x 102.8 cm, *c* 1648
Tate Gallery

Provenance: 3rd Earl of Craven by 1739; by descent to Cornelia, Countess of Craven, from whose Trustees it was purchased; presented through the National Art Collections Fund (E. Cremetti Fund) to the Tate Gallery, 1966
Literature: Pennant 1811, p. 247; Toynbee, 1927-28, p. 10, p. 63; Collins Baker, 1912, vol. 1, p. 196 (as Soest); Millar, 1978, p. 41

Lely was in England by 1643, and his first known portraits in this country date from 1647, when he was employed by Charles I. This picture may have been purchased around this time by the first Earl of Craven (1608-97), a prominent patron of Van Dyck and the young Lely. It therefore forms a useful link between Flemish seventeenth-century art and the eighteenth-century fancy picture. Of all Lely's early works in England, none is more closely allied to the traditions of the Utrecht Caravaggisti other than its companion, the *Man playing a Flute* (also now Tate Gallery). Even so, as early as the 1730s both pictures were credited to Frans Hals, although the resemblance to the latter's work is at best superficial.

The picture was first recorded in an inventory of 17 September 1739 as one of 'Five Italian Musicians by Francis Halls [*sic*]' in the collection of the 3rd Earl of Craven, Combe Abbey, Warwickshire. Horace Walpole, who saw the pictures in 1768, also attributed them to Hals, while earlier this century they were attributed to Gerard Soest (*c* 1600-81). The other three pictures in the series were a man playing a violin, a young man playing a lute, and a woman playing a theorbo-lute (Christie's, 20 November 1992 (6-8)). A sixth, related, picture of a man playing a violin is in the Sarah Campbell Blaffer Foundation, Houston, Texas. It has been plausibly suggested (Millar, 1978, p. 42) that the picture of the young man playing the lute is a self-portrait and that the other sitters were individuals who formed the artist's circle of friends during his earliest years in England. The pictures may have been commissioned, although given their air of casual intimacy it is more likely that they were done for pleasure or to demonstrate the artist's skills to potential patrons. Indeed, although the *Boy with a Jew's Harp* is painted on the scale of life it is not a straightforward portrait, but a character study. Its initial owner, quite possibly the 1st Earl of Craven – who may have known the musicians – may have

Note: A number of catalogue entries on engravings are by David Alexander. These entries and those on which he has assisted are initialled 'DSA'

purchased their pictures with the specific intention of hanging them in a suite where music was played.

Musicians, either playing or carousing, were popular subjects among the Utrecht Caravaggisti during the earlier decades of the seventeenth century, notably Hendrick ter Brugghen, Gerrit van Honthorst, and Dirck van Baburen, whose *Young Man Playing a Jew's Harp* of 1621 (Utrecht, Centraal Museum), was produced the year he returned from Italy (see Spicer and Orr, 1997, no. 37). These single-figure musical images rapidly gained popularity throughout the Dutch Republic, spreading to Leiden and to Haarlem, where Lely worked as a young apprentice in the late 1630s.

2 *The Musical Boy*
JAMES WATSON (*c* 1739-90), after Frans Hals

Mezzotint, 37.6 x 27.6 cm
LETTERED: '*Francis Halls* [sic] *pinxit/James Watson Sculpsit./THE MUSICAL BOY/Done from the Original Picture of the same size, in the Collection of the Right Honourable Lord Stewart./Published July 24*[th] *1777 by John Boydell Engraver in Cheapside London*'
The Trustees of the British Museum
Literature: Chaloner Smith 1883, vol. 4, p. 1547, no. 159

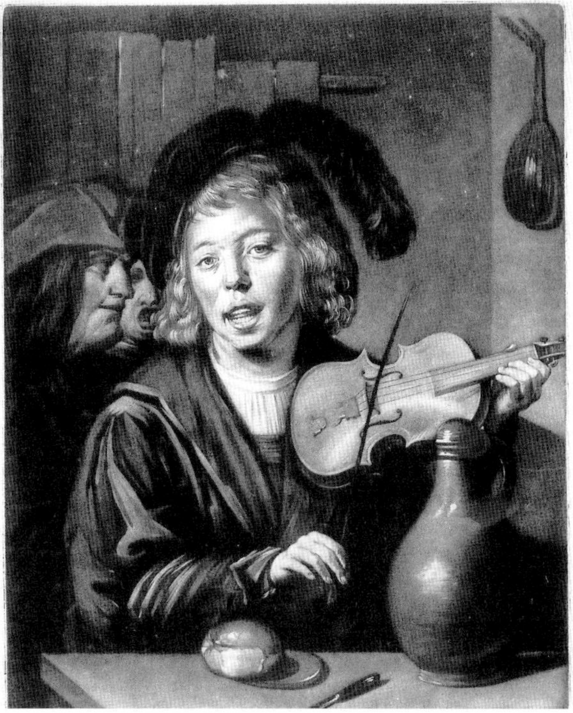

Like Murillo, Frans Hals (*c* 1582/3-1666) was influential upon the development of the fancy picture in eighteenth-century England. And while his reputation was no where near so secure as Rembrandt's in Georgian England, Hals was widely admired and collected. Reynolds, for example, owned six works attributed to 'Frank Halls', as he was known in England. These included a *Man with a Beer Jug* (Henry Reichhold Collection, New York) and a *Woman with a Medal* (Kiev, State Museum) – although the latter is now attributed to Jacob Backer (see Broun, 1987, Hals, nos. 1 and 2). In the sixth *Discourse* Reynolds criticized Hals's lack of finish, but he appreciated the 'strong-marked character of individual nature' in his works (Wark, 1975, p. 109). The present picture is typical of the kind of work for which Hals was most admired, and which he produced mainly during the earlier part of his career, up to *c* 1640. These figures, who often combine their interests in music with a cheerful indulgence in drink, were in part allegorical, representing the pleasures of the Senses, Hearing and Taste. These paintings of the Senses were popular in Hals's own lifetime, and exerted a powerful influence upon later artists, not least Mercier, whose youthful *Drinker* of *c* 1730 (Louvre) approaches as closely to Hals's pattern without quite descending to the level of pastiche.

3 *Moor playing a Pipe* (Plate 4)

SIR JOSHUA REYNOLDS (1723-92)

(painted over a painting once variously attributed to Velázquez and Veronese)

Oil on canvas, 96.5 x 76.2 cm (shown unframed), *c* 1776 (Reynolds's contribution)

Private Collection

Provenance: Purchased by James Northcote on behalf of Sir Joshua Reynolds (possibly 'A negro playing on the flute by P. Veronese', J. Got de Grote sale, Christie's, 30 March 1776 (24)); Reynolds's old-master sale, Christie's 17 March 1795 (33) as 'P. Veronese, A NEGRO PLAYING ON THE FLUTE, study from Nature, a grand design, painted with freedom and spirit. A capital picture, esteemed by Sir Joshua as one of the best in his collection'; bought Wilson for 100 guineas, sold by him to Samuel Whitbread for 110 guineas; by descent

Exhibited: 'Burlington Fine Art Club Winter Exhibition' 1934-35; 'Burlington Magazine X-ray Exhibition', Agnew's, March 1969

Literature: Northcote, 1818, vol. 2, p. 190; Leslie and Taylor, 1865, vol. 2, pp. 140; Graves and Cronin, vol. 4, p. 1457; Millar, 1951, p. 48; Broun, 1987, 'Italian School', pp. 73-5.

'It was a particular pleasure to Sir Joshua,' said his pupil James Northcote, 'when he got into his hands any damaged pictures by some eminent old masters; and he very frequently worked upon them with great advantage, and has often made them, both in effect and colour, vastly superior to what they had ever been in their original state' (Northcote, 1818, vol. 2, p. 189). Northcote cites two instances: one is a portrait by Velázquez of the Infante Don Baltasar Carlos, probably the picture now in the Wallace Collection; the other is *Moor Playing a Pipe*.

Northcote was a first-hand witness to Reynolds's restoration of the present picture, not least because he purchased on his behalf at auction: 'When he got it into his painting room he painted an entire new back ground to the picture, a sky instead of what was before all dark without any effect; but with this and some few other small alterations, it became one of the finest pictures I ever saw' (Northcote, op. cit., p. 190). When the picture was sold at auction after Reynolds's death Benjamin West confirmed that 'when Sir Joshua bought [*sic*] it had a dark drapery sketched in and a dark back ground. Sir Joshua painted the present drapery &

background' (Farington, 24 March 1795). X-ray photography has since shown not only that Reynolds had overpainted the picture of the Moor but that the Moor itself was painted over a composition containing several figures – possibly a sketch for a painting of the stoning of St Stephen. In his original account Northcote stated that the picture of the *Moor Playing a Pipe* which he purchased for Reynolds was by Velázquez, although, as Francis Broun has noted, that was probably a slip of the pen, since he had just been discussing a picture by Velázquez (Broun, 1987, Veronese, no 2). It is more likely that the picture was then attributed to Veronese, the name under which it was sold in 1795, and the artist linked to the sale of a negro playing a pipe at auction in 1776 (the very time that Northcote would have been buying pictures for Reynolds).

Reynolds's alterations to the present picture extended from the addition of the sky background to the figure's red cap and coat, and possible even to parts of the flesh areas. In the opinion of Sir Ellis Waterhouse, who thought it 'an unusually good *amorosi*', the Moor was 'pretty well all Reynolds' (Waterhouse, MS notebook, 2 October 1932). In the early 1950s Sir Oliver Millar stated that 'as it is seen today there is little to suggest Velázquez or Veronese, to indeed, anything earlier than Reynolds's (Millar, 1951, p. 48). Professor Michael Jaffé told the picture's owner in 1975 that he could see 'nothing but Reynolds', and certainly no trace of Velázquez, Rubens or Veronese. The *Moor* may have been made by an Italian, although it could have been by a Flemish seventeenth-century painter (Rubens, for instance, painted a number of character studies of black sailors around the port of Antwerp).

4 *Piping Shepherd* (Plate 3)

SIR JOSHUA REYNOLDS (1723-92)

Oil on canvas, 83.8 x 62.2 cm, *c* 1771-3

Private Collection

Provenance: Bequeathed by the artist to his niece, Mary Palmer, later Marchioness of Thomond; her sale, Christie's, 18 May 1821 (70), bought George Phillips; Sir George Richard Phillips, Bart.; 1883 passed to his daughter Juliana, Lady Camperdown; Lord Camperdown sale, Christie's 21 February 1919 (145), bought W.S.M. Burns; passed to his daughter Lady Carew Pole; by descent

Exhibited: British Institution, 1813 (3); 1823 (7); 1843 (7); Royal Academy, 1882 (185); Plymouth, 1951 (62)

Literature: Leslie and Taylor, vol. 2, p. 7, note 1, p. 54, note 1; Graves and Cronin, vol. 3, pp. 1203-4; Cotton 1856, p. 199; Waterhouse, 1941, p. 64; Pope, ed., 1960-63, vol. 2, p. 337; Waterhouse, 1973, p. 26, pl. 62; Postle, 1995, p. 72, pl. 26

Engraved: J. Spilsbury, 1786; Stipple by J. Barney, 1788, as 'A Shepherd Boy'; S.W. Reynolds; anon., as 'a vignette'; F.T. Palgrave, 1858 (in reverse)

The *Piping Shepherd* remained in Reynolds's family's possession until the death of his niece, Lady Mary Thomond, in 1821. At the auction of her pictures it was described in the catalogue as 'The Piping shepherd boy with his dog, in the distance a clear, illumined landscape with a flock of sheep'. A more memorable account of the picture appears in the diary of Benjamin Robert Haydon, who attended the auction: '*The Piping Shepherd* is in my estimation one of his finest emanations of his sentiment. The look of his eyes, the tone of his complexion, the grace of his motion, the pressure of the upper lip on the flageolet, the actions of the fingers, the tone of the background fill the mind with those associations of solitude and sound which are so affecting in Nature when the melancholy strain of a flageolet comes to my ear across a meadow or dell. The colour of this exquisite harmony with the idea of a yellow leaf in Autumn opposed by a dark sky, fills the mind with associations of melancholy and music I think it the most complete hit in expression and colour that he ever made' (Pope, ed., 1960-63, vol. 2, p. 337). Haydon communicated his love for the picture to Sir George Phillips, who purchased it at the sale for the phenomenal sum of £430 10s, a sum surpassed only by those paid for Reynolds's large subject pictures and his designs for the *Nativity* at New College, Oxford.

Reynolds probably painted this picture during the early months of 1773, when he recorded a sitting in his pocket book for a 'Shepherd Boy'. (These cannot have been for Lord Halifax's picture of the same title, which had already been purchased by Lord Irwin.) The *Piping Shepherd*, like Reynolds's slightly earlier *Shepherd Boy*, looks back to the Arcadian figures of Giorgione, Titian and Savoldo, as exemplified by the *Piping Boy* in the Royal Collection, presently attributed to Titian. It is also reminiscent of Nathaniel Hone's *Piping Boy* (National Gallery of Ireland). Hone had been producing fancy pictures of this kind, often modelled on his own children, since the late 1760s.

5 *Shepherd Boy (The Young Shepherd)* (Plate 2)
SIR JOSHUA REYNOLDS (1723-92)

Oil on canvas, 76.2 x 63.5 cm
The Halifax Collection

Provenance: Bought from the artist 1772 by Lord Irwin; by descent
Exhibited: International Exhibition, London, 1862 (66); 1926-31 on loan to the National Gallery, London
Literature: Leslie and Taylor, 1865, vol. 1, p. 465, note 5, vol. 2, p. 175; Graves and Cronin, 1899-1901, vol. 3, p. 1205; Waterhouse, 1941, p.62; Cormack, 1970, p. 156; Postle, 1995, pp. 69, 72, pl. 25
Engraved: James Scott 1863 as 'The Young Shepherd'

The *Shepherd Boy* was among the first of many fancy pictures featuring young children in allegorical roles painted by Reynolds during the 1770s and eighties. It was probably painted sometime either towards the end of 1770 and the spring of 1771, when Reynolds recorded a series of sittings with unidentified child models in his pocket books. The picture was probably already hanging in Reynolds's gallery by July 1771 when Lord Irwin, who purchased it the following year, visited Reynolds to have his own portrait painted. Interestingly, Lord Irwin paid Reynolds 50 guineas for the *Shepherd Boy*, although the artist was then only charging 35 guineas for portraits of the same size.

Reynolds's *Shepherd Boy* was, according to Sir Ellis Waterhouse, 'in all but name, a Christ Child as The Good Shepherd' (Waterhouse, MS essay, p. 3). He also suggested that Reynolds's picture was in part inspired by the 'Murillo' of *The Good Shepherd* (see cat. 7) imported into England in 1772. Even though Reynolds painted this picture before he saw that picture, the belief that he had been looking at Murillo – possibly the *Infant St John* recently acquired by the Duke of Montagu – remains strong.

6 *A Shepherd*
RICHARD EARLOM (1743-1822), after Thomas Gainsborough

Mezzotint, 40.1 x 27.9 cm
LETTERED: '*Gainsborough pinx^t/R^d Earlom Sculp/J. Boydell Excudit, Published, Oct.^br 1st 1781*'
Trustees of Gainsborough's House, Sudbury

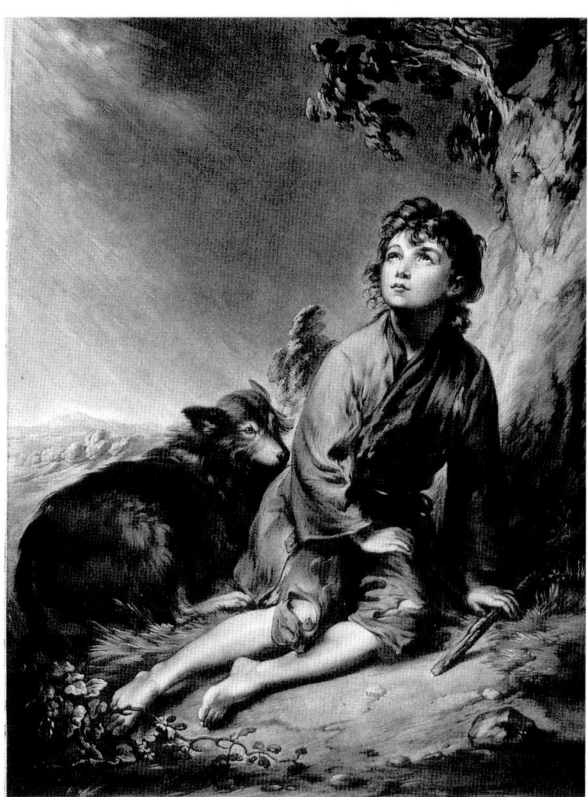

Earlom's engraving is after the painting of the same title exhibited by Gainsborough at the Royal Academy in 1781, and destroyed by fire at Exton Park in 1810, along with his *Woodman* (see cat. 86). The composition, for which a drawing of the child's head survives (Hayes, 1970, p. 301, no. 828), was based upon the figure of a seated urchin in Murillo's *Invitation to the Game of Pelota* (Fig. 17), which was then probably owned by the London based French art dealer Noel Desenfans (1745-1807) from whom Gainsborough later purchased his *St John in the Wilderness*, also ascribed to Murillo. *A Shepherd* was trumpeted by Henry Bate in the pages of the *Morning Herald* as 'the *chef d'oeuvre* of this great artist, a composition in which the numberless beauties of design, drawing, and colouring are so admirably blended as to excite the imagination of every beholder' (Whitley, 1915, p. 173). A rival publication, the *London Courant*, disagreed, preferring the 'wanton frenzy' of Reynolds's *Thais* and the 'domestic elegance' of his *Waldegrave Sisters* to Gainsborough's *Shepherd* – or 'the Beggar Boy of St James's Street', as he disparagingly referred to it (op. cit., pp. 174-5). The beggar boy in question, named Jack Hill, was apparently found by Gainsborough in St James's Street and modelled for the artist, and others, over the next few years (see cat. 81)

7 *The Good Shepherd* (Plate 5)
THOMAS GAINSBOROUGH (1728-88), after Murillo

Oil on canvas, 175.9 x 132.6 cm, *c* 1778-80
Private Collection

Provenance: Gainsborough's studio sale 1789 (50); bt. soon after by Samuel Whitbread (at Southill by 1815); by descent.
Exhibited: Agnews, London, 1969
Literature: Waterhouse, 1946, p. 137; Waterhouse, 1958, p. 125, No. 1025; Murillo, 1982, pp. 71 and 176

This copy of Murillo's *Christ Child as the Good Shepherd* was apparently made from memory by Gainsborough when he saw a version of the picture at Christie's in 1778. The version in question (Fig. 5) had been acquired by the engraver Thomas Major (1720-99), who sold it in 1773 to the Duchess of Bridgewater. At the time it was thought to be by Murillo, although in the nineteenth century, when Murillo's original picture (Lane Collection) came to England, it was discovered to be by the French artist Alexis Grimou (1678-1733) and probably painted in Paris during the 1730s. Thomas Major made an engraving from Grimou's picture, which he exhibited at the Royal Academy in 1776 (184), accompanied in the catalogue by lines from Milton's *Il Penseroso*, 'Looks commercing with the skies, Thy wrapt soul sitting in thine eyes.' Grimou's painting was next seen in public in the summer of 1778 when it was offered for sale at Christie's by the Duchess of Bridgewater. At this time Gainsborough, whose house was next to James Christie's auction house, made his own copy (presumably using Major's engraving as an aide-memoire). The present work bears an inscription on the back, signed by Gainsborough Dupont: *'The Good Shepherd painted from memory by Mr Gainsborough in 1780, after having seen the original in the possession of the Duke of Bridgewater'*. Given Gainsborough's evident fascination with Murillo's composition it is interesting to note that both this picture and its companion, *The Infant St John the Baptist and the Lamb* (National Gallery, London) have been singled out for their 'charming anticipation of eighteenth-century sensibility' (Murillo, 1982, p. 176).

In the seventeenth century, knowledge of Murillo's art outside his native Spain was chiefly related to his paintings of urchins and Madonnas which were exported by Dutch and Flemish merchants. By the late 1600s his work was also becoming known in England, but it was not until the mid-eighteenth century that his reputation really grew, owing to the importation of works by merchants, diplomats and aristocrats (notably the *Flight into Egypt*, bought at auction in 1756 by Sir Sampson Gideon and the *Infant St John*, which belonged to the Duke of Montagu by 1770). This influx of works by Murillo accounts for the fact that he was increasingly influential on the form and content of Reynolds's and Gainsborough's fancy pictures during the 1770s and '80s.

The present painting is one of two known copies by Gainsborough after Murillo. The other, *Abraham and Isaac*, originally belonged to the Cartwrights of Aynoe Park, Northampshire. (The tradition dating back to the nineteenth century that a copy of Murillo's *Urchin mocking an Old Woman eating Polenta* at Dyrham Park, Gloucestershire, was painted by Gainsborough is unfounded; see Laing, 1995, cat. 53, p. 144 and note 19.) An indication of the high regard in which Gainsborough held Murillo was his purchase for five hundred guineas of the painting *St John in the Wilderness* from the dealer Noel Desenfans. Until the present century the work was accepted as being by Murillo, although since entering the National Gallery it has been ascribed to an anonymous follower of the artist (see MacLaren and Braham, 1988, no. 3938).

8 Two Shepherd Boys with Dogs Fighting (Plate 6)
THOMAS GAINSBOROUGH (1727-88)

Oil on canvas, 223.5 x 157.5 cm, 1783
The Iveagh Bequest, Kenwood

Provenance: Wilbraham Tollemache, later 6th Earl of Dysart, by *c* 1786; passed to his collateral John, 1st Baron Tollemache; A. de Rothschild; Agnew; Earl of Iveagh, 1888
Exhibited: Royal Academy, 1783 (35), 1928 (209); Suffolk Street, 1833 (58); British Institution, 1845 (154); Manchester, 'Art Treasures', 1857 (92), 1928 (61), 1957 (201); Paris 1972 (125)
Literature: Leslie and Taylor, 1865, vol. 2, p. 410; Whitley, 1915, pp. 195, 204, 262; Waterhouse, 1946, vol. 88, pp. 134 ff.; Woodall, 1949, p. 109; Waterhouse, 1958, pp. 36, 103, no. 800; Woodall, 1961, pp. 29 and 43
Engraved: Mezzotint by Henry Birche, 1791; Henry Dawe 1824; Normand *fils*

Before the Royal Academy exhibition of 1783, Gainsborough was anxious about how his works would be displayed at Somerset House, writing to Francis Newton (1720-94), Secretary of the Academy: 'God bless you hang my Dogs and my Landskip in the great Room' (Woodall, 1961, p. 29). Gainsborough's request was granted although owing to an altercation with the Academy's Hanging Committee the following year, 1783 was to be the last year he displayed his works there. Gainsborough's love for fancy pictures of this kind, which he valued far more highly than his portraits, is revealed in a letter which he wrote to to Sir William Chambers on 27 April 1783, shortly after the exhibition opened: 'I sent my fighting dogs to divert you. I believe next exhibition I shall make the boys fighting & the dogs looking on – you know my cunning way of avoiding great subjects in painting & of concealing my ignorance by a flash in the pan. If I can do this while I pick pockets in the portrait way two or three years longer I intend to turn into a cot & turn a serious fellow; but for the present I must affect a little madness. I know you think me right as a whole, & can look down upon Cock Sparows as a great man ought to do, with compassion' (Woodall, 1961, p. 43).

The picture was received favourably by critics at the exhibition who, like Gainsborough, clearly preferred his fancy pictures to his portraits. 'These are the Scenes,' it was observed, 'in which the Friend of Gainsborough and the Art will wish to see him always occupied – in which he works evidently and successfully *con amore*. – Portrait Painting he seems to struggle through with the Impatience that indicates it to be considered as a Task of Duty' (*Public Advertiser*, 2 May 1783). Another critic perceived the particular influence of Murillo in the boys and that of Snyders in the fighting dogs, adding that the viewer should also 'not overlook the preservation of characteristic appearance, so well descriminating both the Boys and the Dogs – the one being a Shepherd and a Shepherd's Dog: the other, a Butcher's boy and a butcher's dog!' (*Morning Chronicle*, 10 May 1783).

The picture is, as John Hayes has admitted, 'one of the strangest and most difficult to explain of all Gainsborough's pictures' (Hayes, 1975, p. 222). The distinct impression is that Gainsborough was disguising some of his most profound thoughts on art in this enigmatic work. The painting is, after all, immensely suggestive, brimming with provocative pictorial allusions and formal contrasts: the dark haired boy and dark haired dog (the butcher's boy and dog?) set against the red-haired boy and the red-haired dog (the shepherd boy and dog?); the red-jacketed boy with the stick and the green-jacketed boy restraining him; the contrasting facial features of the two boys, with expressions that take on the emblematic appearance of the masks of Comedy and Tragedy.

While Murillo was mentioned as an influence upon the present painting, the subject-matter and colouring relate more closely to Gainsborough's interest in Venetian and Flemish art. Certainly, the dogs, as was noted at the time, were modelled on those of Snyders, whose work Gainsborough collected. Moreover, we know that Gainsborough made at least one trip to Flanders in the autumn of 1783 (Asfour et al. 1997, pp. 27ff.). A slightly smaller version of the picture, possibly (although there is no evidence) by Gainsborough Dupont, was exhibited at the Grosvenor Gallery in 1885 (130) by Lord Bateman. It has since disappeared.

9 *Shepherd Boy Listening to a Magpie* (Plate 7)
GAINSBOROUGH DUPONT (1754-97)

Oil on canvas, 190 x 137.2 cm, 1794
Private Collection

Provenance: Artist's sale, 11 April 1797 (100), unsold; possibly acquired *c* 1800-15 by Lord Ennismore (later 1st Earl of Listowel) for Kingston House; Lord Blakenham, sold Christie's, 15 July 1983 (40)
Exhibited: Royal Academy 1794 (179); National Loan Exhibition 1909/1910 (5)
Literature: Waterhouse, 1946, p. 140; Hayes, 1970, p. 301; Hayes, 1982, pp. 152, 218, pl.253

This magnificent full-length was shown at the Royal Academy in 1794 as 'A young gentleman in the character of a shepherd's boy', a title which suggests that it was conceived as a portrait rather than a fancy picture. While the features of the boy may have been based on those of a portrait sitter rather than a hired model, the figure of the shepherd boy is based upon a chalk study by Gainsborough (Victoria and Albert Museum). As the drawing indicates, Dupont, who inherited his uncle's studio, has reversed the pose of the figure in Gainsborough's drawing. He may also have adapted the drawing itself, for according to John Hayes the sheep to the left of the figure and the shepherd's crook are not by Gainsborough, and may have been added later by Dupont (Hayes, 1982, p. 8, no. 829).

Gainsborough Dupont, born 24 December 1754, was the son of Thomas Gainsborough's sister Sarah and her husband Philip. According to Gainsborough's friend Henry Bate, the young Dupont was 'fostered under his uncle's wing from a child'. On 12 January 1772 he was formally apprenticed to Gainsborough for seven years to learn 'The Art or Mystery of a Painter'. In 1774 he accompanied Gainsborough to London, entering the Royal Academy Schools the following spring. As Gainsborough's sole studio assistant Dupont was employed in making replicas, reduced oil copies and mezzotints after his uncle's fancy pictures, including the *Two Shepherd Boys with Dogs Fighting* (see cat. 8). He was also quite an accomplished landscape painter. Gainsborough, while he complained of his nephew's laziness, evidently had great affection for Dupont. In 1782 they toured the West country together and on one occasion, as a reward for his services, Gainsborough offered him the choice of any picture in his studio. Dupont selected the *Haymaker and Sleeping Girl* (Museum of Fine Arts, Boston), despite pressure from Gainsborough to take his own favourite, *The Woodman* (see cat. 86).

After Gainsborough's death in 1788 Dupont, who remained a life-long bachelor, continued to live and work in Gainsborough's house in Pall Mall, gaining the patronage of the Duchess of Devonshire and William Pitt, as well as various members of the Royal family. In addition to the present picture he exhibited one other fancy picture, a *Cottage Girl*, shown at the Royal Academy in 1790. Dupont's work, as contemporaries noted, closely emulated Gainsborough's own. A visitor to Dupont's studio in 1794, noted that, like Gainsborough, he painted by artificial light: 'On the door of the back drawing-room opening I was surprised, and not a little shocked to see the room darkened (daylight shut out); and lighted by a large lamp hanging from the centre of the ceiling there stood a man half-naked... Gainsborough Dupont was painting him. I heard it was the custom of Dupont to paint much by lamplight' (Whitley, 1915, pp. 395-6).

Dupont was shy and retiring by nature, and it was not until 1790, when he was aged thirty five, that he began to exhibit at the Royal Academy. Hitherto, he may have feared that his own work would appear a pale imitation of his uncle's.

It was remarked how closely Dupont's style resembled that of Gainsborough. Dupont continued to exhibit at the Royal Academy until 1795, at the end of which year he failed at his third attempt to be elected as an Associate Royal Academician. By that time Dupont had left Schomberg House, the lease having expired in 1792. Gainsborough's widow moved with her daughters to Sloane Street while Dupont went to Grafton Street. There he remained until his death on 20 January 1797, aged forty-two.

10 *Beggar Boy*
PHILIP DAWE (b. 1750), after Bartolomé Esteban Murillo

Mezzotint, 38.8 x 28 cm
LETTERED: '*Murillio [sic] pinx.*/*P. Dawe fec.*/*Published as the Act directs Aug. 26 1769/Printed for John Bowles at N°. 13 in Cornhill*'
The Trustees of the British Museum

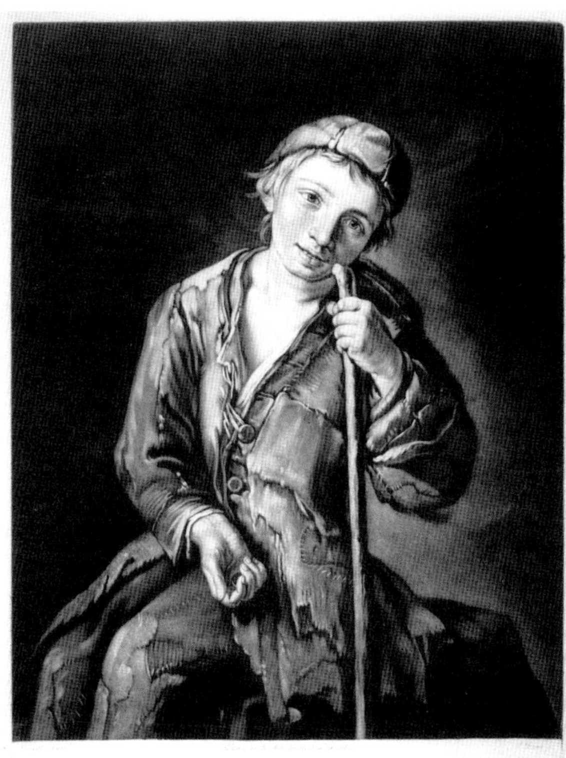

Philip Dawe studied engraving under Henry Morland during the 1760s. The owner of the painting on which Dawe's print was based is unknown, although we can assume that it was probably a popular image, contributing to the emergence of the cult of the 'picturesque' beggar in rags and tatters exemplified by Kitchingman's *Beggar and his Dog* of the mid-1770s (see cat. 93).

11 *The Maid in Rural Happiness* (Plate 11)
PETER VAN BLEEK (1695-1764) after Bartolomé Murillo

Mezzotint, 28 x 32 cm
LETTERED: '*Murillo pinxt — P. V. B. 1757*', with verses
David Alexander

The painter P[i]eter van Bleek was born in Flanders and in 1733 went to England, where he made his name as a pioneer of the theatrical conversation piece. George Vertue noted that he took up mezzotint engraving in 1735 because of his dissatisfaction with John Faber's print of his portrait of Mrs Clive. He engraved and published a number of his own pictures, and some fancy pictures such as this one. Murillo (1617/8-82) was primarily a painter of religious paintings, but his subject pictures, especially those of urchins, were sought after for their charm and vitality. This is one of the earliest paintings by Murillo to have been engraved in England; no owner is acknowledged and so the picture may have belonged to a dealer who hoped that the picture would sell better if it was engraved. Van Bleek added verses to add a moral to the print

> The maid in Rural Happiness,
> Pursues her innocent Employ
> And is her Pretty Care to bless
> Accosted by the Blithsom Boy.
> Her soft Intention to emprove,
> He makes an Offring on his Part
> An Emblem of their future Love,
> And with it tenders her his Heart.

DSA

12 *St John and the Lamb*
VALENTINE GREEN (1739-1813) after Bartolomé Esteban Murillo

Mezzotint, 49.5 x 35.5 cm
LETTERED: '*Morellio pinxt./Val. Green sculp.*'
The Trustees of the British Museum

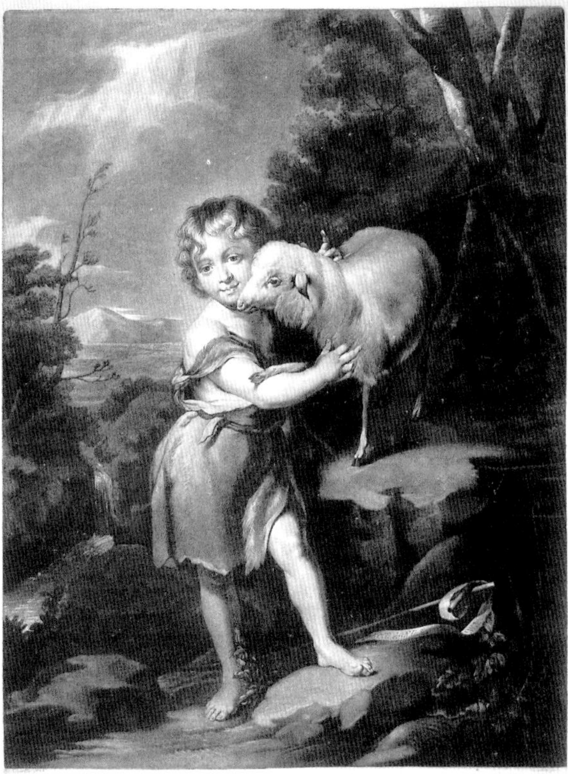

Green's engraving was taken from a copy of Murillo's *St John and the Lamb*, painted between 1660 and 1665 for Justino de Neve, Murillo's patron and patron also of the parish of Santa Maria la Blanca, Seville, where the painting was first shown as part of an altarpiece. Since 1840 it has been in the National Gallery, London. St John was painted frequently by Murillo as a young child holding a lamb, a subject deriving partly from the story in St Luke's gospel that the Baptist had gone to live in the wilderness during boyhood, and from renaissance depictions of the Virgin with the Infant Baptist and Christ Child. And while other artists before Murillo had painted the Infant Baptist,

it was the example of Murillo which impinged most on eighteenth-century sensibility.

Murillo's original picture was made as a pendant to the *Infant Christ as the Good Shepherd*, a copy of which was made by Gainsborough in the late 1770s (cat. 7). We do not know who painted the copy of *St John* upon which Green based his engraving. This picture, now in the collection of the Earl of Lovelace, was said in the late nineteenth century to have been acquired by the Hon. Thomas King (later 5th Baron Lovelace) in 1734. (MacLaren and Braham, 1988, no. 176, p. 66 and note 5). Murillo's original painting, along with the *Infant Christ as the Good Shepherd*, was then probably in Paris, suggesting that the copy in question may have been made in France. It is tempting to wonder whether this picture was made by Alexis Grimou, who had also made the copy of the *Infant Christ as the Good Shepherd* copied by Gainsborough, although such speculation should be tempered by the fact that at least five other copies of *St John* have been identified, any one of which may or may nor have been by Grimou or one of his contemporaries. In any event, Green's engraving of *St John* would certainly have been studied with great interest by Gainsborough and Reynolds, who made several of his own paintings of the infant Baptist at the time (see cat. 13 below).

13 *The Child Baptist in the Wilderness (St John)*
JOSEPH GROZER (*fl* late 18th century), after Sir Joshua Reynolds

Mezzotint, 44.7 x 35.5 cm
PROOF BEFORE LETTERS
The Trustees of the British Museum

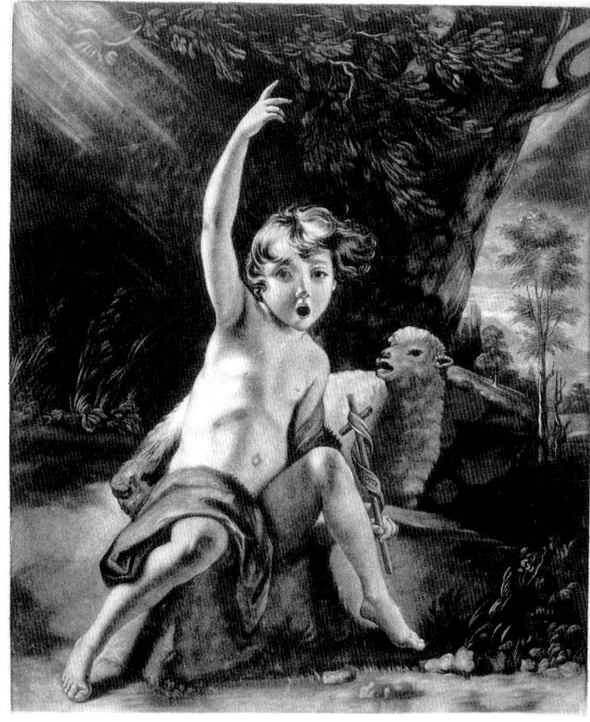

Reynolds exhibited the painting upon which the present mezzotint engraving is based at the Royal Academy in 1776. It was among the artist's most popular works. Hannah More, who saw it on Reynolds's easel, remarked that it 'bids fair for immortality' (Postle, 1995, p. 90). Shortly afterwards the picture was bought, along with a painting of *Samuel* (see cat. 14), by the Duke of Rutland, for 100 guineas each. (By comparison, a portrait by Reynolds of similar dimensions then cost only 70 guineas.) Despite Hannah More's aspirations for the picture, *The Child Baptist* was not destined for immortality, and perished alongside *Samuel* in a fire at Belvoir Castle in 1813. Three other prime versions have survived, including one in the Wallace Collection and an unfinished work in the Minneapolis Institute of Art. It is not entirely clear which version Grozer used to make his engraving, although it was most likely to have been either that in the Wallace Collection, or Lord Rutland's picture. The compositional source for *The Child Baptist*, it has been suggested, was a painting by Battista Franco, which Reynolds had sketched in Italy (Perini, 1988, pp. 163-4). Equally, he could have been inspired by Guido Reni's painting of the Baptist, now in Dulwich Picture Gallery. Ultimately, however, the artist uppermost in Reynolds's mind was Murillo, who had the previous century visualised the saint not merely as a youth but as a sweet-faced infant. In this vein, Reynolds would have known the *Infant St John* (then belonging to the Duke of Montagu) and a similar painting engraved by Valentine Green after a copy of Murillo's picture in the collection of Lord Lovelace.

The disparity between the elevated iconography of the image and the reality experienced by urchins who sat to Reynolds for such pictures was wonderfully captured by the Victorian painter William Powell Frith. Frith believed that he had found the model for Reynolds's *Infant Baptist*, a model who was, of course, now an old man. The old man recalled that the earlier artist had been a 'deaf gent' with an ear trumpet, whom he had to shout at. Upon agreeing to act as Frith's model, the old man supposed that Frith too would want him to remove his shirt 'as the deaf gent did'. Frith explained that would not be necessary. 'Then why,' said the man, 'did the old gent make me take off all but my trousers, and give me a crook to hold? There was a lamb in the picture as the old gent done' (quoted in Postle, 1995, p. 89). This incident apparently took place in 1838, by which time Reynolds's model would have been in his late sixties. Perhaps there was a grain of truth in Frith's story.

14 *The Calling of Samuel* (Plate 8)
SIR JOSHUA REYNOLDS (1723-92)

Oil on canvas, 90.2 x 69.8 cm
Private Collection

Provenance: Bought from the artist by John Frederick Sackville, 3rd Duke of Dorset, 1776; by descent
Exhibited: ?Royal Academy 1776 (244); British Institution, 1817 (44); Grafton Gallery, 1895 (140)
Literature: Waagen, 1837, Supp. p. 340; Leslie and Taylor, 1865, vol. 2, pp. 148, 156; Graves and Cronin, 1899-1901, vol. 3, p. 1201-2, vol. 4, p. 1461; Waterhouse, 1941, p. 67; Cormack, 1970, p. 150; Postle, 1995, pp. 90-93
Engraved: mezzotint by J.R. Smith 1783 as 'The Calling of Samuel'; mezzotint by S.W. Reynolds as 'The Infant Samuel'

In 1776 Reynolds exhibited a picture entitled *Samuel* at the Royal Academy. The picture was either the present work, later engraved as *The Calling of Samuel*, or another quite different, and slightly larger, composition known as *The Infant Samuel*. *The Calling of Samuel* was bought from Reynolds by the 3rd Duke of Dorset in 1776. The same year the Marquess of Granby, also a keen connoisseur of Reynolds's fancy pictures, purchased *The Infant Samuel* (destroyed in a fire at Belvoir Castle in 1813). Both paintings, replicated by Reynolds's pupils and followers in full size and in miniature, were among his most popular fancy pictures.

Hannah More, a woman with strong Christian convictions, saw *The Calling of Samuel* in Reynolds's studio shortly after it was completed. 'Sir Joshua tells me,' she wrote to a friend, 'that he is exceedingly mortified when he shows this picture to some of the great – they ask him who Samuel was? I told him he must get someone to make an Oratorio of Samuel, and then it would not be vulgar to confess they knew something of him. He said he was glad to find that I was so intimately acquainted with the devoted prophet' (Roberts, 1834, vol. 1, pp. 71-2). More's admission that it was considered unfashionable to betray a knowledge of religious subject-matter when unconnected, for example, to an oratorio, underlines the predominantly secular sphere in which Reynolds's religious fancy pictures were viewed, and explains why it was not possible for an artist working in England to concentrate upon sacred art. It may also explain why, when Reynolds's *Samuel* was exhibited at the Royal Academy, it was described in several editions of the catalogue as 'Daniel'.

Reynolds, himself the son of a clergyman, was familiar with the Bible. He was not, however, remotely interested in generating enthusiasm for Hannah More's evangelical revival through fancy pictures such as *The Calling of Samuel*. He never went to church and had no interest in organised religion. His sister Elizabeth wrote in 1776 to inform him that his soul was 'a shocking spectacle of poverty' (G.B. Hill, *Johnsonian Miscellanies*, 1897, vol. 2, pp. 455-6, note). Ultimately, he was far more interested in promoting the Old Masters than the Old Testament, in works such as the *Calling of Samuel* which capitalised on the current vogue in England for Murillo's infant saints (see cat. 7). Indeed, of all Reynolds's child saints, it is *The Calling of Samuel* and the *Infant Baptist in the Wilderness* (see cat. 13) that most closely emulate the art of Murillo, notably in his sentimental depiction of the *Infant St John*, a picture which he would have inspected in the collection of the Duke of Buccleuch.

15 *The Calling of Samuel* (Plate 9)
JOHN OPIE (1761-1807)

Oil on canvas, 127 x 99.5 cm, *c* 1803
University of Manchester (Tabley House Collection)

Provenance: Purchased from the artist by Sir John Fleming Leicester, 8 February 1806; by descent to Lt.-Col. John Leicester-Warren; bequeathed by his executors in 1976 to the Victoria University of Manchester
Exhibited: Heim Gallery, London, 1989, no. 15
Literature: Hall, 1962, p. 87; Cannon-Brookes, ed., 1989, pp. 56-7, rep.

Opie's *The Calling of Samuel*, both in terms of the young boy's attitude and dress, strongly recalls Sir Joshua Reynolds's *Infant Samuel* of 1776 (rather than Reynolds's *Calling of Samuel*, exhibited here). The *Infant Samuel* had been among Reynolds's most popular fancy pictures, and versions belonged to the Duke of Rutland (destroyed), Sir Charles Long, later Lord Farnborough (Tate Gallery), and Reynolds's friend Antony Chamier, who exported his picture to France (Musée Fabre, Montpelier). In addition to Opie's painting, Reynolds's composition inspired a number of related compositions, including a French patriotic print, '*Je prie Dieu pour mon père et pour la France*', which showed a kneeling child praying for the safe return of her father from the Napoleonic Wars. *The Calling of Samuel*, which is more sentimental in mood than Opie's fancy pictures of the 1780s, probably dates from the early 1800s.

Sir John Fleming Leicester's own interest in the present painting may well have stemmed from Sir Charles Long's ownership of a version of Reynolds's *Infant Samuel*: both men admired Reynolds and were fervent patrons of contemporary British art. Leicester's relationship with Opie, however, seems only have started around the time he purchased this picture. It coincided with the completion of his picture gallery at 24 Hill Street, London.

16 *The Spartan Boy*
JOHN RAPHAEL SMITH (1752-1812), after Nathaniel Hone

Mezzotint, 37.7 x 27.8 cm
LETTERED: '*Painted by N. Hone R.A./Engrav'd by J.R. Smith/THE SPARTAN BOY/Having stolen a cub Fox, conceal'd it under his Garment, when being observ'd, he suffr'd it to bite him Mortally, rather than undergo the disgrace of a discovery./Published 18 July 1775 by T. Bradshaw, James Street Covent Garden, & J.R.Smith, N⁰ 10 Batemans Buildings, Soho Square*'
The Trustees of the British Museum

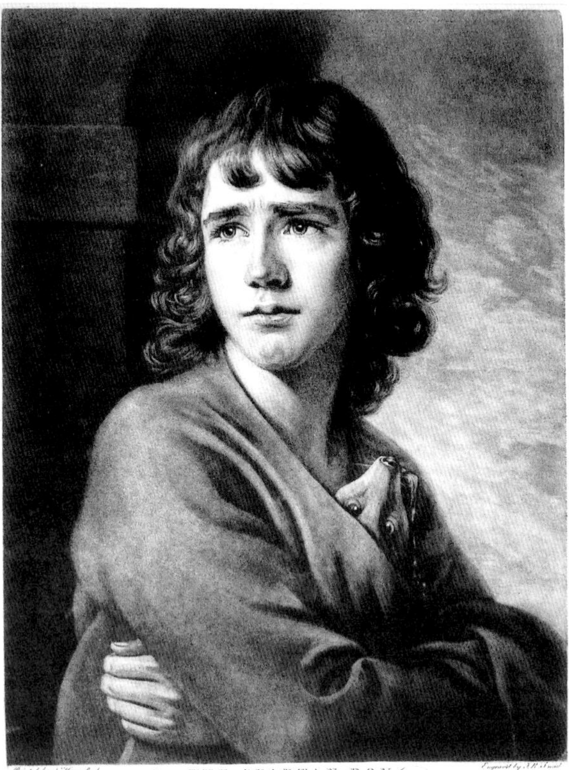

The original painting of the *The Spartan Boy* (private collection) was exhibited by Nathaniel Hone at the Royal Academy in 1775, perhaps in competition with Reynolds's compositions featuring mythological and biblical children and infants. The model used by Hone was his son Camillus, who sat for a number of other examples of Hone's fancy pictures, including the *Boy Deliberating his Drawing* (whereabouts unknown), shown at the Society of Artists in 1766. Although Hone is best remembered as the author of *The Conjuror*, his wonderfully scurrilous satire on Reynolds, during the 1760s Hone had also pioneered the single-figure fancy picture, with works such as *The Brick-dust Man* (see cat. 58) and the *Piping Boy* (National Gallery of Ireland). There can be little doubt that Reynolds, always aware of potential rivals, kept a close eye on Hone's experimental fancy pictures during the 1760s and early 1770s.

17 *Euphrosyne (also known as 'Terpsichore' and 'Comedy')*
SIR JOSHUA REYNOLDS (1723-92)   (Plate 12)

Oil on canvas, 127 x 101.6 cm, *c* 1762
Private collection

Provenance: The artist's niece, Mary Palmer, later Marchioness of Thomond; her sale, 26 May 182 (14), 'Large sketch for the portraits of the Marquis of Rockingham, and Mr. Burke (Fitzwilliam Museum, Cambridge), and ditto of Euphrosyne', bought Coles for £11 0s 6d; Sir Digby Neave by 1863; his sale, Christie's 6 June 1868 (121) as 'Terpsichore'; bought in by owner for £220 10s; by descent
Exhibited: British Institution 1863 (150)
Literature: Leslie and Taylor, 1865, vol. 1, p. 479; Graves and Cronin, 1899-1901, vol. 3, p. 1151; Postle, 19995, p. 20ff

The present study is closely related to the figure of Comedy in Reynolds's allegorical portrait *Garrick between Tragedy and Comedy* (private collection), exhibited at the Society of Artists in 1762. The exhibited picture was intended to advertise allegorically Garrick's versatility as an actor, as one capable of taking on both comic and tragic roles with equal ease. In *Garrick...* Reynolds shows the figure of Tragedy declaiming to the actor while the sylph-like Comedy seductively pulls him in the opposite direction. The image was based upon the ancient tale told by Prodicus of Hercules at the crossroads between Virtue and Pleasure, although Reynolds appears to have based his own interpretation principally upon the satirical account in Ovid's *Amores* and Lord Shaftesbury's pedagogical essay, 'A notion of the historical draught or tablature of the Judgement of Hercules' (see Postle, 1995, pp. 20ff.).

The narrative in *Garrick...* revolved around the skills of the actor. Reynolds also had a secondary agenda, which concerned the choices faced by the artist. Tragedy is painted in the manner of the Bolognese master Guido Reni, an artist devoted to the didactic aspects of High Art, while Comedy echoes the soft-edged manner of Correggio. These two artists in turn represent the intellect and the heart, Guido obeying the constraints of line while Correggio is seduced by the nuances of colour and light.

The present figure differs from that of Comedy in the arrangement of her garments and in the addition of the cymbals, which occupy her hands and transform her into Euphrosyne. In this respect she resembles another unfinished sketch by Reynolds (Art Museum, Stockholm). These two figures are in turn related to a life drawing of a female nude holding an arrow, which belonged to Reynolds (although I am no longer convinced that it is actually by him, see Postle, 1995, pl. 11). Taken together, the drawing, the oil sketch, and the picture under discussion suggest that the figure of 'Comedy' either evolved as an independent subject before it was incorporated into the painting of *Garrick*, or that Reynolds re-used the figure at some later stage for a fancy picture.

18 *Venus Chiding Cupid for Learning to Cast Accounts*
SIR JOSHUA REYNOLDS (1723-92)   (Plate 13)

Oil on canvas, 101.6 x 97.8 cm, 1771
The Iveagh Bequest, Kenwood

Provenance: Purchased from the artist by James Caulfeild [*sic*], 1st Earl of Charlemont, 1774; passed to the widow of the 2nd Earl; Wertheimer; Agnew by 1888; purchased from Agnew by the Earl of Iveagh
Exhibited: Royal Academy, 1771 (156); Dublin Industrial Exhibition 1853 (695); Royal Academy, 1928 (208); Manchester 1928 (27)
Literature: Leslie and Taylor, 1865, vol. 1, p. 399, note 1, vol. 2, p. 54 note 4; Graves and Cronin, 1899-1901, vol. 3, pp. 122526, vol. 4, p. 1464, p. 1480 BBB; Waterhouse, 1941, pp. 61, 67, 76; Cormack, 1970, p. 148; Kenwood, 1978, p. 26; Postle, 1995, pp. 85-7, 103
Engraved: Stipple by Francesco Bartolozzi, 1784 (not this version); R.J. Collyer, 1786; mezzotint by S.W. Reynolds (?not this version)

Reynolds showed the picture at the Royal Academy in 1771, with the title '*Venus chiding Cupid for learning to cast accompts*' [*sic*]: 'Charming, but the drawing faulty: better coloured than usual' (Walpole). One critic said of Venus that 'one would imagine the painter had drawn her from some girl in low life of thirteen or fourteen years of age' – which was probably true (Postle, 1995, pp. 86-7). The picture was perhaps displayed in Reynolds's gallery among his various Old Masters until it was spotted by Lord Charlemont, who gave £100 for it three years later. The subject does not derive from a classical source, although it was common among French eighteenth-century artists, including Etienne Falconet who made a marble statuette of the subject around 1760 (Wallace Collection). Reynolds was aware of trends in French art, and visited Paris in the autumn of 1768. He was friends with prominent French artists including Falconet.

The subject brims with sexual innuendo. Venus holds before him Cupid's inverted arrow, while the grinning putto points to his own sharp and upwardly mobile weapon. Clearly Cupid's attempt at financial wizardry is sapping his prowess as a legendary lover. In this sense it prefigures the risqué pendants painted a few years later, *Cupid as a Link Boy* and *Mercury as a Cutpurse* (see cats. 39 and 40). Reynolds's decision to address the subject of Venus chiding Cupid, just after he had assumed the Presidency of the Royal Academy, was prompted, we can assume, by a desire to produce art which conformed with sophisticated, cosmopolitan taste. Nor is it a coincidence that the majority of patrons who purchased his racier fancy pictures were aristocrats, like Lord Charlemont, schooled in contemporary continental art as well as the Old Masters.

Reynolds's principal compositional source for *Venus chiding Cupid* appears to have been a painting by the Bolognese artist Alessandro Tiarini (1577-1668), a detail of which Reynolds had sketched during his Italian sojourn some twenty years earlier. Stylistically, *Venus chiding Cupid* is a conflation of the styles of a number of artists, including Correggio as well as Van Loo, Amigoni and Boucher.

Ten years after selling *Venus chiding Cupid* Reynolds made a second version of the painting for Brooke Boothby (Lady Lever Art Gallery, Port Sunlight). It differs in a number of significant ways from the present work, and was not simply a copy of the earlier composition. In any event, since Reynolds no longer owned the first version, and it had yet to be engraved, he presumably relied on memory to make the second version. It was this picture that Bartolozzi engraved in stipple in 1784. Bartolozzi too made some changes to the composition, notably substituting the sums on Cupid's scroll with the word 'pinmoney', a pun relating to the little pin-like arrows held by Venus and the putto teasing the tearful Cupid about his own blunt instrument.

19 *A Snake in the Grass*

JOHN RAPHAEL SMITH (1752-1812), after Sir Joshua Reynolds

Stipple engraving, 25.5 x 20.5 cm
LETTERED: '*Painted by Sir Joshua Reynolds/Engrav'd by J. R. Smith/A SNAKE in the GRASS./*[… 22 lines of verse, signed 'R. B. Cooper', beginning: 'Fann'd by the summer's gentlest wind …'] *London, Pubd Septr 24, 1787 by I. R. Smith, No 31 King Street, Covent Garden.*'
David Alexander
Literature: Frankau 326, Hamilton, p. 158; Alexander 1993, 13.

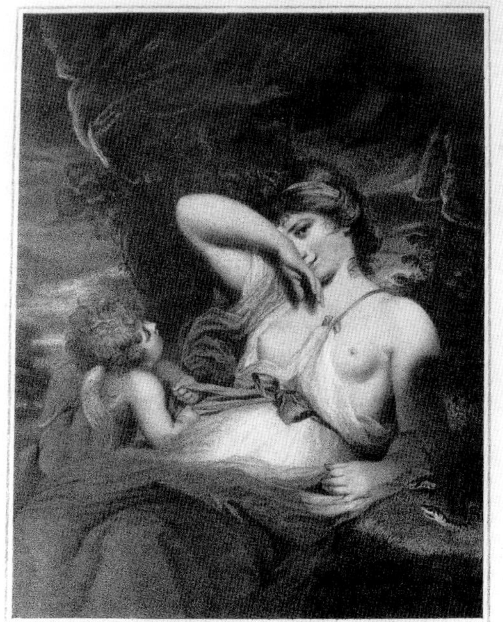

Reynolds exhibited his *Nymph and Cupid*, the painting upon which the present stipple engraving is based, at the Royal Academy in 1784, when it was acquired by Lord Carysfort. Another version, retained by Reynolds, was later acquired by Sir John Soane (Sir John Soane's Museum). A third version was solicited from Reynolds by Lord Carysfort for presentation to Prince Potemkin (The Hermitage, St Petersburg). Lord Carysfort's version was later acquired by Sir Robert Peel at Christie's for £1260, and eventually found its way into the National Gallery in 1871. It is now in the Tate Gallery.

The painting and the associated print became known as 'The Snake in the Grass' owing to the presence of a serpent in the lower right hand corner of several (but not all) versions. It was also known as 'Love untying the zone of Beauty' – a reference to Cupid who tugs at the nymph's girdle.

The picture exemplifies Reynolds's desire by the mid-1780s to appeal to the cosmopolitan, racy tastes of sophisticated young connoisseurs, although the bashful gesture of the nymph (which Reynolds called 'the half consenting') was actually derived from a drawing he had made of a much younger, and fully-clothed model (see Herrmann, 1968, p. 65, repr.; Postle, 1995, p. 198). The sensuous subject-matter was also ideally suited to the soft-focused effects produced by stipple engraving which was then replacing mezzotint as the favoured medium for popular furniture prints. The verses appended to the print were by R.B. Cooper, who, as David Alexander has suggested, may have been a young lawyer named Robert Bransby Cooper (born 1762).

DSA

20 *Guardian Angels*

CHARLES HODGES (1764-1837), after Sir Joshua Reynolds

Mezzotint, 36 x 34.5 cm
LETTERED: '*Painted by Sr Joshua Reynolds PRA/Engraved by C H Hodges/GUARDIAN ANGELS/London Publish'd March 30th 1786 by J.R. Smith No 83 Oxford Street*'
The Trustees of the British Museum

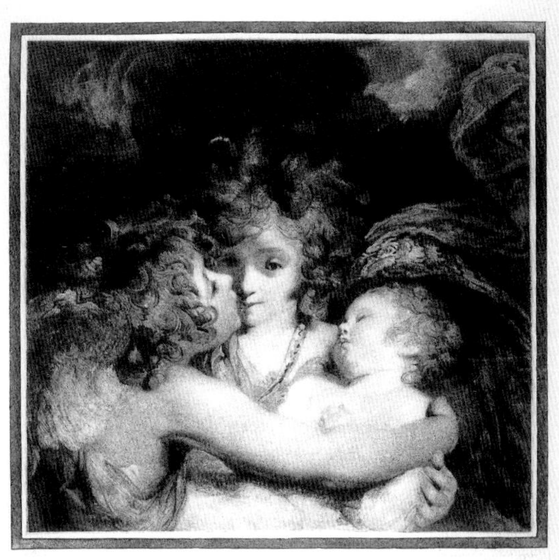

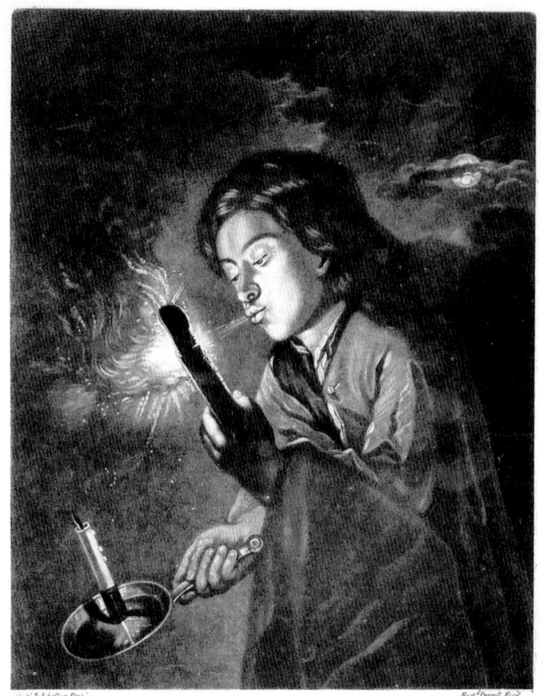

Reynolds's painting upon which this print is based was exhibited at the Royal Academy in 1786 as 'A Child with Guardian Angels'. Hodges's print was published prior to the painting's exhibition, which was slightly unusual, if not unique. Reynolds had been painting infants and small children since the early 1770s, although it was in the course of his work on the *Nativity* for New College Oxford towards the end of that decade that his interest in such subjects intensified. During the 1780s he painted a number of allegorical pictures featuring babies, the closest to the present composition being the portrait of Miss Frances Gordon of 1787 (Tate Gallery), in which the little girl's head is viewed from five different angles, to resemble a cluster of cherubim. Although *Guardian Angels* is to all intents and purposes a fancy picture, another state of the present engraving in the British Museum (1839-10-12-59) is inscribed '*portrait of Master Dunning as a sleeping infant held by two angles* [sic]', which suggests that it may have been related to a portrait commission. However, it would have been unusual for Reynolds to have painted such a young child's portrait without including its mother. Also, the painting's owner was subsequently the Duke of Leeds, whose family name was Godolphin and who had, in any case, a penchant for Reynolds's fancy pictures.

21 *Night (Boy Blowing Charcoal)*
RICHARD PURCELL *(fl* 1746-66), after Godfried Schalcken

Mezzotint, 35.3 x 25 cm
LETTERED: '*Godf.*ʸ *Schalken Pinx*ᵗ.*/Rich*ᵈ. *Purcell Fecit*/NIGHT. */Boy Blowing Charcoal.* / *London Printed for Rob*ᵗ. *Sayer at the Golden Buck near Serjeants Inn Fleet Street*'
The Trustees of the British Museum

Godfried Schalcken (1634-1706) was trained in Leiden by Gerard Dou, who had been a pupil of Rembrandt. Most of Schalcken's career was spent in the Netherlands, although between 1692 and 1697 he lived in London. His influence upon British artists of the eighteenth century centred upon his nocturnes, of which the *A Boy Blowing on a Firebrand to Light a Candle* is a prime example. As has been noted the image of a figure blowing on a firebrand goes back to Jacopo Bassano, although perhaps the most famous

sixteenth-century work was El Greco's *Boy Blowing on a Firebrand*, of 1570-75 (Museo e Galleria Nazionale di Capodimonte, Naples). In the early seventeenth century it was widely exploited by Utrecht painters, notably Ter Brugghen and Honthorst. Honthorst's *Soldier and a Girl* (Braunschweig, Herzog Anton Ulrich-Museum) brings out quite explicitly the phallic symbolism of the burning ember as an emblem of lust fanned by the air blown upon it (see Spicer and Orr, 1997, no. 36). Symbolism of a similar kind was later employed by Reynolds in his painting *Cupid as a Link Boy* (see cat. 39).

The painting upon which Purcell's print is based (see Fig. 18) is of particular interest to British art since it was actually painted during Schalcken's time in London, rather than being exported into the country. Purcell's engraving is undated, but it was probably made sometime during the 1750s or early sixties. The clearest indication of Schalcken's influence on Brititish artists is to be found in the work of Joseph Wright and, to a lesser extent, Henry Morland. At the very time that both artists began to produce nocturnes in the early 1760s, a detailed description of what purported to be Schalcken's method for working by night was published (see cat. 27). Although there were many artists experimenting with tenebrist techniques in Holland and Flanders in the seventeenth century, Schalcken's name was synonymous with the technique. One of Francis Wheatley's very first mezzotint engravings, the *Boy Lighting a Candle* engraved around 1770, was inscribed as being after a painting by Schalcken, although it is now known to be by Rubens (see Webster, 1970, no. E3, p. 158).

As David Alexander notes, Richard Purcell was a pupil of John Brooks in Dublin. He went to London in about 1755, where he was mostly employed in making copies of mezzotints by fellow Irishmen such as James McArdell for the print-seller Robert Sayer. He also engraved a number of mezzotints under the pseudonym 'C.Corbutt'.

22 *The Mischievous Girl*   (Plate 10)
JOHN RAPHAEL SMITH (1752-1812) after William Tate

Mezzotint, 57.5 x 71.5 cm

David Alexander

Literature: Chalmer Smith, 1883, vol. 3, p.1319, no. 195; Frankau, 1902, No 44 as after Wright; Nicolson, 1968

During the eighteenth century there were several attempts to produce prints which would pass as oil paintings. The experiments of Le Blon with three-colour printed mezzotints of old master pictures are well-known. In the late 1770s a number of contemporary paintings were engraved in a process, called 'mechanical painting', which was developed in Birmingham by Edward Jee and Eginton in conjunction with Boulton and Fothergill. This method, by which large aquatints printed in colours from several plates were transferred to canvas, touched up by hand and then varnished, was later adopted by Joseph Booth; this entrepreneur established the Polygraphic Society, which for many years held exhibitions of in its premises in Pall Mall. The engraver and artist John Raphael Smith, son of the landscape painter Thomas Smith, ran a very successful print-publishing business in the 1780s and 1790s, but in the 1790s he also began to work in earnest as a portraitist in crayons, and in 1802 he put himself forward, without success, for election as an Associate of the Royal Academy. Like most publishers he found business much more difficult after war broke out with France in 1793, but he continued to engrave and publish prints. He engraved a number of mezzotint plates on a larger scale and in 1803 he exhibited prints at the British Institution which were described as 'specimens of a new process of painting prints in oil by which invention they will bear cleaning and treating in every respect like pictures and are rendered equally durable'. Like this print they were mezzotints, coloured with oil paints, mounted on canvas, which could be strained onto a stetcher. He applied the process to a number of large prints, and advertised, for example, a large mezzotint of Bonaparte after Appiani as 'Plain Prints, One Guinea; in Colours, two Guineas, and prints Coloured in oil, three Guineas. These last will roll up or keep in a portfolio like other prints; any soil may be washed off with a sponge and clean water, and may be framed at any time, oil pictures not requiring a glass' (*Morning Chronicle*, 27 Jan. 1800).

William Tate (d. 1806) was a member of a Liverpool family with whom Wright of Derby was friendly from the late 1760s. He became a pupil and friend of Wright, painted in his style and owned a number of his pictures.

DSA

23 *Old Woman Plucking a Fowl*   (Plate 15)
RICHARD HOUSTON (1722-75) after Rembrandt

Mezzotint, 35.5 x 25.5 cm

PROOF BEFORE LETTERS

David Alexander

Literature: Chaloner Smith 1883, vol.2, p.701, no.148; Charrington 1923, 85, i/2; New Haven 1984, no. 95

The painting upon which this fine mezzotint is based was acquired by the collector and dealer John Blackwood. He may have commissioned the print from Richard Houston, who made mezzotints of several pictures in his possession, probably in order to increase their saleability. By the time the plate was finished the picture had passed, probably in Blackwood's sale of 1757 (lot 57), to the Hon.

Francis Charteris (1723-1808), later 7th Earl of Wemyss. Its present whereabouts are unknown. The print, or possibly the painting, may have been the inspiration for Henry Walton's *Girl Plucking a Turkey* (see cat. 60).

DSA

24 *Old Woman*
THOMAS FRYE (*c* 1710-1762)

Mezzotint, 50.1 x 35.3 cm

PROOF BEFORE LETTERS

The Trustees of the British Museum

Literature: Chaloner Smith, 1883, vol.2, p.520, no.15; Wynne, 1972, pp. 79-84

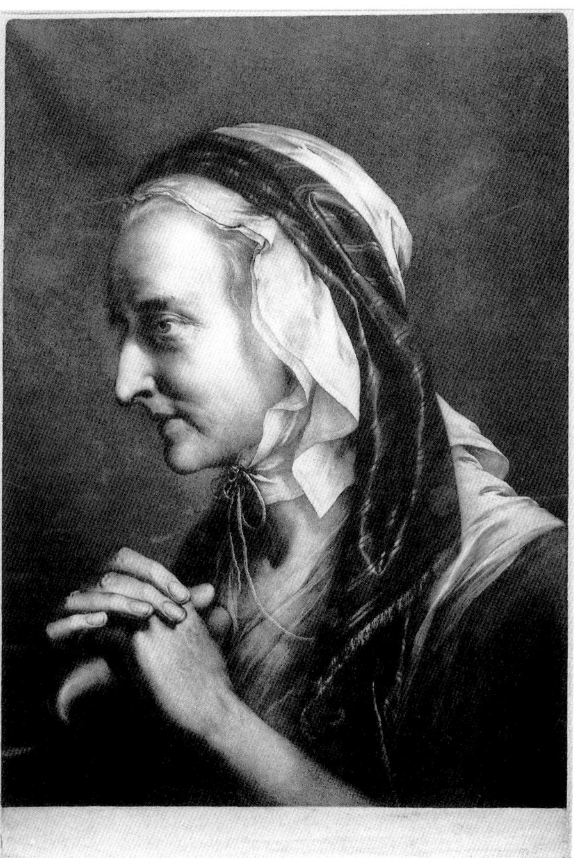

Thomas Frye is one of the most intriguing and original artists to have emerged in Britain during the mid-eighteenth century. Frye was Irish by birth. He had settled in England by 1735, where he painted portraits in crayons, oil and in miniature. A man of many parts, he was also instrumental in setting up the Bow porcelain factory, which he managed until 1759. Frye's most celebrated achievement, however, is the fascinating series of heads which he produced in mezzotint from 1760 to 1762, of which the *Old Woman* is one of the finest. Although all the heads are almost certainly modelled on the artist's friends and family they are not straightforward portraits but life-size character studies. And while these heads are virtually unique in eighteenth-century British art (although there are parallels with later similar studies by John Hamilton Mortimer) they may well have been influenced by chalk studies, which were then much in vogue, by the Italian artist Giovanni Piazzetta (1683-1754). They are also reminiscent of the heads or 'tronies' made by Flemish painters in the seventeenth century for insertion into larger historical compositions and, in the instance of painters such as Bloemaert, as works of art in their own right (see Spicer and Orr, 1997, no. 33). Frye's heads, which he exhibited at the Society of Artists during the early 1760s, were in turn influential upon Joseph Wright, who adapted them for use in his paintings such as *A Philosopher giving a lecture on the Orrery* and *An Experiment on a Bird in the Air Pump* (see Nicolson, 1968, vol. 1, pp. 42-44). The old woman in the present engraving was said to be Frye's wife.

25 *The Captive* (Plate 14)

SIR JOSHUA REYNOLDS (17923-92)

Oil on canvas, 76.2 x 63.5 cm, *c* 1770-73
Private collection

Provenance: Marchioness of Thomond sale, Christie's 18 May 1821 (19) as 'Study for the head of an aged character, The Captive'; bought Lord Lambton; by descent.
Exhibited: Manchester 1857 (45)
Literature: Graves and Cronin, vol. 3, pp. 1136-7, 1217; *Country Life*, 5 May 1966, p. 1084 (repr.); Postle, 1988, p. 742, fig. 13; Postle, 1989, catalogue, pp. 19-20; Postle, 1995, pp. 128, 130, 132 (repr.).
Engraved: J.R. Smith; S.W. Reynolds (as 'A Study from Nature).

The subject of *The Captive* is derived from an episode in Laurence Sterne's *Sentimental Journey* of 1768. Here Sterne sympathises with the plight of a prisoner incarcerated in the bowels of the Bastille: 'As I darkened the little light he had, he lifted up a hopeless eye towards the door, then cast it down – shook his head and went on with his work of afflictions.' Sterne's imaginary captive proved a very popular subject for British artists in the 1770s. John Hamilton Mortimer, Benjamin West and Joseph Wright all produced works based on the subject. The captive had become by the late eighteenth century a leading emblem of pathos in an age of burgeoning sensibility. Typically, however, Reynolds's study remains ambiguous in terms of its relationship to the literary source, there being no means of knowing whether Reynolds actually intended the figure to relate to Sterne's narrative.

Reynolds's studies of old men's heads – notably the series based on the pavior George White – were generic, and took their lead from character studies of ageing patriarchs and prophets by Domenico Feti, Rubens and Guido Reni, which were popular among connoisseurs in eighteenth-century England. They were also extensively copied and faked, Hogarth remarking that Kneller's pupil, John Peters 'could sh-t old mens Heads with ease… ' (Postle, 1988, p. 735). Reynolds himself made at least one 'companion' to an old man's head, after *A Hermit*, imported into England by his friend Lord Palmerston. Reynolds's pendant is known as *Joab*. As a rule, however, Reynolds did not give his own studies of old men historical or religious identities, except in the case of major history paintings such as *Ugolino and his Children in the Dungeon*. We can assume, therefore, that most titles were invented by the engravers who made prints after his paintings. For Reynolds such studies were a means by which he could measure his own achievement against the Old Masters. The present study may have been inspired by a drawing which Reynolds hade made in Rome of Raphael's *Repulse of Attila* in the *Stanza d'Eliodoro* (Penny, 1986, no. 160, repr.).

Reynolds, who kept the picture in his studio, allowed his pupils to make copies. George Engleheart, who worked in Reynolds's studio in the late 1770s, made a miniature of *The Captive* (private collection), along with a number of other Reynolds fancy pictures. An inferior full size replica

in the Ashmolean Museum, Oxford, has been described as 'a portrait of George White, an Artist's model' but the likeness, when compared to other known paintings featuring White, is unconvincing. Also, a slightly reduced version (50.8 x 50.8 cm) in oils was in a private collection in Newquay in the 1930s, at which time it was described as the head of 'an extremely ugly man' (*Daily Express*, 27 November 1933).

The present work, which was engraved variously as *Caius Marius* and a *Study from Nature*, has also been confused with a similar study of a younger bearded man by Reynolds, which was engraved by J.R. Smith as *The Banished Lord*, after Thomas Warton's *The Pleasures of Melancholy* (prime version, Tate Gallery). *The Captive* is clearly the name by which this picture was known to Reynolds's family.

II

Innocence and Experience

26 *Girl with a cat* (Plate 16)

PHILIP MERCIER (?1689-1760)

Oil on canvas, 91.4 x 71.1 cm, *c* 1755
National Gallery of Scotland, Edinburgh

Signed: '*PM*' (monogram)

Provenance: bequeathed by Lady Murray to the National Gallery of Scotland, 1861
Exhibited: Kenwood and York, 1969 (67)
Literature: Waterhouse, 1952, p. 128, fig. 27b; National Gallery of Scotland, 1957, p. 169 (433); Raines, 1964, p. 30, fig. 8; Kenwood and York, 1969, p. 52, no. 67; Ingamells and Raines, 1978, no. 158
Engraved: mezzotint by James McArdell, 1756

The *Girl with a cat*, which has been dated to around 1755, is typical of Mercier's later fancy pictures, which 'tended towards a more "classical" simplicity, often showing a single female figure against a plain background' (Ingamells and Raines, 1976-8, p. 7). The subject-matter of a young girl with a cat is common in seventeenth century Dutch art (see Spicer and Orr, 1997, no. 39), although here any allegorical meaning is bolstered by a more direct appeal to sensibility, the cat being perceived as a domestic pet as much as an emblem of unrequited love. Even so, the girl's engaging smile, her servants' cap and apron, her semi-exposed bosom, and above all the black cat, suggest that the image was intended to convey a strong sexual innuendo. Stylistically, the *Girl with a Cat* is closer to eighteenth-century French prototypes than Dutch examples, most especially the 'fancy' figures of child pilgrims by Alexis Grimou (1680-1740).

The muted colours and marked use of *chiaroscuro* underline the fact that the image was intended to serve as the basis for McArdell's mezzotint engraving. By this time in his career, Mercier, who had recently returned to London, was concentrating almost exclusively on fancy pictures for the print market. In 1756 – the year in which the engraving of the *Girl with a Cat* was published – McArdell published a total of four new engravings after Mercier, while no less than eight plates by John Faber II after Mercier were also reissued (Ingamells and Raines, 1976-8, p. 6).

27 *Two Girls Dressing a Kitten by Candlelight*   (Plate 18)
JOSEPH WRIGHT (1734-97)

Oil on canvas, 90.8 x 72.4 cm, *c* 1768-70
English Heritage, Kenwood

Provenance: Sold by a 'nobleman', Christie's, 24 January 1771; bought Lord Palmerston, £7 7s; 2nd Lord Palmerston; with Leger, then Agnew's; on loan to Kenwood, 1972-96 from private collection; bt 1996 with help of grants from the National Heritage Memorial Fund, NACF, London Houses Museum Trust and The Friends of Kenwood
Exhibited: Winchester, 1938 (50)
Literature: Nicolson, 1968, vol. 1, pp. 48, 106, 240, cat. 212, vol. 2, p. 49, plate 75
Engraved: Mezzotint by Thomas Watson, as 'Miss Kitty Dressing', published 20th February 1781.

Joseph Wright's niece left an invaluable account of how her uncle achieved the captivating effects of light and shade in pictures such as *Two Girls Dressing a Kitten by candlelight*: 'His mechanical genius… enabled him to construct an apparatus for painting candlelight pieces and effects of fire-light. It consisted of a framework of wood resembling a large folding screen, which reached the top of the room, the two ends being placed against a wall, which formed two sides of the enclosure. Each fold was divided into compartments, forming a framework covered with black paper, and opening with hinges, so that when the object he was painting from was placed within the proper light, the artist could view it from various points from without' (Nicolson, 1968, vol. 1, p. 48).

It may have been more than mere coincidence, says Nicolson, that shortly before Wright began to produce such pictures, an account of a very similar method used by Godfried Schalcken (1643-1706) to produce nocturnes was published (Paris, 1762). The point not only underlines the technical similarities between the two artists' methods but the formal debt which Wright's paintings owed to seventeenth-century masters such as Schalcken, Ter Brugghen, Honthorst and other artists of the Utrecht School. As Nicolson observes, 'The reddish-mauve sleeve of the girl on the left masking the candle, the dull dark red colouring of the faces, the saucy curl to the lips, the slanting shadow on the nose of the other girl, her eyes and eyelids, can all be paralleled in Honthorst's work even if the subject cannot' (loc. cit.).

The subject-matter of *Two Girls Dressing a Kitten by Candlight* – children teasing a small animal – is the quintessence of the fancy picture. The picture immediately brings to mind Mercier's well-behaved *Girl with a Cat* (cat. 26), which had been around for ten years in the form of an engraving, or indeed Gainsborough's unfinished study of his own daughters squeezing the tail of a snarling cat (National Gallery). It also recalls countless pictures by seventeenth-century Dutch artists of children and small animals, such as Judith Leyster's *Two Children with a Kitten and an Eel*, now in the National Gallery, London, and the *Girl Teasing a Cat* by Jan van Bijlert (Walters Art Gallery, Baltimore, USA), where an impish little girl pinches a kitten's ear while grasping its paws – a pictorial equivalent to the Dutch proverb, 'whoever plays with a little cat will be scratched' (Spicer and Orr, 1997, p. 248)

Like its Dutch precursors, Wright's picture trades on the ambiguities in the child's world, Wright's children also having, to borrow Simon Schama's phraseology, 'within them from birth the seeds of both goodness and wickedness, a blessed or cursed life' (Schama, 1987, p. 552). The children have tired of playing with their doll, which is what they ought still to be doing according to normal rules of play. Instead, they have removed the doll's headress and fitted it upon the head of the hapless kitten, which, we assume is about to receive additional unwelcome garments from the doll. The picture is comic, but the comedy involves a degree of cruelty. The girls may adopt the expressions of angels, but they can also be little horrors.

The picture, which dates probably from the late 1760s, was bought by Lord Palmerston, who, although he did not in this instance buy directly from the artist, was a patron of Wright's (he purchased, for example a version of Wright's *Iron Forge* in 1772). Palmerston was also a friend and patron of Reynolds, and later acquired his *Infant Academy* (cat. 45).

28 *Muscipula*   (Plate 17)
SIR JOSHUA REYNOLDS (1723-92)

Oil on canvas, 73.7 x 61 cm, *c* 1785-6
Private Collection

Provenance: Purchased from the artist by Count d'Adhémar; D'Adhémar sale, Christie's 17 March 1788; bought by Charles James Fox for £50; by descent.
Exhibited: Grosvenor Gallery, 1884 (29)
Literature: Leslie and Taylor, 1865, vol. 2, p. 3; Liechtenstein, 1875, p. 222; Graves and Cronin, 1899-1901, vol. 3, p. 1176; Waterhouse, 1941, p. 76; Postle, 1995, pp. 112, 115, 117.
Engraved: Stipple by John Jones, 1786; mezzotint by S.W. Reynolds; Samuel Cousins, RA, 1879

Muscipula is one of a series of fancy pictures painted by Reynolds in the 1780s featuring little girls clutching pet birds and animals. Others include *Felina* (holding a kitten) *Robinetta* (holding a robin), and *Lesbia* with a sparrow. All are allegorical depictions of captive love in the tradition of seventeenth century Dutch art, of which Reynolds had seen a great deal on a recent visit to the Low Countries. He would also have been steeped in the iconography of Dutch art, notably through works such as Jacob Cats's *Book of Emblems*, which he had known since boyhood. *Muscipula* shows a girl gloating over a caged mouse, which is in turn being eyed up by a predatory cat. As Peter Sutton notes, 'For classical authors the trapped mouse was a metaphor for unpunished moderation, an idea that was given a more specifically amorous meaning in Dutch literature: as the mouse sacrifices its life for treats, the man pays for stolen kisses with his heart' (Sutton, 1984, p. 357).

In January 1785 a visitor to Reynolds's gallery noted that he had 'finished a fancy picture for the ensuing exhibition, of a peasant girl, with a mouse trap in her hand and a cat on a stool looking up at it, in the manner of Rembrandt'. (*Public Advertiser*, 12 January 1785). *Muscipula* was not exhibited at the Royal Academy, but purchased by the French Ambassador, Count d'Adhémar, the *Morning Herald* (29 May 1785) joking that a 'trap baited with a girl, is surely sufficient to catch the Viceroy of the kingdom of gallantry'. A few years later the French Ambassador sold the picture, which was purchased by the notoriously 'gallant' Whig politician Charles James Fox, who was in turn a close friend of Reynolds and a connoisseur of exotic ephemera.

29 *Attainment* (Plate 22)
RICHARD MORTON PAYE (1750-1821)

Stipple engraving, printed in colours, 25 x 25.6 cm
LETTERED: '*Drawn & Engraved by R. M. Paye./ATTAIN-MENT./[verses]/— London Publish'd Octr 1st 1792 by Freeman & Co corner Beaufort Buildings, Strand.*'
David Alexander

Richard Morton Paye was trained as a chaser before turning to painting. He exhibited paintings and wax models at the Royal Academy between 1773 and 1800. Many of his pictures show the influence of Joseph Wright of Derby in the use of striking light effects. From the beginning most of his works were fancy pictures, notably of children. He attracted the attention of Dr John Wolcot, famous for his satirical writings as Peter Pindar and, after he fell out with his protégé John Opie. Pindar then took up Paye. They apparently quarrelled after Paye painted a son of Wolcot as *The Sulky Boy*, a picture shown at the Royal Academy in 1785 and subsequently engraved in mezzotint by John Young. Many engravings of Paye's pictures of children were issued from 1783 by printsellers such as J. R. Smith, and later by Young (see cat. 38). Paye also engraved a number of his own drawings of children in the dotted manner; this is one of two plates which he must have sold to the firm run by Tristram B. Freeman, a specialist colour printer, who later emigrated to the United States. The verses attached to the print seem, sadly, to have been applicable to Paye, for whom life became very difficult in the 1790s. He got into financial difficulties, and was later handicapped by suffering a stroke:

The Rich with ease their utmost wish obtain,
The Poor may Sigh alas! but Sigh in vain.

Despite being well-known, Paye received no recognition, and when he put himself forward for election as an Associate of the Royal Academy in 1795 he did not receive a single vote.

DSA

30 *Conjugal Peace* (Plate 21)
THOMAS BURKE (1749-1815) after Angelica Kauffman

Stipple engraving, scratched letter proof, before title, 37.5 x 31.2 cm (oval 24.8 x 31)
LETTERED: '*Angelica Kauffman Pinxt/W. W. Ryland Excudt/Thomas Burke Fecit/Published May 3 1779 by W W Ryland London.*'
David Alexander

Provenance: Nathaniel Smith (Lugt 2296-8)
Literature: Alexander 1992, p. 158, fig. 134

The line engraver William Wynne Ryland, who learned the crayon manner first used to reproduce drawings in France, established the popularity of 'stipple' engravings after the drawings and paintings of Angelica Kauffman. Between 1774 and 1779 years he published twenty-two of these prints, generally ovals printed in colours or in sanguine, which were aimed at the market for 'furniture prints'. Although the plates were signed by him it is likely that they were mostly engraved by Thomas Burke, a young Irishman who had trained as a mezzotint engraver under John Dixon. Burke went to work for Ryland after Dixon retired in 1775 and did not sign any prints for the next four years. This is the first print in the dotted manner which has his signature.

The prints published by Ryland were generally framed and the publisher has placed his name immediately under the engraved area, between the names of the painter and the engraver, so that it would be visible even when framed as an oval. Proofs, which generally cost double the price of lettered impressions, were available for collectors who kept their prints in portfolios. This print belonged to the sculptor and print-dealer Nathaniel Smith, father of John Thomas Smith, author of the amusing memoir *Nollekens and his Times*, who was Keeper of Prints and Drawings in the British Museum.

DSA

31 *The Dog's First Sight of Himself* (Plate 19)
NICCOLO SCHIAVONETTI (1771-1813) after John Russell

Stipple engraving, 31.5 38 cm.
LETTERED: '*Painted by J. Russell Crayon Painter to his Majesty and their Royal Highnesses the Prince of Wales and Duke of York/London. Published April 1 1797 by Messrs Schiavonetti No 10 Michael's Place Brompton/Engraved by N. Schiavonetti junior*'
David Alexander

John Russell, who was appointed Crayon Painter to the King in 1790, is remembered now as one of the finest portrait painters working in pastel. In the 1780s and 1790s, when the print publishers were clamouring for pictures which could be turned into engravings, several of his portraits were engraved in the dotted manner, some with 'fancy' titles: thus Emily de Vismé playing the harp was engraved by William Bond as '*St Cecilia*'. Russell also painted a number of fancy pictures of children to be engraved, of which *Tom and his Pidgeons* and *The Favorite Rabbit*, engraved and published by Charles Knight in June 1792, were the best known, and which were copied by engravers on the Continent.

Niccolo Schiavonetti was the younger brother of Luigi Schiavonetti (1765-1810), who came from Bassano, where the well-known firm of Remondini engraved copies of popular Italian, French and English prints which circulated very widely. Luigi worked on his arrival in England in about 1790 for Francesco Bartolozzi, the leading engraver in the dotted or stipple manner, and subsequently engraved plates for leading publishers such as Colnaghi. He later sent for his brother and between 1798 and 1814 they ran a publishing business. When Christie's sold their stock in 1814 it included the pastel on which the present picture was based together with that of its pendant, *Betsey in Trouble*, which showed a child with a dead canary. The two prints were copied for Remondini by A. Zaffonato and G. Venzo.

DSA

32 *The Envied Glutton* (Plate 20)
JOSEPH GROZER (*fl* 1755-97) after Henri-Pierre Danloux

Mezzotint, 38 x 28 cm
LETTERED: '*H. P. Danloux Pinxt/Publish'd as the Act directs by H. P. Danloux No 50 Leicester Square/Grozer Sculpt/The Envied Glutton*'
David Alexander

Literature: Baron Roger Portalis, *Henri-Pierre Danloux… et son Journal durant l'Emigration*, Paris, 1910, p. 83

The painter Henri-Paul Danloux was one of the French
artists who fled the French Revolution and settled in
England. On his arrival in London he realised that a way in
which he could earn some money and also draw attention to
himself was to publish prints. He drew a small boy eating a
piece of cake and had it engraved by Joseph Grozer in mezzotint with this title. Grozer, who was an engraver in mezzotint and stipple with a shop in Castle Street, Leicester
Square, also engraved his portrait of a Macao Chinese visitor, A'kao, another undated mezzotint (Chaloner Smith, CS
10) which Danloux also published.

DSA

33 *A Girl leaning on a Pedestal ('The Laughing Girl')*
SIR JOSHUA REYNOLDS (1723-92)   (Plate 23)

Oil on canvas, 91.5 x 71.2 cm, *c* 1775-85
The Iveagh Bequest, Kenwood

Provenance: Purchased from the artist by Henry Temple, the 2nd Viscount
Palmerston for 75 guineas [not at Christie's in 1791, as has been stated]; the
3rd Viscount Palmertson; passed to William Cowper-Temple; passed to the
Hon. Evelyn Ashley; sold by him, *c* 1890, to Agnew; purchased from Agnew
by the Earl of Iveagh
Exhibited: British Institution 1813 (35), 1824 (152), 1843 (9); Royal Academy,
1872 (85), 1928 (32)
Literature: Graves and Cronin, vol. 3, p. 1166-67, vol. 4, p. 1456; Waterhouse,
1941, p. 76; Connell, 1957, p. 254; Cormack, 1970, p. 161; Iveagh Bequest,
1978, p. 29; Dulwich, 1993, no.9; Postle, 1995, pp. 104-6, 112, 120, 326
Engraved: J.F. Bause, 1784; S.W. Reynolds (both reversed).

In December 1791, Lord Palmerston, who was then in
London socialising with Reynolds, wrote to his wife, 'Sir
Joshua has just sent me home a picture of his own which I
agreed for some time ago and which I think you will like. It
is a girl leaning forward on both her arms… ' (Connell, 1957,
p. 254). The picture referred to by Lord Palmerston, exhibited here, is one of two quite distinct versions. The other
version (Postle, 1995, p. 105, repr.), which also shows a
young, smiling girl leaning on a pedestal, is painted from a
quite different model with curly hair, wearing a white blouse
and a white skirt. An indication of the popularity of this latter image was its reproduction, along with Joseph Wright's
Boy Blowing a Bladder by Candle-light (see cat. 36), as a polygraph, a type of mechanically maufactured oil painting
which was in great vogue towards the end of the 1780s.

It is not known exactly when Reynolds first conceived of
either composition, although a comparison with *A Fortune-
Teller* of 1777 (cat. 78), suggests that the laughing girl in that
picture is the same model used by Reynolds in the present
work. (The location of Lord Palmerston's payment of 75
guineas in Reynolds's ledger – although not dated – suggests it was originally paid for sometime in the mid-1770s.)
The Kenwood version of the *Girl leaning on a Pedestal* was
not exhibited by Reynolds during his lifetime. However, it
is almost certain that he exhibited the other version at the
Royal Academy in 1782. It was described at the time as a
'sweet picture. The arch and comic look of the girl is pecu-
liar to Sir Joshua's pencil' (see Postle, 1995, p. 104-5).

The 'arch and comic look' of the girl (which led to the
picture's being known as the *Laughing Girl*) was certainly a
speciality of Reynolds, as one can see by comparing the
present work with his *Infant Academy* (cat. 45). The facial
expression was derived ultimately, however, from Coreg-
gio's cherubic infants. For the overall composition, with its
pronounced contrasts of light and shade and heavily impas-
toed surface, Reynolds had looked to Rembrandt, a source
which takes on an added significance in the knowledge

that Reynolds's exhibited version of the *Girl leaning on a
Pedestal* may have been painted as a pendant to Rembrandt's celebrated *Girl at a Window*, now at Dulwich Picture Gallery (see Fig. 21) (Postle, 1995, p. 106 and note 37).
The Rembrandt may have been in England by the mid-
1770s. It was certainly in the country by 1786, when it
belonged to the dealer Noel Desenfans. My own belief is
that Desenfans had acquired it from John Campbell, 1st
Baron Cawdor, since not only was the exhibited version of
Reynolds's *Girl leaning on a Pedestal* known to have been
painted 'as a companion' to a Rembrandt then owned by
'Mr Campbell', but that Reynolds's *Girl* still belongs to a
branch of Campbell's family. This speculation is strength-
ened by the fact that Reynolds is thought to have made a
copy of Rembrandt's picture in 1780, an early nineteenth-
century copy of which is in the Hermitage, St Petersburg
(Dulwich, 1993, pp. 35-6).

34 *A Piping Boy*   (Plate 24)
HUGH ROBINSON (1756-96)

Oil on canvas, 99 x 124.5 cm, before 1787
Private Collection

Provenance: By descent from the artist
Exhibited: Royal Academy 1881-82
Literature: *Athenaeum*, 12 March 1881; *Magazine of Art*, February 1882, pp.
156-7; Simon, 1987, p. 225

A *Piping Boy* and the *Boy Flying a Kite* (cat. 35) are among
only a handful of works by Hugh Robinson to have survived. Together, they reveal that this little-known British
painter was among the most promising talents of his generation, before his untimely death in Italy at the age of forty.
Robinson, who was born in Malton, Yorkshire, entered the
Royal Academy Schools in 1779. It was probably around
this time that he made several self-portraits in the manner
of Rembrandt as well as copies of Reynolds's portrait of
Giuseppe Baretti (probably from the Watts engraving of
1780) and Van Dyck's *Madonna and Child* (Fitzwilliam
Museum, Cambridge). Robinson exhibited his first work at
the Royal Academy (a male portrait) in 1780. His only other
exhibited works were shown in 1782, the head of a beggar
(Fig. 43) in the manner of Rembrandt, and a second
unidentified male portrait. The *Piping Boy* and its pendant
were probably painted around this time, and certainly
before the artist's departure for Italy in 1787.

A Piping Boy and the *Boy Flying a Kite* remained in the
artist's family. Both pictures were in all likelihood made for
pleasure and improvement, as exercises, and to impress
potential clients. The status of the present work as a fancy
picture rather than a portrait is enhanced not not only by the
casual pose but also by the fact that the subject was apparently an unnamed boy who worked with Robinson as a studio assistant, somewhat in the manner of Gainsborough's so-
called '*Pitminster Boy*' (private collection, on loan to Gainsborough's House Museum). The motif of the piping boy
goes back to the Renaissance although Robinson may have
been more directly influenced by more recent treatments of
the subject in fancy pictures by Reynolds (see cat. 4) and
Nathaniel Hone (National Gallery of Ireland).

Robinson's style is highly reminiscent of number of
artists then making an impact on the London art world,
among them Joseph Wright, the young Cornish painter
John Opie, and the American John Singleton Copley
(although the latter's influence is perhaps more apparent in

the more dramatically posed *Boy Flying a Kite*, cat. 35). Wright's influence on Robinson is particularly discernable in a number of paintings dating from the late 1770s and early '80s, notably the pendant pictures of *Edwin, from Dr Beattie's Minstrel* (RA 1778) and *Maria, from Sterne*, which Wright exhibited at the Royal Academy in 1781, along with his recumbent portrait of Brooke Boothby (Tate Gallery). The sylvan setting of Robinson's painting and the pose of the boy, leaning against the rock by a pool, is imbued with the spirit of Wright's deeply poetic and innovative portrait. It may have acted as a specific inspiration upon Robinson, an artist who was renowned by contemporaries for his 'Melancholy Sensibility' (see Ingamells, 1997, p. 815).

Hugh Robinson worked in London principally as a portraitist. His ambition, however, was to become a history painter, and in 1787 he left for Italy, sponsored in part by Reynolds's protégé, the budding connoisseur Sir George Beaumont. Robinson resided principally in Rome working on historical compositions (including a *Cupid and Psyche*), and supplemented his income through portraiture. In October 1796 he was reported as having died of consumption on his return journey to England. This tragedy was compounded by the loss at sea of the works he had made in Italy.

35 *Boy Flying a Kite*   (Plate 27)
HUGH ROBINSON (1756-96)

Oil on canvas, 124.5 x 99 cm, before 1787
Private Collection

Provenance: By descent from the artist
Exhibited: Royal Academy 1881-82 (1); Tokyo 1975 (33) (British Council exhibition 'English Portraits from Francis Bacon the Philospoher to Francis Bacon the Painter')
Literature: *Magazine of Art*, February 1882, pp. 156-7; Athenaeum, 12 March 1881; Simon, 1987, p. 225, repr.
Engraved: Mezzotint by S.W. Reynolds

According to family tradition the model for the *Boy flying a Kite* was the artist's nephew, Thomas Teesdale of Malton, Yorkshire. As with *The Piping Boy*, Robinson painted this picture not as a commissioned portrait but a character study, or fancy picture. The physical energy of the boy and the windswept open landscape contrast with the languid pose, contemplative expression and secluded environs of the piping boy.

The *Boy Flying a Kite* belongs to a tradition of children at play explored extensively by artists of the seventeenth century, where the kite was often used at as a metaphor for hubris (in pendant pictures of a high-flying kite and a subsequent image of the kite with a broken cord). Robinson's painting may, for example, be compared with antecedents such as the *Boys Flying Kites* at Upton House, Warwicksire (National Trust), presently attributed to Godfried Schalcken (1643-1706), although that is not a picture Robinson would have known. What distinguishes Robinson's *Boy Flying a Kite* from earlier works is its sheer exuberance, which is matched only, in this genre, by Gainsborough's portrayal of his young daughters chasing a butterfly (National Gallery, London).

The picture plane, stripped of all extraneous detail – including the kite itself – is bisected by the diagonals formed by the boy's arms and legs as he strains at the string, his hair tossed by strong gusts of wind. The energy contained in the boy's form, together with his dramatic

contrapposto, is far more suggestive of history painting than the altogether more passive, contemplative sphere of the fancy picture. Indeed, the artist who most springs to mind is John Singleton Copley, the American painter who was at the very time making a series of innovative forays into modern history painting, including *Watson and the Shark* (RA 1778) and *The Death of Major Pierson* of 1783 (Tate Gallery, London). In these paintings Copley successfully married the language of high art with dramatic portrayals of individuals, including in *Brook Watson* the wind-tossed young man with the harpoon silhouetted against the sky, and in *Major Pierson*, the figures of fleeing women and children. The dramatic characterisation of the boy's head in Robinson's painting combined with his dramatic pose, also suggests the influence of Copley and hints at Robinson's desire to move beyond portraiture and other lesser genres towards high art.

Boy with a Kite was poorly restored earlier this century. At that time the boy's chest was overpainted with a yellow shirt, while the kite string – perhaps in attempt to heighten the drama of the piece – was improbably repositioned around the boy's neck. Although most of the damage inflicted was reversed by a subsequent restoration, there are traces of the earlier damage on the picture's surface.

36 *Boy Blowing a Bladder*   (Plate 26)
37 *Girl Looking through a Bladder*   (Plate 25)
JOSEPH WRIGHT 'OF DERBY' (1734-97)

Oil on canvas, 76.2 x 63.5 cm
Private Collection

The *Boy…* is signed and dated: '*I. Wright pinx·ᵗ/1790*'
Provenance: Richard Arkwright Jr; by descent
Exhibited: International Exhibition, 1862 (54 & 55); Derby, 1883 (68 & 76); Graves Galleries, 1910 (38 & 41); Derby, 1934 (97 & 121); Sotheby's, *Childhood*, 1988 (56)
Literature: Nicolson, 1968, vol. 1, pp. 66, 118, 169, 240, cats. 210 & 211, vol. 2, plates 320 & 321

Wright began painting pictures of children with bladders (the precursor of the modern toy balloon) in the late 1760s, beginning with the dramatic *Two Boys Fighting over a Bladder* (private collection) and its pendant (untraced) which shows, we may assume, the same two boys minutes earlier, blowing up the bladder. These pictures, like Wright's studies of figures reading, studying and working by candlelight, were just one aspect of his investigation into the effects of artificial light. Yet, while earlier paintings of children with bladders are remarkable for their sharp contrasts of light and shadow, and the later *Boy Blowing a Bladder* and its pendant, the *Girl Looking through a Bladder*, are more reticent and tonally more even, the accent being as much on the expressions of the children, the boy with puffed cheeks inflating the bladder while the girl peers at the reflections of light upon its translucent surface.

According to Benedict Nicolson these two pictures were probably not painted as pendants. Even so, considering that they are the same size, have similar subject-matter, belong to the same owner and have always been exhibited together, they can be considered as a pair. Nicolson also noted the popularity of the *Boy Blowing a Bladder*, commenting upon the proliferation of copies of these subjects in private houses in the Midlands, which 'represented the popular conception of Wright from the nineteenth century down to the second world war' (Nicolson, 1968, p. 66).

The popularity of the subject of children playing with bladders at the time is reflected by the exhibition of several pictures by Wright during the 1780s, including an unidentified *Boy Blowing a Bladder*, shown at the Free Society of Artists in 1783 and the so-called *Boy and Girl Engaged with a Bladder* (also unlocated) which was exhibited at the Royal Academy in 1789. The present pictures, which were not exhibited, were painted the following year, and purchased by Richard Arkwright Jr, son of the inventor and industrialist Sir Richard Arkwright. It was also around this time, in 1791, that an exhibition of works by the Polygraphic Society, included a *Boy Blowing a Bladder by Candle-light* by Wright. The Polygraphic Society had been founded in 1784 by Benjamin Booth, who had devised a mechanical means of reproducing oil paintings by stretching a silk screen across them, tracing the design, and squeezing colour through the screen onto a blank canvas – the resulting 'oil painting' being called a 'polygraph'. At the 1791 exhibition (the eighth to be held) Booth exhibited original oils, including works by Reynolds, Opie, Greuze, Claude Lorrain and Rubens, alongside polygraphs made from them. The polygraphs could be purchased for the princely sum of seven guineas. The precise identity of Wright's picture has not been established. However, if it was the present picture, then it might possibly explain why there appears to be an inordinate number of versions of the composition.

38 *The Little Volunteer*   (Plate 33)
JOHN YOUNG (1755-1825) after Richard Morton Paye
Mezzotint, 58.5 x 43 cm
LETTERED: '*Painted by R. M. Paye./Engraved by Jno Young Engraver in Mezzotinto to his R. H. the Prince of Wales/THE LIT-TLE VOLUNTEER/London Publish'd June 22th 1799, by John Young No 58 Upper Charlotte Street Fitzroy Square.*'
David Alexander

John Young engraved a number of Paye's fancy pictures during the 1790s, notably *The Boy Discovering the Golden Eggs*, shown at the Royal Academy in 1795, and its pendant. The print here is after one of a pair of pictures which survive in a private collection, the other showing children playing with model warships. Earlier this century both pictures were attributed to Opie, although it was also thought they might be by Opie's 'rival', one R.M. Page [*sic*] (see Earland, 1911, pp. 338-9). The images reflect the background of the war with France which led to the popularity of prints of battles or ones with military overtones. Young was a good friend to Paye and he published most of the stipples which Paye engraved himself. He was active in the Artists' Benevolent Fund and in 1812 he called on Joseph Farington on Paye's behalf, relating that the painter had had a stroke and was in very poor circumstances.

                                                        DSA

39 *Cupid as a Link Boy*   (below left)
JOHN DEAN (*c* 1750-1805), after Sir Joshua Reynolds
Mezzotint, 38.8 x 27.5 cm
LETTERED: '*S*ʳ. *Ioshua Reynolds Pinxit/Iohn Dean Fecit*' [inscribed in ink, '*Published by Sayer & Bennett August 15th 1777*']
The Trustees of the British Museum

40 *Mercury as a Cutpurse*   (below right)
JOHN DEAN (*c* 1750-1805), after Sir Joshua Reynolds
Mezzotint, 39.1 x 27.5 cm
LETTERED: '*Sir Joshua Reynolds Pinxit/Iohn Dean Fecit/Published April 16th 1777 by In Dean*'
The Trustees of the British Museum

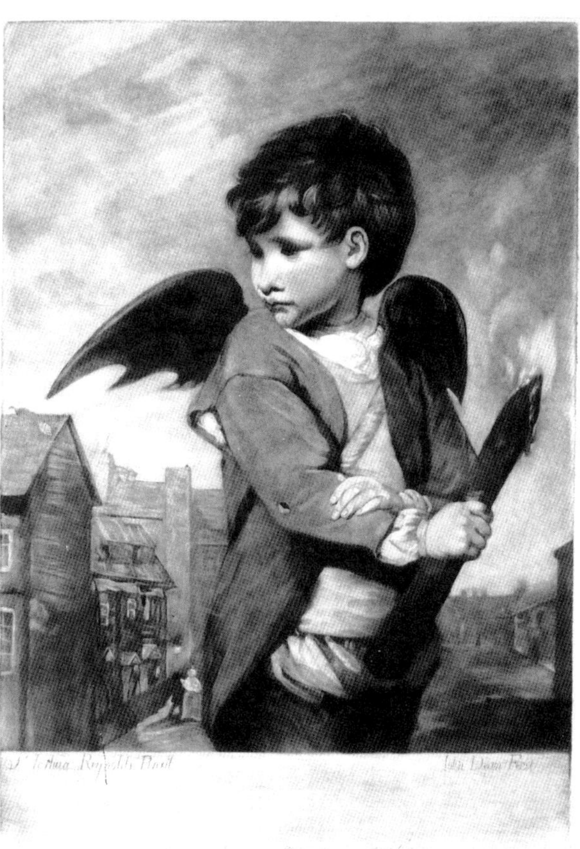

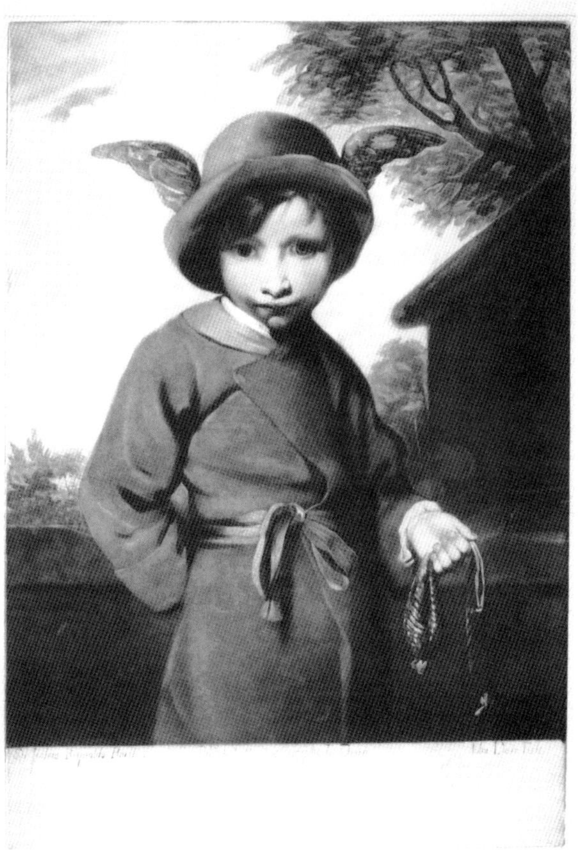

Mercury as a Cutpurse and *Cupid as a Link Boy* (cat. 39) were painted as pendants, and purchased from Reynolds by John Frederick Sackville, 3rd Duke of Dorset, who was one of the greatest admirers of the artist's fancy pictures. The paintings, which may well have been a private commission, were not exhibited during Reynolds's lifetime, although engravings were made in 1777, some three years after Lord Sackville had bought the paintings. Reynolds, in a technical memorandum on these pictures, referred to them simply as 'Blackguard Mercury and Cupid', although their present titles provide a more precise interpretation. (Incidentally, the boy who modelled for these pictures would have been oblivious of Reynolds's intention, especially as it was his practice in such paintings to paint the model's head only, adding the body at a later stage.)

In *Cupid as a Link Boy* Reynolds depicts the little god of love brandishing a 'link' or flaming torch, which was used by boys to light people's way through the city streets. Link boys, as David Mannings notes, 'were notorious little thieves, and those most likely to suffer at their hands were the very people who trusted them as guides – an obvious parallel to the traditional role of Cupid (Penny, 1986, p. 264). Cupid's role as a mischievous sexual icon is confirmed by the phallic nature of his torch and the obscene arm gesture. In similar fashion Mercury, at once the god of commerce and a little thief, holds a purse, of a suggestively limp and tubular form, indicating, as Mannings says, that he is 'in a double sense "spent"'. Given the thinly disguised sexual allusions in these pictures Reynolds may have considered it prudent not to show them at the Royal Academy.

---

41 *Felicity*   (Plate 30)
WILLIAM PETHER (1731-1821)

Mezzotint, proof before title, 35.5 x 25.5 cm
LETTERED: '*Wm Pether Pinxt et sculpt/Publish'd… Mar 12 1791 by Darling & Thompson N. 3 Great Newport Street, London.*'
David Alexander

Literature: Chaloner Smith 1883, vol.3, p. 995, no. 150, unrecorded proof

William Pether, painter and engraver, learned mezzotint from Thomas Frye, whom he assisted with the large heads which Frye drew and engraved in 1760-2 (see cat. 24). Between 1762 and 1793 Pether signed over 60 mezzotints, mostly between 1762 and 1793, which included some of the finest prints after Wright of Derby. Pether was, however, primarily a portrait painter in oil, crayons and in miniature. He was of a restless temperament, and at various times left London to visit provincial centres such as Exeter and Nottingham; in about 1804 he settled as a drawing-master in Bristol, where he died. At the time that this picture was engraved it belonged to Dr James Chelsum, DD, a collector of prints who wrote a small *History of the Art of Engraving in Mezzotinto*, Winchester, 1786. If the picture is the version sold at Sotheby's, London, 6 July 1973 (lot 234 as Nathaniel Hone) it was a painting in oil.

DSA

---

42 *Young Artist*   (Plate 28)
PHILIP MERCIER (?1689-1760)

Oil on canvas, 76 x 64 cm, 1740-45.
Signed: '*PM*' (monogram)
Cannon Hall Museum, Cawthorne, Barnsley

Provenance: Christie's 4 November 1960 (185) as Chardin; Agnew
Literature: Raines, 1967, p. 136, pl. XI, I; York, 1969, no. 61; Ingamells and Raines, 1976-78, no. 136

The depiction of children learning to draw and read was a common motif in French and British art by the mid-eighteenth century. Among those who had pioneered the genre was Chardin, to whom the present work was attributed as recently as 1960. Chardin's work was becoming increasingly well known in England by the later 1730s through engravings after his works, including John Faber's *Youth with a Port-Crayon* of 1740 (cat. 43).

The subject of the picture concerns the education of the young artist, who draws from an Antique bust. The self-absorbed attitude of the boy, intent upon his studies, marks the work out as a fancy picture rather than a commissioned portrait. In terms of artistic education Mercier's *Young Artist* addresses the first stage of academic training: the young artist beginning with antique fragments, before graduating to the entire figure, and ultimately the living model. By the 1740s this form of education was standard in European academies. It had been pioneered by the Académie Royale in Paris in the 1640s, and adopted elsewhere, including the Royal Academy of Frederick I in Berlin, where the young Mercier had studied.

On another level the picture reveals the changing attitudes towards children's education and childhood sensibility by the mid-eighteenth century. Here, unlike a work such as Van Loo's *Allegory of Painting* (Fine Arts Museum of San Francisco) or Reynolds's *Infant Academy* (cat. 45), where children ape the activities of adults, the boy is treated as an individual in his own right, engaged in activity appropriate to his age. Mercier's image, like so many other similar works of the period (notably Reynolds's *Boy Reading* of *c* 1746 (Private Collection) or Greuze's *Boy with a Lesson-book* (National Gallery of Scotland), embraces an Enlightenment approach to education, respecting the unformed mind of the child while at the same time helping him to learn through the use of the senses. Of these senses sight was regarded as of fundamental importance for it was through observation that experience was accumulated, and knowledge was gained.

---

43 *Youth with a Port-Crayon*   (opposite)
JOHN FABER the Younger (*c*1695-1756) after Chardin

Mezzotint, 32.6 x 22.3 cm
LETTERED: '*Chardin pinxt 1737/J. Faber fecit 1740/The happy Youth whom Strength of Genius fires;/Who smit with Science, to fan Fame aspires,/Thro' all her Windings, Nature must pursue;/Sold by Faber at the Golden Head, Bloomsbury Square*'
The Trustees of the British Museum

The Parisian artist Jean-Baptiste Simeon Chardin (1699-1779) was among the foremost painters of genre and still-life in France during the first half of the eighteenth century. More than any other artist of his generation Chardin exploited a growing interest in Dutch and Flemish artists of the seventeenth century. He was also an important influence upon the evolution of the fancy picture in England, not least because of the impact of his work on Philip Mercier. The link between Mercier and the present mezzotint is underlined by the fact that it was made by John Faber the Younger, the Dutch-born engraver, who was then making prints after Mercier's fancy pictures.

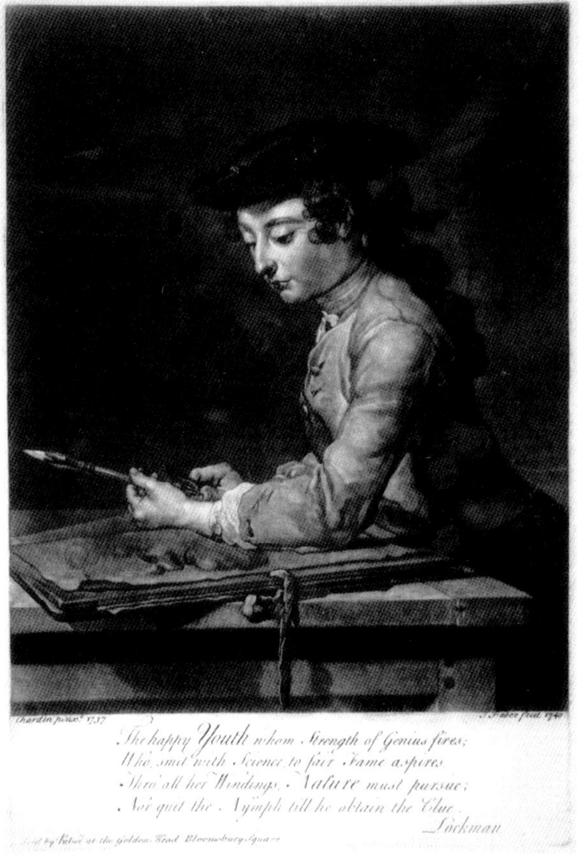

44 *The School Boy* (Plate 29)

JOHN DEAN (1750-98), after Sir Joshua Reynolds

Mezzotint, engraving, 35.5 x 25.5 cm

LETTERED: '*Sir Joshua Reynolds Pinxit./Published Octor 31st 1777, by J. Dean, Church Street, Soho/John Dean Fecit./A School Boy*'

David Alexander

The model used by Reynolds here is the same boy who posed for the *Boy with Cabbage Nets*. According to William Mason, who met the boy, the painting upon which the present engraving is based was 'almost his absolute portrait' (Mason in Cotton, ed., 1859, p. 57). The subject of a boy engaged in an aspect of study had first been explored by Reynolds in the mid-1740s in the quasi-autobiographical fancy picture, a *Boy Reading*, a painting which had strong formal parallels with contemporary French artists, notably Mercier and Jean-Baptiste Greuze. The present picture, which has, as Mason observed, the air of a portrait rather than a fancy picture, recalls more closely Reynolds's 1754 portrait of the eight-year old Lord George Greville, later Earl of Warwick (Private Collection), in which the young aristocrat holds a book containing lessons on grammar (see Penny, 1986, no. 22). The irony, of course, was that, unlike those bourgeois and aristocratic children brought by their parents to sit for their portraits, Reynolds's young model would not have gone to school or had any semblance of an education. Mason recalled (see cat. 67) that he was in reality an orphan who sold cabbage nets to support himself and his younger siblings. *The School Boy* was painted by Reynolds probably around 1776 to 1777, at which time it was engraved by John Dean, a pupil of Valentine Green. As David Alexander notes, this was one of several fancy pictures which Reynolds allowed Dean to make as he was starting out as an independent engraver.

Although never exhibited in public Reynolds probably hung the painting in the picture gallery annexed to his house in Leicester Square, where its Rembrandtesque aura would have allowed it to blend comfortably with the artist's assembled old-master collection. In 1779 Lord Warwick, reminded perhaps of his own portrait of some twenty-five years earlier, bought *The School Boy* for fifty guineas. Suitably, he hung it in the library at Warwick Castle.

45 *Infant Academy* (Plate 31)

SIR JOSHUA REYNOLDS (1723-92)

Oil on canvas, 111.7 x 137.1 cm, 1782

The Iveagh Bequest, Kenwood

Provenance: Bequeathed in 1792 to Henry Temple, the 2nd Viscount Palmerston; the 3rd Viscount Palmerston; William Cowper-Temple; the Hon. Evelyn Ashley; sold by him, *c* 1890, to Agnew; purchased from Agnew by the Earl of Iveagh

Exhibited: Royal Academy, 1782, as 'Children'; British Institution, 1813 (101), 1823 (53), 1833 (40), 1843 (21); RA, 1872 (47); Grosvenor Gallery, 1883-4 (62); Manchester, 1928 (38); Birmingham, 1961 (79)

Literature: Graves and Cronin, vol. 3, pp. 1158-60, vol. 4, p. 1455, p. 1480 AAA; Waterhouse, 1941, p. 73, 125 and plate 229.

Engraved: Stipple by Francis Haward, ARA, 19 April 1783; mezzotint by S.W. Reynolds; etching by J. Bromley; W.T. Fry, 4 June 1823; J. Walker, 1854

In the late 1770s and '80s Reynolds began to produce a series of allegorical pictures based upon very young children and babies. These included *A Cupid Asleep*, *A Child Asleep*, *Moses in the Bullrushes*, and *A Child with Guardian Angels* (see cat. 20). Of these pictures the most ambitious was the *Infant Academy*. Reynolds exhibited the picture at the Royal Academy in 1782. It subsequently went on display in his picture gallery, where it remained until his death. At the Royal Academy the picture had simply been entitled 'Children', although Francis Haward's engraving of 1783 bore the title by which the work is now universally known. In the later 1780s it was asserted that the picture's popular name of the *Infant Academy* had been given by Dr Johnson (see Postle, 1995, p. 103). The motif of the Infant Academy was already well established in the iconography of Western art (see below). Even so, the idea that Johnson provided the picture's title is worth recording, especially in the light of the existence of another similar fancy picture of a seated baby known as the *Infant Johnson*. If Reynolds painted an infant Johnson, might not the child-artist in the *Infant Academy* have been conceived as an infant Reynolds?

The idea that the *Infant Academy* was a satire upon the occupation of Reynolds and his fellow portraitists is supported by the elaborate and fashionable bonnet propped upon the otherwise naked sitter's head. The egregious presence of the hat was noted at the time as 'too violent an approach to caricature to be tolerated as representative of infancy', which another critic believed that 'a wreath of flowers on the girl's head would have been better than a cap, as the fashion of caps is perpetually changing (Postle, 1995, p. 104). That, of course, was the whole point of Reynolds's satire. 'The witty mixture of high-seriousness and the true-life facts of the learned artist confronted with the perpetual demand for high-style portraiture is virtually a comment, couched in French Rococo language, on the amusing disparity between the lofty pretentions of the Royal Academy and the realities of British patronage and practice' (Rosenblum in Penny, 1986, p. 47).

The *Infant Academy* was painted just after Reynolds returned from his first visit to Flanders, a factor which prompted contemporaries to compare its rich colour with Rubens and other Flemish masters. The picture, however, was far closer, as Rosenblum notes, to the language of the French Rococo, and may have owed a specific iconographic debt to Carle Van Loo's *Allegory of Painting* of 1753 (Fine Arts Museum of San Francisco), or an untraced *Infant Academy* by Jacopo Amigoni. A link with the Amigoni is intriguing since that picture not only belonged to the Earl of Wemyss by the 1770s but was later described as having been 'painted upon' by Reynolds. In other words it was yet another work which Reynolds had restored or 'improved' (see cat. 3).

In his will Reynolds gave Henry Temple, 2nd Viscount Palmerston second choice of any of his own works. Lord Palmerston chose the *Infant Academy.* It remained at his seat Broadlands until the late nineteenth century, when it was acquired by the Earl of Iveagh. Although the original was sold, at some point a full-scale copy was made which remains at Broadlands. Reynolds also made a separate study of the central figure in the painting, which became known as *The Mob Cap.*

newly introduced dotted manner. It is engraved in an oval although the painting is an upright rectangle, and it was issued without title, establishing it as a fancy print rather than a portrait. John Boydell later acquired the plate, and reissued it with the title *Reflections on Clarissa Harlowe* in 1785, at the same time altering the engraver's name to 'Scorodomoff', the anglicised version by which he had become known.

Garril Ivanovitch Scorodumov trained in Russia under the French engraver Antoine Radig. At the age of twenty he was awarded the right to study abroad for three years, and enrolled in the Royal Academy Schools in London in October 1772. He must have applied to Reynolds, who was helpful to several young engravers at the start of their careers, for a picture to engrave and allowed access to this one. He appears to have learned stipple engraving from the French-born V. M. Picot, a pioneer of the technique in England, who issued some of the young Russian's earlier prints. He was able to prolong his stay in London on the grounds that 'the best engravers in Europe are to be found in London' and he did not return to Russia until 1782. Boydell presumably acquired the plate from the engraver on his departure.

DSA

---

46 *The Good Mother Reading a Story* (Plate 32)

CHARLES WILLIAM WHITE (1751-85) after Emma Crewe

Stipple engraving, 28.5 x 30.5 cm
LETTERED: '*Emma Crewe Delint/C. W. White sculpt/*THE GOOD MOTHER READING A STORY*/[2 lines of verse]/Publishd by C. W. White March 1783, Kemps Row, Chelsea'.*
David Alexander

During the last quarter of the eighteenth century increasing numbers of fancy prints were designed by ladies. Emma Crewe was one of the most active, designing well over twenty plates, of which the majority were engraved by Charles William White. In the early 1780s White engraved a number of subject prints in the dotted manner, some after Daniel Gardner and other professional artists, but many after amateurs such as Ladies Spencer and Lincoln.

A high proportion of Emma Crewe's drawings were of children; this print carries lines which reflect the progressive attitudes towards education at the end of the century:

Insinuate Truth disguis'd by Fiction's Veil
They'll leave their Play & listen to ye Tale

DSA

47 *Girl Reading (Reading Clarissa Harlowe)* (Plate 34)

GARRIL SCORODUMOV (1752-92) after Sir Joshua Reynolds

Stipple engraving, 33 x 27 cm (oval 30 x 25).
LETTERED: '*Sir Joshua Reynolds pinxt. — G. Scorodoumow sculpt./Published March 10, 1775, by V. M. Picot, No 16 in the Strand.*'
David Alexander

Literature: Cross, 1980, pp. 212-5; Hamilton 1884, p. 149; Alexander, 1993, pp.7-8

Reynolds exhibited this portrait of his niece Theophila Palmer reading Samuel Richardson's *Clarissa Harlowe* at the Royal Academy in 1771 (158). It was engraved in the

48 *Serena*

JOHN RAPHAEL SMITH (1752-1812), after George Romney

Mezzotint, 47.1 x 35.2 cm
LETTERED: '*Painted by G. Romney/Engraved by J R Smith/Serena vide Hayley's triumphs of temper/London Publishd Semptem^r 28th 1782 by J J Smith N° 83 opposite the Pantheon Oxford Street*'
The Trustees of the British Museum

Literature: Chaloner Smith 1883, vol. 3, p. 1316; Ward & Roberts 1904, vol. 2, pp. 146-8

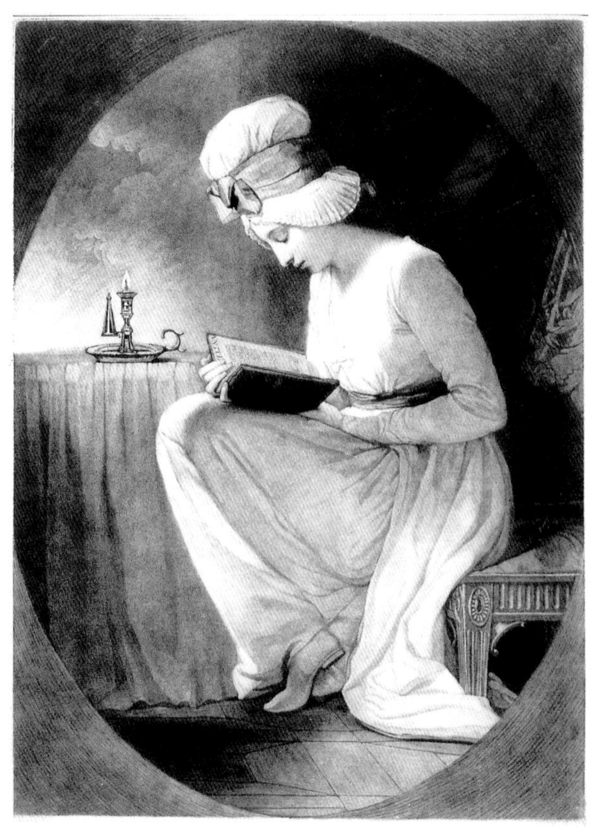

Smith's print is based upon one of several paintings Romney made of a girl reading by candlelight, apparently based upon Miss Honora Sneyd. As Miss Sneyd had married in 1773, aged 20, it has been supposed that the original painting dates from before Romney's departure for Italy in March 1773. Nor does it appear to have been originally inspired by William Hayley's poem *The Triumph of Temper*, which was not published until 1781, the year after Miss Sneyd's death. In Smith's print the girl is shown reading *Evelina*, Fanny Burney's debut novel, which had appeared to universal acclaim in 1778. Later impressions also carry lines from the first Canto of Hayley's poem, which was in turn inspired by Burney's novel:

> Sweet *Evelina*'s fascinating power
> Had first beguilíd of sleep her midnight hour;
> Possesst by Sympathy's enchanting sway,
> She read, unconscious of the dawning day.

It was not only young fictional heroines such as Serena who indulged in nocturnal readings from *Evelina*: Sir Joshua Reynolds was reported to have stayed awake all night in order to finish it.

49 *Female Lucubration* (Plate 35)

PHILIP DAWE (*c* 1750-1809) after John Foldsone

Mezzotint, *c* 1775, 46.5 x 35.5 cm
David Alexander
Literature: Chaloner Smith, 1883, vol.1, no.15a

'Lucubration' – a word little used today – connotes study, especially by lamplight. John Foldstone (*fl* 1769-84) was a minor portrait painter who also painted a number of fancy pictures, exhibiting between 1769 and 1783. Philip Dawe trained under Henry Morland, a painter who became known for his fancy pictures, several of which were engraved in mezzotint by Dawe and exhibited at the Society of Artists 1769-85 and again in 1782. He exhibited this print at the Society in 1775. The publication line on this impression of the plate, which was 20 by 14 inches, a standard size, has been cut off; mezzotints were very often 'close framed', that is with the picture frame close to the edge of the print.

DSA

50 *Attention* (Plate 37)
51 *Inattention* (Plate 36)

ROBERT MEADOWS (1763-1812) after John Raphael Smith

Stipple engravings, 37 x 30 cm
LETTERED: '*Painted by J. R. Smith – Engraved by R. M. Meadows./Published Novr 28th 1791 by I. R. Smith King street Covent Garden.*'
David Alexander
Literature: J. R. Smith's Catalogue, 254-5

This pair of prints, which is shown here framed close to the subject as was usual with furniture prints, was accompanied by a pair of verses:

> INATTENTION — L'ATTENTION
> Read Fox's Martyrs to Sixteen
> How dull how stupid it must prove!
> How it would brighten up her mien
> Would Granny read her those of love

P.P.

> INATTENTION — L'ATTENTION
> When Loves the theme what eye can close
> The Minutes steal the Lightnings wings
> Adieu at once to dull repose.
> For who can Sleep when Ovid sings.

P.P

Robert Meadows was a highly regarded stipple engraver, who was principally engaged on subject pictures, notably those by Richard Westall.

DSA

III

Love Songs and Matches

52 *The Oyster Girl* (Plate 39)
PHILIP MERCIER (?1689-1760)

Oil on canvas, 91.5 x 71.2 cm, *c* 1750-55
Private Collection
Provenance: Probably the picture formerly owned by Viscountess Galway; Chichester Antiques, 1961; Sir Albert Richardson; by descent
Exhibited: Kenwood and York, 1969 (64)
Literature: York, 1969, no. 64; Webster, 1970, p. 70, fig. 85; Ingamells and Raines, 1978, no. 164, pp. 43-44
Engraved: Mezzotint by Richard Houston, *c* 1756, entitled 'Native Meltons'; mezzotint by Richard Houston, entitled 'The Fair Oysterinda'

There are at least two other oil versions of the picture, including one with minor variations, including the replacement of the basket with a wooden receptacle (see Ingamells and Raines, 1978, no. 165). The replication of the work suggests that this composition was among Mercier's most popular fancy pictures, a suggestion which is supported by the fact that it was engraved twice by Richard Houston; once under the title *Native Meltons* (cat. 53) and again as *The Fair Oysterinda* (fig. 35). Of the two prints *The Fair Oysterinda* is technically a cruder print than *Native Meltons*, with verses to match:

> The Oysters good – The Nymph so fair!
> Who would not wish to taste her Ware?
> No need has she aloud to Cry 'em,
> Since all who see her Fare must buy 'em.

These lines, with their heavy-handed innuendo, suggest that female vendor was not simply selling oysters, but her own sexual favours. The point is especially pertinent given that the oysters, here prized open suggestively by the girl, were renowned for their legendary aphrodisiacal properties.

The iconography of Mercier's picture, although it derives in part from the European tradition of portraying street vendors, including the characters popularised by Marcellus Laroon's *Cryes of the City of London*, also relies upon themes explored in Dutch seventeenth-century genre painting, where the preparation of food was often associated with the stimulation of sexual appetites. There are clear parallels between the verses which appear in *The Fair Oysterinda* and those to be found in French eighteenth-century engravings after seventeenth-century Dutch paintings. On a print, for example, after Gerard Dou's *Girl Chopping Onions* (Her Majesty The Queen), Pierre Louis Surugue inscribed a caption to the effect that the girl in question was far more appetising than the meal she was preparing (see Sutton, 1984, p. 185).

53 *Native Meltons* (Plate 38)

RICHARD HOUSTON (1722-75) after Philip Mercier

Mezzotint, 33 x 23 cm
Proof before all letters, published by Robert Sayer *c* 1756
David Alexander
Literature: Chaloner Smith 1878-83, 138 i/2

This picture is of a young woman opening oysters, which were very plentiful at the time and considered to be food for the poor rather than a delicacy. It was was one of Mercier's most popular pictures; several versions are known (see cat. 52 above), and Houston engraved a similar plate with the title *The Fair Oysterinda* for Sayer's rival John Bowles. Mercier's work became extremely well-known through engravings: a total of about fifty of Mercier's fancy pictures were engraved in mezzotint, and there were many unauthorised copies of the prints. According to Chaloner Smith (loc.cit.), a version of this print has been inscribed with the name 'Lady Falmouth'.

DSA

54 *The Shrimp Girl* (Plate 40)

WILLIAM HOGARTH (1697-1764)

Oil on canvas, 63.5 x 52.7 cm, after 1740
Trustees of the National Gallery, London

Provenance: Jane Hogarth; her sale, 24 April 1790 (51); George Watson Taylor sale, Erlestoke, 24 July 1832 (47); Sir W. Miles by 1854; bt. by the Trustees of the National Gallery (Wheeler Fund) at Leigh Court (Sir Philip Miles) sale, 28 June 1884 (31)
Exhibited: International Exhibition, South Kensington, 1862 (40); Royal Academy 1875 (31); Paris 1938 (68); Chicago, New York and Totonto, 1946-7 (4); Manchester, 1954 (39); Tate Gallery, 1997
Literature: Nichols, 1781, p. 59; 2nd edition, 1782, p. 325; Nichols and Steevens, 1817, vol. 2, p. 268, vol. 3, p. 270; Beckett, 1949, pp. 72-73, pl. 197; Davies, 1959, pp. 68-69; Gowing, 1971, p. 53, no. 129; Paulson, 1971, vol. 2, p. 246, pl. 266; Lindsay, 1977, pp. 134-5, 225; Webster, 1979, p. 119 and p. 133, repd.; Bindman, 1981, pp. 7, 149, fig. 120; Einberg, 1997, pp. 28-29, no. 8
Engraved: Stipple by Bartolozzi, 1781, untitled; 1782 by Bartolozzi with the title '*Shrimps!*'.

The existence of this oil sketch was first noted by John Nichols in 1781, when it was in the possession of Hogarth's widow Jane. At the same time it was also engraved in stipple by Francesco Bartolozzi (cat. 55). In the first edition of his *Biographical Anecdotes* Nichols described the work as 'a most spirited sketch in oil of a young fishwoman', while in the second edition of 1782 he referred to it as *The Shrimp Girl*, the title by which it is known today. Although the picture has been cut down, the extent to which the canvas has been cropped suggests that it was originally only slightly larger, and was tidied up rather than cut from a larger composition. 'Its purpose', according to one recent commentator, 'is hard to make out. It is too big for use in a modern history meant for engraving; it would not have suited any sublime history' (Lindsay, 1977, p. 134).

The painting is almost the only example of such a picture in Hogarth's oeuvre. Yet it does relate, as Frederick Antal has noted, to several characters to be found in the artist's small-scale satirical compositions, notably the milkmaid in the engraving *The Enraged Musician* and the fisherwoman in *Beer Street* (see Antal, 1962, p. 117). According to Antal, *The Shrimp Girl* should not be seen as 'a work on its own account' but as a study for one of the above figures. That may be so. However, the present composition, even though it is unfinished, relates more broadly to fancy pictures of female street traders by Mercier and Henry Morland.

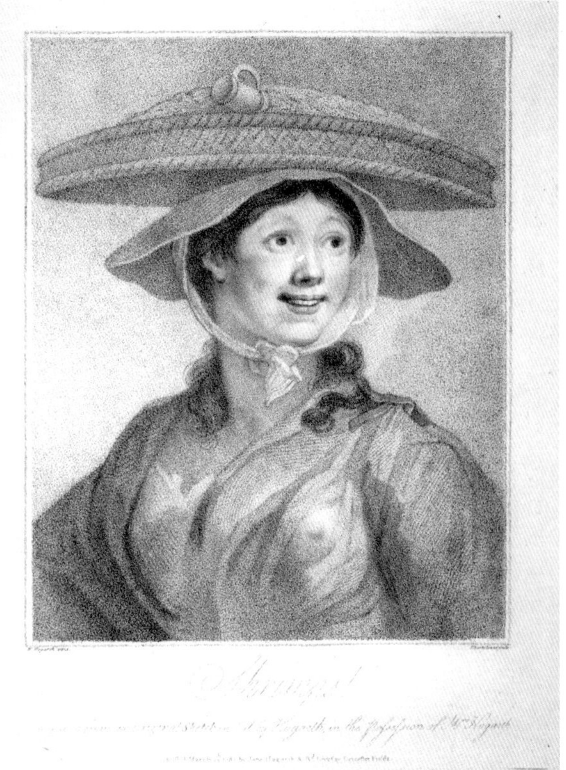

The *Shrimp Girl*, in terms of its pictorial icongraphy, harks back to several characters to be found in Marcellus Laroon's popular *Cryes of the City of London Drawne after the Life* (1st edition 1687). Indeed, earlier in his career Hogarth had painted a *Savoyard Girl* or *Hurdy-Gurdy Player* (see Beckett, 1949, p. 72), which was highly reminiscent of Laroon. The Shrimp Girl, however, in terms of its subject, most closely resembles Laroon's *Crab Crab any Crab* and *Buy my Dish of great Eeles* (fig. 33). As has been noted, of the seventy four street traders in Laroon's *Cryes*, six are fishmongers, seafood being an important part of the diet of Londoners in the eighteenth century. Although the 'Abstinence' statute – which encouraged the eating of fish at regular intervals, on vigils, and throughout Lent – had lapsed by the late seventeenth century, fish remained a staple foodstuff (see Shesgreen, 1990, p. 116). Hogarth's *Shrimp Girl*, while it is clearly based upon a life study, is formally similar to Laroon's eel seller, with her basket jauntily balanced upon her head and her cheerful, casual demeanour. The difference between the two women's wares is singled out only by the measuring jug resting on the shrimp girl's basket and the plate used by the eel girl to dispense her fish. They were, observed Donald Lupton in 1632, 'Crying, Wandring, and Travailing Creatures [who] carry their shops on their heads, and their Storehouse is ordinarily *Bilingsgate*' (quoted in Shesgreen, p. 92). Most itinerant fish vendors in London were women, although they did not specialise, selling one day fish, another fruit, and – as popular mythology would have it – even their own bodies.

According to one tradition (see Lindsay 1977, p. 134) the present oil sketch was known by the artist's family simply as 'the *Market Wench*'. Jane Hogarth, who clearly revelled in its down-to-earth liveliness and vigor, told visitors: "They say he could not paint flesh. There's flesh and blood for you — them!'. As David Bindman states, the *Shrimp Girl* perfectly illustrates Hogarth's adherence to the living model above the example of the Antique, preferring as his model a 'blooming young girl of fifteen' to 'the stony features of a venus' (Bindman, 1981, p. 149).

55 Shrimps! (opposite)

FRANCESCO BARTOLOZZI (1727-1815), after William Hogarth

Stipple engraving, 27 x 20.5 cm

LETTERED: '*W. Hogarth pinx./F. Bartolozzi sculp./ Shrimps!/Engrav'd from an Original Sketch in Oil by Hogarth, in the Possession of Mrs Hogarth/Publish'd March 25th 1782 by Jane Hogarth & Rd Livesay Leicester Fields*'

The Trustees of the British Museum, London

Francesco Bartolozzi was among the foremost engravers in stipple during the later eighteenth century, engraving many works after Cipriani and Angelica Kauffman. Bartolozzi, who was born in Florence and trained as an engraver in Venice, arrived in England in 1764, the year of Hogarth's death. He continued to etch and engrave in line, notably his series of prints after drawings by Guercino in the Royal Collection. At the same time Bartolozzi became aware of the potential of stipple engraving. In the present instance – his only engraving after Hogarth – Bartolozzi has subverted the healthy vitality of the *Shrimp Girl*, by the softening of girl's form and through the carefully crafted addition of an exposed nipple. In this context, the print's title, *Shrimps!*, takes on a distinct air of ambiguity.

In his 1785 catalogue of Hogarth's works, John Nichols criticized Bartolozzi's choice of stipple as the medium for this print: "This plate, which is executed in the dotted manner so much at present in fashion, should have been etched or engraved like those excellent performances by Bartolozzi after the drawings of Guercino. Spirit rather than delicacy, is the characteristic of our artist's *Shrimp Girl*' (Nichols, 1785, 3rd edition, p. 411).

Thomas Gainsborough, while he confessed to admire his work as an engraver, commented upon Bartolozzi's libidinous nature, even late in life: 'Why will Bartolozzi', he asked, 'spend his last precious moments in f—g a young Woman, instead of outdoing all the world with a Graver; when perhaps all the world can outdo Him in the former work!' (Woodall, 1963, p. 181).

56 Oyster Woman (below left)

PHILIP DAWE (b. 1750) after Henry Morland

Mezzotint, 50.9 x 35.4 cm

PROOF BEFORE LETTERS

The Trustees of the British Museum, London

Literature: Chaloner Smith, 1883, vol. 1, p.158, no. 17

Henry Morland's *Oyster Woman* (Glasgow Art Gallery) was exhibited at the Free Society of Artists in 1769 ('An oister girl), shortly before the publication of Dawe's mezzotint, shown here. The *Oyster Woman* is a small, meticulously worked picture, painted – unusually for the artist – on tin-plate. Equally unusual is the fact that it is smaller than the engraving made from it by Dawe. The subject is similar to, and may indeed have been influenced by, Mercier's *Oyster Girl* (cat. 52) which had been engraved by Richard Houston in the 1750s. Unlike Mercier's oyster-seller, however, the emphasis here is less upon the woman's personal charms than the dramatic play of light and shadow. In this respect it is formally closer to the nocturnes which Joseph Wright was simultaneously exhibiting at the Society of Artists. The *Oyster Woman* was one of over half-a-dozen prints made by Dawe after Morland's fancy pictures, including the *Girl Singing Ballads by a Lanthorn*, *A Laundry Maid Ironing*, and *A Lady's Maid Soaping Linen* (cats. 64, 69, 70). Philip Dawe, although he worked subsequently as an engraver, trained under Henry Morland. He was also the friend and biographer of Henry's profligate son, the artist George Morland.

57 The Watercress Girl (below)

JOHN RAPHAEL SMITH (1752-1812), after Johan Zoffany

Mezzotint, 38 x 27.5 cm

LETTERED: '*Painted by J. Zoffany R.A./Engraved by JR Smith/Jane Wallis/London Publishd Septem the 9th 1780 by JR Smith No 10 Bateman Buildings Soho & Birchall No 473 Strand*'

The Trustees of the British Museum

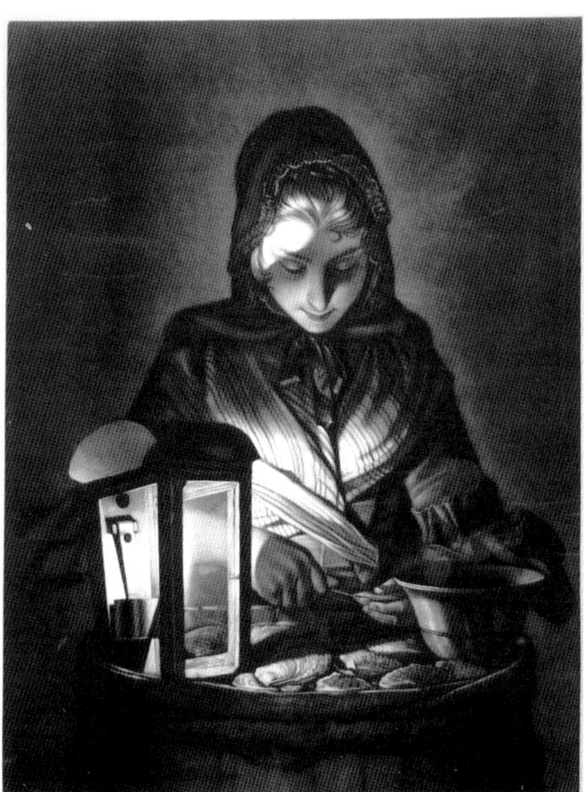

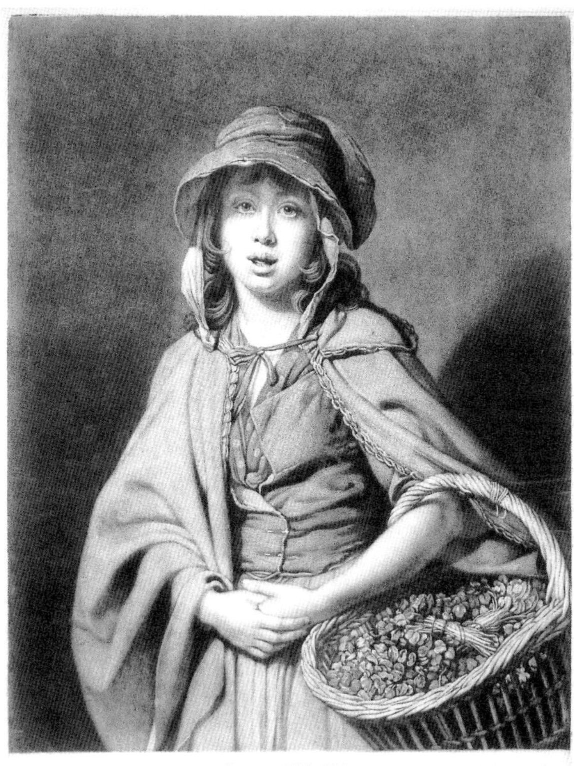

The subject is identified via a penned inscription '*Jane Wallis*', although Zoffany's painting, on which Smith's mezzotint is based, was shown at the Royal Academy in 1780 merely as an anonymous 'Girl with water-cresses'. Zoffany's other contribution to that year's exhibition, the *Tribuna of the Uffizi*, could not have been more different. But perhaps that was the point: Zoffany, after his extended absence from the country and the public exhibition wished to demonstrate his versatility, and his commitment to popular themes as well as High Art. *The Watercress Girl* and its pendant *The Flower Girl* (engraved in 1785, but probably painted earlier) are in the tradition of street vendors of Marcellus Laroon, and their 'speaking likenesses' are related to the cries of their trades. In Zoffany's hands, and especially under the graver of John Raphael Smith, these figures take on a refined and sophisticated air. The painting, we know, drew favourable responses, not least because of the attractiveness of Zoffany's model: 'The Artist has been very fortunate in a choice of a most beautiful Girl for his subject and he has copied nature so exactly, that it is not easy to determine whether it is real life or a painting.' Real, yet unreal: Zoffany's image at once brought the viewer into intimate contact with a figure with whom they would not in life encounter other than casually on the streets. As he does so Zoffany transforms the girl from a common vendor into an acceptable icon for domestic consumption, anticipating the sanitised figures found in Wheatley's *Cries of London* in the mid-1790s.

58 *The Brickdust Man*

JAMES WATSON *(c* 1739-90), after Nathaniel Hone

Mezzotint, 34.5 x 25.2 cm

LETTERED: '*Nathl Hone pinx^t Ja^s Watson fecit/The Brickdust Man/Printed for Henry Parker & Elizth Bakewell opposite Birchin Lane in Cornhill London*'

The Trustees of the British Museum

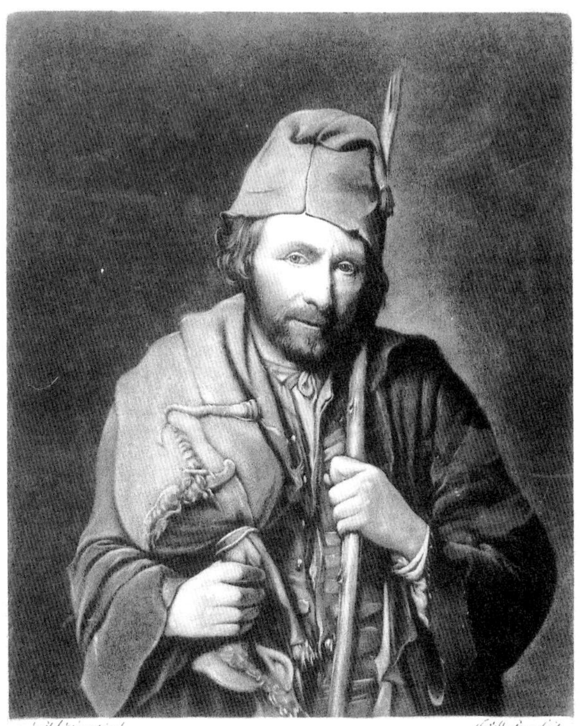

The subject of Hone's picture probably earned his living by selling brick dust to domestic households, where it was used as a scouring agent. Alternatively, he may also have worked collecting ashes from homes to resell to brickmakers, who mixed them with clay in the manufacturing of bricks. In any event, whether he was selling brick dust or collecting ashes to make bricks, he must have been a common site on the city streets, one of many individuals gleaning an income from the recycling industry, collecting bones, rags, and household refuse for resale. Nathaniel Hone was one of the first artists to make such a lowly individual the subject for a fancy picture. The painting upon which the present engraving is based was exhibited at the Society of Artists in 1760, and again at his one-man show in 1775. *The Brickdust Man* also appeared in Henry Bromley's *Catalogue of British Engraved Portraits* of 1793, alongside miscellaneous lamplighters, ballad singers and others classified as 'Phaenomena'. James Watson, who also engraved fancy pictures for Reynolds among others, was one of a small group of Irish print makers who brought the art of mezzotint to a state of near perfection during the middle decades of the eighteenth century. *The Brickdust Man* is among his finest productions, and exploits to the full the nuances of light and shadow of which the medium was capable.

59 *Porter with a Hare* (Plate 41)

JOHAN ZOFFANY (1733-1810)

Oil on canvas, 76.2 x 63 cm
Inscribed on the label attached to the hare: '*Zu Zaffaly*'; on the back of the stretcher '*Zafani*'

Herbert Art Gallery and Museum, Coventry

Provenance: Messrs. Gooden & Fox; Ernest Cook; bequeathed by Ernest Cook to the National Art Collections Fund, 1955, and presented to the Herbert Art Gallery and Museum, Coventry
Exhibited: ? Society of Artists, 1769 (213); Walker Art Gallery, Liverpool, 1968 (97); National Portrait Gallery, London, 1976 (45)
Literature: Manners and Williamson 1920, pp. 19-20, 177, 196; Webster, 1976, p. 44, no. 45
Engraved: Mezzotint by Richard Earlom, 1774

Zoffany arrived in London sometime during 1760, at which point he was still Johannes Josephus Zauffaly, the name under which he was baptised in Frankfurt in 1733. He had come to England by way of Regensburg, where he was apprenticed and worked for a while, and Italy, where he studied under Agostino Masucci (1692-1768). In London he was taken up by David Garrick, and quickly gained popularity through a series of theatrical paintings and meticulously worked conversation pieces. *The Porter with a Hare*, however, stands out as quite different from the rest of the artist's work during his first decade in England.

It is not known precisely when Zoffany painted *The Porter with a Hare*, nor to whom it originally belonged. Like his *Florentine Fruit Stall* of the late 1770s, it may have remained in his studio, although the existence of at least one other version, together with the fact that it was engraved in 1774, suggests the picture attracted a buyer. It was either the present picture or a similar version, now in a private collection, which Zoffany exhibited at the Society of Artists in 1769. Aside from stylistic variations, the principal difference between the two versions is that the present picture is inscribed '*Zu Zoffaly*', whereas the label in the other version reads 'Mr Zoffany L[incoln's] Inn Fields', i.e. the Anglicized version of his name and his London address since 1765.

Zoffany painted only a few fancy, or domestic genre, pictures. They include the pendant *Watercress Girl* (see cat. 57) and *Flower Girl*, and *Beggars on the Road to Stanmore* (cat. 89). All of these pictures are a world away from the sweet, playful conceits of Mercier and Morland, or the allegorical infant saints of Reynolds. Rather, they recall the stark, sharply focused documentaries of Henry Walton, who was, so we understand, a pupil of Zoffany's around the time he painted *A Porter with a Hare*. That Zoffany exercised some influence on the young Walton through this picture cannot be doubted, when viewed next to a picture such as *The Cherry Barrow* (cat. 61).

Because *A Porter with a Hare* is unique in Zoffany's oeuvre it is tempting to speculate on the circumstances surrounding its creation. An unreliable tradition, recorded earlier this century, was that Zoffany witnessed the scene from his window and immediately set about painting it (Manners & Williamson, 1920, p. 19). At the time it was first exhibited a newspaper stated that the picture showed 'two School Boys reading the direction on a Hare to a Porter', the implication being not simply that the porter is disoriented but that he cannot read. According to another tradition, the two boys in the picture were sons of the Baskerville family of Crawley Park, who by implication may have commissioned the work. Certainly, the boys do resemble well-dressed sons of the gentry. The boy to the left points out directions to the porter, suggesting that they live in the neighbourhood (Lincoln's Inn) and are telling the porter where the hare is to be delivered – '*Zu Zaffaly*', that is to Zoffany ('zu' meaning both 'by' and 'to', depending on its usage).

One final point, which suggests that the picture may originally have had a meaning which is now lost, concerns the fact that the boy giving directions to the puzzled porter is also eating. Horace Walpole, in his exhibition catalogue, stated that he is 'looking up, eating bread and butter'. More precisely, he is eating a sandwich, the celebrated snack invented only a few years earlier by John Montagu, 4th Earl of Sandwich, to keep the pangs of hunger at bay while at the gaming table.

60 A Girl Plucking a Turkey (Plate 42)

HENRY WALTON (*c* 1746-1813)

Oil on canvas, 72.4 x 61 cm, 1776
Tate Gallery

Provenance: acquired from Messrs. Leggat Brothers by the Tate Gallery in 1912
Exhibited: Society of Artists, 1776 (131); Norwich, 1963 (10)
Literature: Collins Baker, 1907, p. 136 ; Farrer, 1909, pp.139-47; Norwich, 1963, p. 12, no. 10
Engraved: J.R. Smith, 1777 as 'Plucking the Turkey'; Unknown, 1797, as 'A Cottage Maid' (with the addition of a cottage and landscape).

A Girl Plucking a Turkey is the first of only a handful of studies exhibited by the artist, depicting figures absorbed in domestic duties and commonplace activities. It is also the picture which, more than any other, demonstrates Walton's familiarity with trends in contemporary French art. As is now clear, Walton had extensive first-hand experience of French art, through his frequent trips to Paris both as a practising artist and as a dealer. We do not know the dates of his visits, nor indeed any other relevant details. Even so, it is intriguing that the present picture was exhibited at the Society of Artists after a gap of three years, before which time Walton had restricted his exhibits to portraits.

Walton's precise interests in Continental art, which may at some time be revealed by the nature of his picture col-

lecting, remain uncertain. Chardin, with his deceptive simplicity and pictorial economy, must have appealed to Walton. Whether he ever met Chardin (whose reputation was already on the decline) is another matter. Among the younger generation of artists, whose work may have influenced him more directly, it is worth singling out Jean-Baptiste Greuze (1725-1805) and Etienne Aubry (1745-81), an exact contemporary of Walton's, who was exhibiting at the Paris salon throughout the 1770s.

The pictorial roots of *A Girl Plucking a Turkey*, while allied to trends in eighteenth-century French art, lie in Dutch art of the 1600s, a compelling comparison being Rembrandt's *Old Woman Plucking a Fowl* (unlocated), which at the time belonged to the Hon. Francis Charteris (1723-1808), and which was engraved in mezzotint by Richard Houston (cat. 23). In Rembrandt's painting, and in Walton's depiction of a younger woman, the subject is treated soberly without reference to anecdote or the intrusion of extraneous detail, despite the fact that the activity in which they are engaged was frequently used as a metaphor for sexual activity or bawdy humour. It is the lack of any allusion beyond the immediate scene in question that takes Walton's pictures out of the realm of 'fancy' and into the domain of domestic genre painting.

61 The Cherry Barrow (Plate 44)

HENRY WALTON (1746-1813)

Oil on canvas, 76.2 x 63.5 cm
Sir Reresby Sitwell, BT, DL

Exhibited: Royal Academy 1779 (339) as 'A group of figures with a fruit barrow'; Norwich, 1963 (14)
Literature: Waterhouse, 1953, pp. 199-200, pl. 186; Norwich, 1963 (14)

Henry Walton remains something of an enigma. He was born in Norfolk, the son of a gentleman farmer. Probably towards the end of the 1760s Walton went to London, where he became a pupil of Zoffany. In 1770 he applied to become a student at the Incorporated Society of Artists' school in Maiden Lane. Two years later he was appointed a Director of the Society. Virtually nothing is known about his life at this time. However, an acquaintance in later life, Dawson Turner, recalled that Walton 'with the view of studying or of buying pictures had made frequent journeys to Paris' (Norwich, 1963, p. 6). Among the fruits of these visits to France were, we can assume, Walton's limited series of domestic genre pictures, in the manner of the French *genre sérieux*. They included *A Girl Plucking a Turkey* (cat. 60), *A Market Girl* (RA 1777), *A Woman Buying a Ballad* (RA 1778) (Fig. 41) and the present work, which Waterhouse considered as 'near perfection in the genre as has been achieved in English painting' (Waterhouse, 1953, pp. 99-100).

Walton's subject-matter, especially his female street vendors, is reminiscent of earlier works by Mercier and Morland, although their low-key matter-of-factness is far more akin to that of Chardin. There are significant differences in approach. In *The Cherry Barrow* a genteel, well-dressed bourgeois woman and her daughter (relatives of Walton?) look out towards the viewer while the little urchins are absorbed in sampling the old fruit seller's wares. The combination of portrait and genre here is similar to that in pictures such as Francis Wheatley's *Family Group in a Landscape* (Mr and Mrs Paul Mellon) of around the same date, where the mother holding a fishing-rod turns to the spectator while her family concentrate upon their various leisure activities. The difference – and what makes Walton original – is that *The Cherry Barrow* is not a 'conversation piece', i. e. an informal group portrait of a bourgeois or aristocratic family. Here and in the *Woman Buying a Ballad* Walton brings together working people, oberved sympathetically, with those middle-class individuals who more usually form the audience for such works. It is also worth remembering that *The Cherry Barrow* was painted nearly fifteen years before Wheatley's fruit vendor pictures, 'Sweet China Oranges, Sweet China!' and 'Round, and Sound Five Pence a Pound Duke Cherrys!' from the *Cries of London*.

1779, the year in which *The Cherry Barrow* was shown at the Royal Academy, marked the end of Walton's public career as an artist, at the early age of thirty-three. No satisfactory explanation has emerged as to why Walton all but surrendered his ambitions in the capital. It may have been connected with his failure to secure election as an Associate Academician in 1778, although it is more likely, given his comfortable circumstances, that he simply did not need to succeed as a professional painter, being more preoccupied with dealing in pictures than painting them (we need only think of Vermeer). In any event, Walton left London in the 1780s in favour of a squirearchical life on his Suffolk farm. He continued to paint (principally portraits), although increasingly he became known as a connoisseur and picture-dealer rather than an artist.

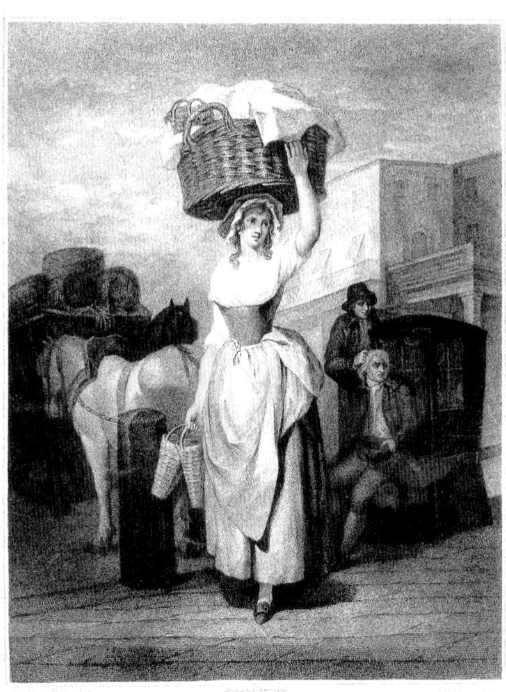

62 *Strawberrys, Scarlet Strawberrys!*)

VENDRAMINI, after Francis Wheatley

Stipple engraving, 43.2 x 33 cm

LETTERED: '*Painted by F. Wheatley* R.A.*/Directed by L. Schiavonetti/Engraved by Vendramini/*CRIES OF LONDON*/Strawberrys, Scarlet Strawberrys!/Fraises, fraises, ma belles fraises/London Publish'd as the Act directs June 25 1795 by Colnaghi & C*^{O} *N*^{O} *132 Pall Mall.*'

The Trustees of the British Museum

This engraving may be compared with Reynolds's *Strawberry Girl* of nearly twenty years earlier, or with Laroon's *Ripe Strawberryes*, to which it bears a far closer formal resemblance. All three prints show the strawberry seller with her distinctive cone-shaped wicker basket, or 'pottle', made to hold exactly two quarts of fruit. Wheatley's strawberry seller is a characteristically genteel character, dressed, as Gillray remarked, 'with great smartness, but little propriety, better suited to the fantastic taste of an Italian opera stage than to the streets of London' (quoted in Webster, 1970, p. 83). The huge basket on her head is borne with deceptive ease, which belies the physical demands placed upon such women. As Richard Philips noted in 1804: 'These women carry upon their heads baskets of strawberries or raspberries, weighing from forty to fifty pounds, and make two turns in the day, from Isleworth to market, a distance of thirteen miles each way; three turns from Brentford, for a distance of nine miles; and four turns from Hammersmith, a distance of six miles. For the most part, they find some conveyance back; but even these industrious creatures carry loads from twenty-four to thirty miles a day, besides walking back unladen some part of each turn!' (quoted in Shesgreen, 1990, p. 84). Behind Wheatley's strawberry girl is a 'conveyance' laden with fruit baskets, and a chairman, resting from his labours while wondering at the young woman's physique and stamina.

63 *A new Love Song only ha'penny a piece!*

ANTOINE CARDON (1772-1813), after Francis Wheatley

Stipple engraving, 42.2 x 33 cm

LETTERED: '*Painted by F. Wheatley R.A./Engraved by A. Cardon/*CRIES *of* LONDON*/A New Love Song only ha'penny a piece!/Chanson nouvelles deux sous la piece/London Publish'd March 1796 by Colnaghi & C*^{O} *N*^{O} *132 Pall Mall*'

The Trustees of the British Museum, London

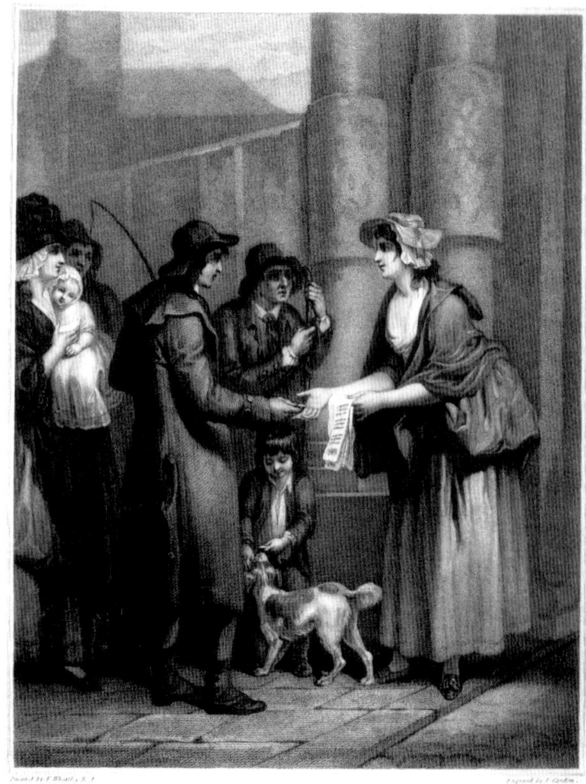

The Belgian-born Antoine Cardon was one of a growing band of engravers who made their living towards the end of the century producing large quantities of popular stipples intended as furniture prints, book and periodical illustrations. Arriving in London in 1792, Cardon found employment engraving bookplates for Colnaghi. His most successful engravings for Colnaghi were the three plates he engraved for Francis Wheatley's *Cries of London*, 'Do you want any Matches?', 'Round, and Sound Five Pence a Pound Duke Cherrys!', and the present engraving which shows a young woman selling ballads to a couple of coachmen, while a well-dressed woman and child look on. The depiction of street vendors crying their trades goes back to the Middle Ages, although it was the seminal series of 74 prints, *The Cryes of the City of London Drawne after the Life*, published in 1687 by Marcellus Laroon, which provided the benchmark for the genre in years to come. Such subjects gained immense popularity in France and England in the form of furniture prints. Mary Webster, citing Binet's *Les Jolies Crieuses* of the early 1780s and Beauvarlet's engravings after Greuze's *La Marchande de Marrons* and *La Marchande de Pommes Cuites*', has observed the influence upon Wheatley of French precedents (Webster, 1970, pp. 82-3). The *Cries of London* were originally sold in paired prints, a total of twelve being published between 1793 and 1796 (plus a thirteenth in 1797). Coloured sets of all thirteen prints were sold by Colnaghi for 16 shillings, monochromes for 7s 6d. As the inscription in French as well as English indicates, they were intended equally for export abroad as well as the home market.

---

64 Girl Singing Ballads by a Lanthorn   (Plate 43)

HENRY ROBERT MORLAND (?1719-97)

Oil on canvas, 75.6 x 62.2 cm, *c* 1765-82

Tate Gallery

Provenance: Bequeathed to the Tate Gallery by Mrs Frances Elinor Pearse 1944
Exhibited: Versions of this composition were exhibited during Morland's lifetime as follows: 'A ballad singer; in crayons', Society of Artists, 1764 (73) ; 'A girl singing ballads; in oyl', Free Society of Artists 1767 (203); 'A ballad singer', FSA, 1768 (166); 'A girl singing ballads by a paper lanthorn' FSA, 1768 (294); 'A ballad singer', FSA, 1774 (197); 'A girl singing ballads', FSA, 1776 (253); 'A girl singing Ballads by a paper lanthorn', FSA, 1782 (59)
Literature: Davies, 1946; Farthing, 1944, p. 101, repr.; Waterhouse, 1981, p. 246, repr.
Engraved: Mezzotint by Philip Dawe as 'The pretty Ballad Singer', 1769

Morland exhibited no fewer than seven versions of this picture at the Society of Artists and the Free Society of Artists between 1764 and 1782, an indication of the popularity of the composition – even after the publication of Philip Dawe's mezzotint in 1769. Five of the oil versions are known today, including one formerly belonging to the Earls of Morley (National Trust, Saltram) and one originally purchased by Lord Charlemont (see Farthing, 1944, p. 102) – an indication that the taste for Morland's fancy pictures was distinctly aristocratic. In 1767 Morland was charging the not inconsiderable sum of 12 guineas for a version of his *Ballad Singer*, which presumably limited such sales to the well-off.

Henry Morland, who was born in London, had a prolific if precarious career. Although constantly active as a painter he also supplemented his fluctuating income by working as a picture restorer, dealer, artist's colourman, and copyist (latterly with the assistance of his son, George Morland). Despite his artistic adaptability Morland was evidently a bad businessman, and was in 1762 declared bankrupt – having two years earlier relinquished the lease on his house in Leicester Square to Joshua Reynolds. It was Morland's own financial difficulties, as well as the popularity of his fancy pictures, which probably compelled him to turn them out as 'potboilers'.

The *Girl Singing Ballads by a Lanthorn* is one of a series of nocturnal fancy pictures by Morland, others including *A Lady reading by Candle-Light* and *A Servant Girl with a Candle*, all of which were engraved by Philip Dawe. In general such works rely on seventeenth-century Dutch models, notably the work of the Netherlandish Caravaggisti, as well as later genre painters such as Gerrit Dou and Godfried Schalcken, whose works were reproduced in engraving by that time (see cat. 21). Apparently, Morland was particularly fond of Dou's work (see Farthing, 1944, p. 102), but Morland's decision to exploit the genre may have in turn encouraged Joseph Wright, the two artists quite probably experimented with the technique quite independently.

Like Mercier's *Oyster Girl*, Morland's *Ballad Singer* also traded on the kind of images already familiar through Laroon's prints in *The Cryes of the City of London*. During the 1760s ballad singers were still familiar figures on the streets of London. They made their living not from singing songs but by selling ballads. These would often be posted in taverns and coffee houses for communal singing. The subject-matter, which was invariably topical, was also often bawdy. Hence, female ballad singers, perhaps more so than other London street vendors, were associated with the distribution of sexual favours. They were also allied in the public imagination to vice, not only through their songs about the activities of celebrated criminals but also through their own dubious connections. As John Gay observed in 1716:

> Let not the Ballad-Singer's Shrilling Strain
> Amid the Swarm thy list'ning Ear detain;
> Guard well thy Pocket; for these *Syrens* stand,
> To aid the Labours of the diving Hand;
> Confed'rate in Cheat, they draw the Throng,
> And *Cambrick* Handkerchiefs reward the Song

(*Trivia: or, The Art of Walking the Streets of London*, London, 1716 quoted in Shesgreen, 1990, p. 100).

It is worth recalling that in Dutch seventeenth-century iconography the image of a woman holding a lantern was linked to prostitution, illustrating the popular proverb that 'a beauteous whore is like a lantern without a light' (see Schama, 1987, p. 452).

---

65 Love Songs and Matches   (Plate 50)

JOHN RUSSELL (1745-1806)

Pastel on paper, laid on canvas, 90.2 x 68.6 cm, 1793
The Trustees of the Holburne Museum, Bath

Provenance: Revd. F.A. Bowles; J. Wentworth Smith, Christie's 14 December 1928 (69); J. Wentworth Smith; Gooden & Fox for E.E. Cook, Bath; presented to the Holburne Museum through the National Art Collections Fund in 1955
Exhibited: Royal Academy 1793 (321); Holburne Museum 1991 (31)
Literature: George C. Williamson, *John Russell, R.A.*, London, 1894, p. 137; A Guide to the Collections, Holburne Museum, Bath, 1979, pp. 18-19, repr.

This picture is one of Russell's finest works and epitomises the late eighteenth-century fancy picture. The boy, as suggested by the title of the work (under which it was first exhibited at the Royal Academy in 1793), is a vendor of popular ballads and matches. Russell's street boy belongs to a popular graphic tradition stretching back to the seventeenth century, notably to Laroon's *Cryes of the City of London*. In Laroon's series the match vendor ('Any Card matches or Savealls') is, as with many other illustrations in the series, represented by a young woman. In Laroon's final engraving the woman is relatively neat and well presented, although in his original sketch she is ragged and scruffy (see Shesgreen, 1990, p. 90). In Russell's picture the boy, despite his engaging smile, is also dressed in rags.

While the rags serve as a picturesque device for the artist, they also underline the grinding poverty endured by such people. In reality match vendors were on the lowest rung of the social ladder, an urban counterpart to Millet's rural gleaners of the 1850s. They were among the poorest of street vendors, being composed of the old, crippled, widows, and abandoned children. Often whole families would work as match sellers, the card matches being cut and trimmed by children in domestic sweatshops. There was little money to be made in selling matches, and their survival depended principally on kitchen scraps, begging and stealing (Shesgreen, loc. cit.).

When Russell's pastel was shown at the Royal Academy, Francis Wheatley was evolving his own *Cries of London* (see cats. 62 and 63), most of the original oils being exhibited at the Royal Academy between 1792 and 1793. Among these was probably 'Do you want any Matches?', which was published as a stipple engraving by Cardon in 1794 (Webster, 1970, p. 175). In Wheatley's picture two vendors are shown: a young woman and a small boy, who is perhaps her younger brother. The representation of the boy, with his broad-brimmed hat, wicker basket and dog, is reminiscent of Russell's figure, although the similarity presumably depended on shared perceptions.

66 *The Strawberry Girl* (Plate 45)

THOMAS WATSON (d. 1781), after Sir Joshua Reynolds

Mezzotint engraving, 37 x 27.5 cm

LETTERED: '*Painted by Sir Joshua Reynolds/Engrav'd by Tho.s Watson/*THE STRAWBERRY GIRL.*/Publish'd* [*Novr 1st 1774, for W. Shropshire No 158 & T. Watson No 142 New Bond Street.*]

Private collection

Literature: Hamilton, 1884, p. 120

Reynolds exhibited his *Strawberry Girl* at the Royal Academy in 1773. According to his pupil James Northcote, Reynolds counted it among his finest and most original works – although the little girl's attitude may have been derived from a painting by the seventeenth-century Bolognese painter, Albani (Prochno, 1990, p. 464). Reynolds's first idea for the work emerged from a painting of around 1767 which he made using his young niece, Theophila Palmer, as model, although he reworked the composition frequently over the next decade. The present engraving is made from the prime version of the composition purchased by Lord Carysfort, and which was almost certainly the picture exhibited by Reynolds in 1773. A slightly different version of the *Strawberry Girl*, retained by Reynolds in his studio, was later acquired by the poet-banker Samuel Rogers and bought at his sale by the Marquess of Hertford: this is the picture now in the Wallace Collection.

The Victorian art critic Tom Taylor described the *Strawberry Girl* as a kind of 'little Red Riding Hood hearing the first rustle of the wolf in the wayside bushes' (Leslie and Taylor, 1865, vol. 2, p. 3). Reynolds's context for the image

was, however, not a fairy tale, but the everyday world of commerce, the term 'strawberry girl' connoting in the eighteenth century either those who sold strawberries in the market place or – as Sir Ellis Waterhouse noted – quite young girls who worked in Strawberry Gardens. These places were popular leisure resorts in the summer and, as Waterhouse observes, the girls who worked there 'must have been considerably dismayed at what went on around them' (quoted in Postle, 1995, p. 82). Whether such dismay can account for the wide-eyed gaze of the girl in Reynolds's picture is, however, open to question – not least because the model was his own niece.

67 *The Boy with Cabbage Nets* (Plate 46)

CHARLES HARDY, after Sir Joshua Reynolds

Mezzotint engraving, 34.5 x 25 cm

LETTERED: '*THE BOY WITH CABBAGE NETS/This Plate from a Picture painted by Sir Joshua Reynolds in the Collection of her Grace the DUCHESS OF DORSET is by Permission respectfully Inscribed to her Grace by her Graces' obedient Servant. Charles Hardy./Published as the Act directs August 10th. 1803 by C. Hardy, 92 Norton Street.*'

Private Collection

Reynolds exhibited the painting upon which Hardy's engraving was based at the Royal Academy in 1775 as 'A beggar Boy and his Sister', by which time it probably belonged to the Duke of Dorset. (The picture is now owned by the Trustees of the Faringdon Collection, Buscot Park.) It is unusual among Reynolds's fancy pictures in that it depicts the child in a role which approximated to his status in life, an impoverished urchin eking out a living by selling cabbage nets on the streets of London. The boy was among Reynolds's favourite child models of the 1770s. He posed for *The Calling of Samuel* (cat. 14) *A Fortune Teller* (cat. 78), the so-called 'School Boy' (see cat. 44) as well as several studies of children reading. He was singled out by William Mason, a frequent visitor to the artist's studio at the time. 'This boy (at the time about fourteen), though not handsome, had an expression in his eye so very forcible, and indicating so much sense, that he was certainly a most excellent subject for his [Reynolds's] pencil... He was an orphan of the poorest parents, and left with three or four brothers and sisters, whom he taught, as they were able, to make cabbage-nets; and with these he went about with them, offering them for sale, by which he provided both for their maintenance and is own. What became of him afterwards I know not' (Mason in Cotton, 1859, p. 57).

David Alexander has suggested that the print, although it bears the name Charles Hardy, may have been engraved by Thomas Hardy (1757-1804 or later: he was at 92 Norton Street from 1796). Charles Hardy may possibly have been the son of Thomas Hardy.

68 *A Girl Sewing (The Sewing Lesson)* (Plate 47)

PHILIP MERCIER (?1689-1760)

Oil on canvas, 76 x 64 cm, *c* 1750

Tate Gallery

Signed '*PM*' (monogram)

Provenance: Dr Robert Jaimeson; his grand-niece, Mrs Gertrude Bell; Sotheby's, 9 December 1964 (114) as 'The Sewing Lesson' by H. Morland, bt.

Sabin; bt. from Sabin by the Tate Gallery 1965
Exhibited: York and Kenwood, 1969 (74)
Literature: Tate Gallery, *Report*,1965-6, p. 20; Ingamells and Raines, 1969, Addenda, no. 74; Ingamells and Raines, 1976-78, no. 227

When sold at auction in the 1960s the picture was attributed to Henry Morland (partly due to the misreading of Mercier's monogram). The subject-matter, if not the style, is far more reminiscent of Chardin, notably his *Young Schoolmistress* in the National Gallery, London (Fig. 4). When it was shown at Kenwood and York in 1969, *A Girl Sewing* was dated to around 1740 although a later date is now preferred (see Ingamells and Raines, 1976-8, p. 53). In terms of Mercier's own *oeuvre*, the present picture, with its air of genteel domesticity, is akin to works such as the *Boy Reading to a Girl Sewing* (private collection) and *The Bible Lesson* (private collection) which was engraved in 1743. The contrast between the small thumb-sucking child and the older girl could also connote innocence and experience.

What may be a sketch by Mercier of the seated girl has recently been identified by Alastair Laing (see MS correspondence, Tate Gallery Archive). The drawing, which belonged at one time to the Goncourt brothers, was formerly attributed to Jacques-Andre Portail (1694-1759), although it does not especially resemble other known drawings by the artist (see Elisabeth Launay, *Les freres Goncourt collectionneurs de dessins*, 1991, no. 260, p. 420). As a comparison between the drawing from the Goncourt collection and Mercier's painting reveals, there are compositional differences between the two images, not least in the angle of the girl's head, her dress, and the object of her attention. Even so, these are the kinds of variations that one would expect to find when a life study is translated into a finished picture. Indeed, the overall similarities between the two works, and the drawing's stylistic resemblance to other known studies by Mercier (notably the drawing for Viscountess Tyrconnel in the painting *Viscount Tyrconnel with his Family*) support the present attribution to Mercier.

Mercier returned to the theme of the present work towards the end of his career with three related pictures showing single figures of young women sewing, washing and knitting. Two of these works, *A Girl Washing* and *A Girl Sewing* were exhibited at the Society of Arts in 1760, which was shortly before the artist's death. All three of them were engraved by J.S. Negges under the collective title *Domestic Employment*, along with a fourth work entitled 'Reading' based on a mezzotint by John Faber II after Richard Wilson.

69 *A Laundry Maid Ironing* (Plate 48)
HENRY ROBERT MORLAND (1716-97)

Oil on canvas, 74.2 x 61.5 cm, *c* 1768-82
Tate Gallery

Provenance: Bought by the National Gallery in 1894 from Colnaghi; transferred to the Tate Gallery in 1919
Exhibited: Versions of this composition were exhibited during the artist's lifetime as follows: 'A servant ironing', Free Society of Artists 1768 (164); 'A girl ironing some sleeves', FSA 1774 (215); 'A girl ironing some shirt sleeves', FSA 1775 (174); 'A girl ironing shirt-sleeves', FSA 1776 (251); 'Laundry Maid ironing', FSA 1782 (40)
Literature: Williamson, 1904, pp. 2-3; Sparrow, 1931, pp. 72-3, repr.; Farthing, 1944, p. 102, repr.; Winter, 1977, pp. 19-20
Engraved: Mezzotint by Philip Dawe, 2 October 1769

70 *A Lady's Maid Soaping Linen* (Plate 49)
HENRY ROBERT MORLAND (1716-97)

Oil on canvas; 70.5 x 62.3 cm
The Trustees of the Holburne Museum, Bath

Provenance: Probably Mr Asher Wertheimer, 1910; Ogden Mills; Parke-Bernet Galleries, Inc., New York, May 12, 1938 (46); Major Edward Bowes; Parke-Bernet Galleries, Inc., New York, 13 November 1943 (167); Schoenemann Galleries; presented by Mrs Inez Murray 1978
Exhibited: Versions of this composition were exhibited during the artist's lifetime as follows: 'A lady's maid soaping linen', Free Society of Artists 1769 (163); 'A lady's maid soaping some fine linen', FSA 1774 (209); 'A lady's maid soaping some fine linen', FSA 1775 (169); 'A lady's maid soaping linen', FSA 1776 (25); 'Lady's maid soaping Linen in a Bason', FSA 1782 (108)
Literature: Sparrow, 1931, pp. 72-3; Farthing, 1944, p. 102 repr. (a version); Fox, 1987, p. 133
Engraved: Mezzotint by Philip Dawe, 2 October 1769

These pictures, published simultaneously as mezzotints by Morland's friend Philip Dawe in 1769, were clearly regarded by the artist as pendants. Altogether Morland exhibited five versions of each picture, all of which, apart from the initial pair, were shown at the same exhibitions at the Free Society of Artists. Along with the *Girl Singing Ballads by a Lanthorn* (cat. 64) they were clearly Morland's most commercially successful images. The immediate inspiration for the paintings was most probably Mercier's series of pictures of women performing household chores, and which were engraved during the 1750s under the collective title 'Domestic Employment'. Even so, they were not simply pastiches of Mercier's work and Morland produced, especially in the *Laundry Maid Ironing*, a work of some individuality.

The market for Morland's ballad singers and serving maids was distinctly aristocratic. Versions of the *Lady's Maid Soaping Linen* were owned at one time or another by the Marquis of Linlithgow (Hopetoun House); Lord Halifax; and the Earl of Mansfield. There was an inferior copy at Badminton House. It is probably owing to their aristocratic pedigree that a myth was propagated in the mid-nineteenth century that Morland's models were the beautiful Gunning sisters, Maria, Countess of Coventry, and Elizabeth, Duchess of Hamilton. (The Earl of Mansfield's pictures were exhibited in 1867 as such.) While it is true that both sisters sat for allegorical portraits it is doubtful that they would have agreed to model for Morland's domestic servants, even in an age when the masquerade permitted a good deal of dressing up – and dressing down.

71 *Air* (Plate 54)
FREDERICK EDWARD ADAMS (*fl* 1760-73) after Jean Raoux

Mezzotint, 35.5 x 25.5 cm, *c* 1768
LETTERED: '*Raoux pinxit./F. E. Adams fecit./AIR. L'AIR/Printed for John Bowles at No* [3 in Cornhill]'
David Alexander

Literature: Chaloner Smith, 1883, vol. 1, p. 2, no. 4

The French painter Jean Raoux (1677-1734) was trained as an historical painter but was best known for his fancy pictures. He visited London in 1720 and was patronised by Sir Andrew Fontaine. Whether this print derives from an engraving or from a picture in England has not been discovered; Chaloner Smith suggested that this print was engraved as a companion to *Earth* and *Water* by Spooner after Pyle, published by Bowles in 1768. Francis Edward

Adams (*fl* 1760-73) received a premium from the Society of Arts in 1760: he signed so few prints that he probably worked for other engravers before setting up briefly as an engraver and printseller in the early 1770s.

The print measures 10 by 14 inches, the usual size for 'posture mezzotints', which could be fitted into frames of a standard size.

DSA

72 *Air* (Plate 53)
73 *Water* (Plate 52)

RICHARD HOUSTON (1722-75) after Philippe Mercier

Mezzotints, 35.5 x 25.5 cm
LETTERED: '*Ph Mercier pinxt/Publish'd according to Act of Parliament, October 1st 1756./Richd Houston fecit/*[verses] *Air [Water]/London Printed for Robert Sayer opposite Fetter-Lane Fleet Street & Elizth Bakewell in Cornhill – Price 1s-6d'*.
David Alexander

Literature: Chaloner Smith, 1883, vol. 2, p. 696, no. 134; Ingamells and Raines, 1976-8, XLVI

The French painter Philip Mercier, who was much influenced by the work of Watteau, moved to London in the 1720s and became Principal Painter to the artistically-inclined Frederick, Prince of Wales, for whom he painted a number of animated portraits. After he lost this post in 1736 he took two initiatives: he moved to York in search of new patrons; and in 1739 he launched a subscription for a set of prints of his fancy pictures, asking a guinea for eight mezzotints by John Faber. This was well enough supported for him to bring out a second set in 1743. For the rest of his life he was able to sell his pictures, or the right to engrave them, to the print publishers, of whom Robert Sayer was one of the most enterprising.

Richard Houston was one of a group of Irish engravers who went to England in the 1740s and dominated mezzotint engraving until 1775. Horace Walpole noted that 'Houston, the best engraver in London, was very idle capricious and extravagant. He… absconded for debt in 1762'. Initially he published prints himself but for the latter part of his career he worked for the publishers, principally Sayer, who is said to have had him confined to the debtors' prison in the Fleet in order to know where to find him.

DSA

74 *A Woman in Bed (Lydia)* (Plate 51)

THE REVD MATTHEW WILLIAM PETERS (1741/2-1814)

Oil on canvas, 61 x 72.4 cm
Tate Gallery

Provenance: Richard, 1st Earl Grosvenor by 1776; Hamilton Rice; Dorothy F. Hill; Michael Fitzsimmons; Christie's, London, 11 July 1986 (53); bt. Tate Gallery 1986
Exhibited: probably Royal Academy 1777 (270) as *A woman in bed*
Literature: Manners, 1913, pp. 54, 62
Engraved: Mezzotint by W. Dickinson, 1 December 1776 as 'Lydia'

The present picture was engraved in December 1776, when it was in the possession of Richard, 1st Earl Grosvenor. The engraving, entitled *Lydia*, was accompanied by lines from Dryden:

> This is the Mould of which I made the Sex.
>
> I gave them but one tongue to say us nay.
>
> And two Kind Eyes to grant.

Although the image was propelled into the public domain by Dickinson's print, Lord Grosvenor kept the picture under wraps to amuse his friends in private, reputedly hiding it behind a curtain – which, following Peters's elevation to the priesthood in 1782, was apparently nicknamed the 'episcopal lawn' (Manners, 1913, p. 6). (The story of the curtain may also explain why in a later impression of Dickinson's print, published in 1824, a curtain was introduced at the left of the image partly concealing the woman's cap and the pillow.) This picture, and others like it, clearly appealed to Lord Grosvenor's set, and a similar work, engraved as 'Sylvia' by John Raphael Smith in 1778, was in the possession of Peniston Lamb, the 1st Viscount Melbourne.

Matthew William Peters was born on the Isle of Wight, where his father worked as a civil engineer. Having spent his youth in Ireland Peters was sent to London to train under Thomas Hudson, making his first trip to Italy in 1763, via a bursary from the Dublin Society. On his return he became a member of Society of Artists, exhibiting portraits in oil and pastel. In 1769 Peters also became a Freemason, which brought him the patronage of the Duke of Manchester and Lord Petrie (who were both Grand Masters). Other prominent aristocratic patrons included Charles, 4th Duke of Rutland, then Marquess of Granby (who later presented him with a number of lucrative livings in Leicestershire), Lord Courtney and Lord Grosvenor. From 1772 to 1776 Peters travelled in France and in Italy. There he copied works by Rubens, Correggio and Barocci. In Paris he became acquainted with the work of Greuze. In Rome he was familiar with the circle gathered around Henry Fuseli, while in Venice he continued to nurture his taste for the exotic, and developed a particular interest in the art of Titian. It was on his return from the Continent that he painted his controversial series of 'pin-ups'.

His first exhibited work at the Royal Academy in this vein was the pastel of *A Lady in an Undress* in 1776. This work may have been related to a print entitled 'Belinda', engraved by Robert Dunkerton. It was followed up in 1777 by *A Woman in Bed*, which may be the present work. Peters's portrayals of women in bed, which is far more frank than earlier 'pin-ups' of Mercier or Morland, are also more extreme than any produced by other artists working in England at that time, although they do prefigure Fuseli's erotic drawings of courtesans of the 1780s and '90s. Certainly, there were plenty of pictures and prints produced which depicted semi- or wholly naked women, but these were invariably presented as nymphs or 'Venuses' and given suitably classical titles.

When *A Woman in Bed* was exhibited it naturally caused a stir, the *Morning Chronicle* (26 April) noting how it 'makes every gentleman *stand* for some time – and gaze at it'. The same critic could not, however, 'help thinking that the inviting leer of the lady, and her still more inviting bosom, ought to be consigned to the bed-chamber of a bagnio, where each would doubtless *provoke* a proper effect; in the present situation they serve to prevent the pictures around them from being so much seen and admired as their merits demand'. Peters himself refrained from exhibiting such works again in public and later renounced them, 'not only because they were degrading to his character, but, as far as I could judge, from sincere moral regret' (Manners, 1913, p. 6).

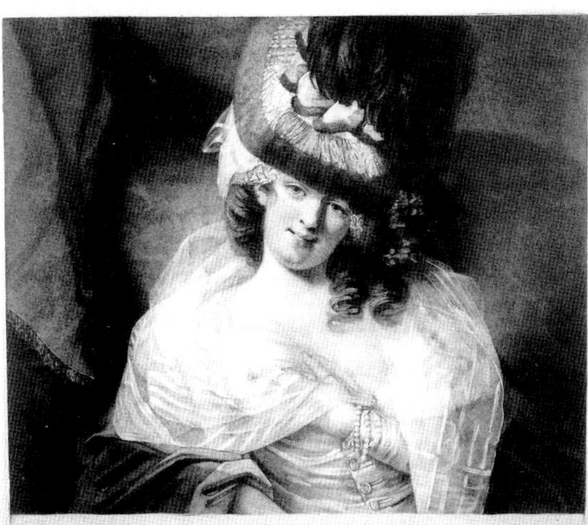

75 *Love in her Eyes Sits Playing*
JOHN RAPHAEL SMITH (1752-1812), after the Revd Matthew William Peters

Mezzotint, 35.5 x 39.6 cm
LETTERED: '*Painted by Wm Peters RA/Engrav'd by J R Smith*'
The Trustees of the British Museum

Love in her Eyes Sits Playing is one of a handful of titillat-ing 'pin-ups' painted by Matthew Peters on his return from Italy, egged on it seems by a knot of like-minded English aristocrats with a penchant for slightly risqué sub-ject-matter. The painting upon which Smith's engraving is based may be identified with 'A lady in an undress; in crayons', exhibited by Peters at the Royal Academy in 1776. It also resembles a work formerly in the J.P. Morgan collection, New York (see Waterhouse, 1981, p. 277), although the painting is less graphic than the print: the woman in the painting is thinly veiled, although she is not fondling herself. The model used in the painting, and pre-sumably the print, was at some later date identified as Kitty Fisher, although the woman here bears no resem-blance to that infamous courtesan, who had in any event died ten years earlier.

Peters's quasi-erotic fancy pictures, and the prints after them, successfully targeted a particular market for those who wanted a sanitised fantasy – the grim realities of eighteenth-century prostitution being far removed from the genteel image presented by Peters. Here, the fash-ionably dressed woman is to all intents and purposes a quite respectable individual, only her gesture and expres-sion differentiating her from those ladies who sat to Peters and his peers for conventional portraits. While these pictures have few parallels in Britain, they are rem-iniscent of Greuze's swooning young women, although Peters, showing comparative *sangfroid*, shies away from the quasi-orgasmic excesses indulged in by his French counterpart. Peters, who went on shortly afterwards to take holy orders, later regarded these pictures as some-what of an embarrassment.

IV

The Deserving Poor

76 *Margaret Gainsborough as a Gleaner* (Plate 55)
THOMAS GAINSBOROUGH (1727-88)

Oil on canvas, 73.7 x 63.5 cm, late 1750s
The Visitors of the Ashmolean Museum, Oxford

Provenance: G Strutt before 1896 ; Anon. sale Christie's 16 July 1909 (119), bt. Peile; bt. from Sir Hugh Lane by Louis Fleischman; Mrs A. Fleischman; pur-chased from Mrs Fleischman by the Ashmolean Museum
Exhibited: Art Council, 1949; British Council 1957/58; Tate Gallery 1953, 1980-81 (68); Gainsborough's House 1988; Birmingham, 1995 (5)
Literature: Waterhouse, 1958, p. 68, no. 283 ; Hayes, 1980, no. 68

The painting, which has been cut down, is traditionally said to show the artist's younger daughter, Margaret Gainsborough (1751-1820), although a comparison with other portraits of Gainsborough's children indicates that the subject could equally well be Mary Gainsborough (1750-1826), who would have been about nine or ten at the time this picture is thought to have been made. As a description in the *Somerset House Gazette* of 1824 reveals, the painting originally contained both Margaret and her elder sister 'in the garb of peasant girls, on the confines of a cornfield, dividing their gleanings. They appear to be of the age of eight or nine, and are the size of life'. The whereabouts of the section containing the other sister are unknown.

Like other similar studies which Gainsborough made of his daughters during the 1750s (notably *The Painter's Daughters Holding a Cat* and *The Painter's Daughters Chasing a Butterfly* in the National Gallery, London, and the smaller study in the Victoria and Albert Museum) this work is unfinished. It dif-fers in that the artist's daughter is portrayed in character, rather like the small rustic figures in the manner of Ruisdael and Hobbema which Gainsborough was already incorporat-ing into his landscapes. The way in which this picture antic-ipates the artist's fancy pictures of the 1780s is emphasised by the girl's dress and makeshift bonnet, and also by the wistful expression she shares with the subject of Gainsborough's *Cot-tage Girl and Pitcher* of 1785 (Fig. 25). The present study is also curiously reminiscent of Ribera's *St Mary of Egypt* (Museo Civico Gaetano Filangieri, Naples), a work which Gainsborough could not have known, although he may have seen something similar. (Coincidentally the model for *St Mary* was traditionally – if probably erroneously – thought to have been Ribera's daughter.) In any event, irrespective of any possible influence by Ribera on Gainsborough, this study of his daughter, tinged with melancholy, was – like Reynolds's portrayals of his nieces of the 1760s – clearly influenced by the artist's interest in the Old Masters, not least the expressive images of sainted ecstasy and self-morti-fication so redolent of the Counter-Reformation.

The painting was made for pleasure and as a means for Gainsborough to experiment with his painting technique. Given that is appears to date from the late 1750s, it was probably made in Ipswich, just prior to the artist's move to Bath in 1759. At that time Gainsborough was attempting to loosen up his technique, despite criticism. As he wrote in the spring of 1758: 'You please me much by saying that no other fault is to be found in your picture than the roughness of the surface; for that part being of use in giving force to the effect at a proper distance, and what a judge of painting knows an original from a copy by' (Woodall, 1961, p. 61).

77 *A Gipsy Girl* (Plate 60)
SIR THOMAS LAWRENCE (1769-1830)

Oil on canvas, 90.2 x 69.2 cm, 1794
The Royal Academy of Arts, London

Provenance: Presented by Lawrence to the Royal Academy of Arts in 1794
Exhibited: British Institution 1855 (114); Manchester 1857 (214); Royal Academy 1884 (201), 1904 (55), 1951 (393), Leicester 1953 (67)
Literature: Gower, 1900, p. 175; Armstrong, 1913, p. 176; Garlick, 1954, p. 209; Garlick,1989, p. 294, no. 889, pl. 43
Engraved: Mezzotint by S.W. Reynolds in 1840

Thomas Lawrence was elected a member of the Royal Academy in 1794. The same year he submitted *A Gipsy Girl* to the Academy as his Diploma work. According to Richard Westall, who was elected RA at the same time as Lawrence, both painters were asked to rework their submissions on the grounds that they were insufficiently finished. Lawrence, who was notoriously slow in completing even his commissioned portraiture, apparently made no effort to do so (Farington, 3 December 1794).

Lawrence, whose principal profession was portraiture, painted few subject pictures. The reason why he submitted the present work to the Academy as his Diploma work was that portraiture was inadmissable. And yet, while *A Gipsy Girl* was put forward as a fancy picture, it is to all intents and purposes a portrait-in-character, the use of the gipsy motif being a convenient way of satisfying the Academy's rubric whilst exploiting the current 'Picturesque' vogue for such subjects.

The attitude, expression and facial features of *A Gipsy Girl* correspond closely to Lawrence's portrait of Maria Siddon of around 1797. Indeed, it is likely – as has been suggested – that Maria Siddons (1779-98) was the model for Lawrence's *Gipsy Girl*. If so, she would have been sixteen at the time. Maria was the younger daughter of the tragic actress Sarah Siddons (1755-1831), whom Lawrence had first painted in 1786. During the later 1790s Lawrence seems to have had brief flirtations with both Mrs Siddons's elder daughters. It was while he was supposedly engaged to the eldest daughter Sally that he also fell in love with Maria. The story that Maria bore Lawrence's love child appears to be without foundation.

When the portrait of Maria Siddons was shown at the British Institution in 1830, the youngest Siddons daughter, Cecilia, vehemently denied that either of her sisters had ever sat to Lawrence (Garlick, 1989, p. 265). Even so, both the portraits of Maria and Sally – and *A Gipsy Girl* – bear a physical resemblance to known portraits of Mrs Siddons.

78 *A Fortune-Teller* (Plate 59)
SIR JOSHUA REYNOLDS (1723-92)

Oil on canvas, 145 x 123.2 cm, *c* 1781?
The Iveagh Bequest, Kenwood

Provenance: the artist's niece, Mary, Marchioness of Thomond; Thomond sale, 18 May 1821 (69); bought Gosling for Colonel Fulke Greville Howard; his nephew, the 3rd Viscount Templeton; Agnew, 1888; bought from Agnew by Lord Iveagh
Exhibited: British Institution, 1813 (124); Royal Academy, 1928 (237); Manchester, 1928 (42)
Literature: Leslie and Taylor, vol. 2, pp. 183, 185; Graves and Cronin, vol. 3, pp. 1153-4, vol. 4, pp. 1454, 1480; Waterhouse, 1941, p. 68; Iveagh Bequest,
1978, p. 27; Postle, 1995, pp. 6-8, 94-95, 98
Engraved: Mezzotint by John Keyse Sherwin, 1784 (after the version at Knole); W. Ward; mezzotint by S.W. Reynolds, 1836 (although probably not from the present version).

A *Fortune-Teller* is one of several versions of a picture purchased from Reynolds by the 3rd Duke of Dorset, and exhibited at the Royal Academy in 1777 (now at Waddesdon Manor). At the time it was described by the self-styled 'Gaudenzio' of the *St James's Chronicle* (17-19 April 1777): 'A Gipsey is telling a young Girl, sitting on her Lover's Knees, her Fortune, and seems to be saying to her that she will soon be married to him, at which she laughs, and is pleased, without well knowing what it means. So I understand the historical part of this Picture'. Others objected to Reynolds's picture being described as an history painting. 'An historical piece,' stated the *London Chronicle*, 'I always understood to be a representation of some particular feat in ancient or modern, real or fabulous, sacred or profane history. But this is a representation of no such fact, and therefore cannot be called an historical piece more than a picture of Jonas shuffling the cards would be' (*London Chronicle*, 29 April-1 May 1777).

A Fortune-Teller was clearly not a history picture; nor would Reynolds have conceived of it as such. Yet, the subject was related to the Old Masters, inasmuch as the composition was based upon Caravaggio's *Fortune-Teller*, then owned by the King of France. That Reynolds knew the Caravaggio there can be no doubt. It may also have been known to the the Duke of Dorset, who was at the time British Ambassador to the Court of Louis XVI, and who, as we have noted, bought Reynolds's *Fortune-teller*. The Duke of Dorset had a particularly soft spot for Reynolds's fancy pictures, owning no fewer than eight of them, including *Cupid as a Link Boy, Mercury as a Cutpurse* (see cats. 39 and 40, *A Boy with a Drawing in his Hand, A Beggar Boy and his Sister* (see cat. 67), *The Calling of Samuel* (cat. 14), and *Lesbia* (also known as *Robinetta*). A number of these – including the present picture – feature Reynolds's favourite boy model, who sat frequently to the artist during the early to mid-1770s, and whom Reynolds nicknamed the 'Net Boy' owing to his trade in life as a maker of cabbage nets.

Reynolds's picture, then, had its roots in a tradition pioneered by Caravaggio in the early seventeenth century, and explored extensively by followers in France, Flanders and the Low Countries over the intervening period. The character of the gipsy fortune teller was also popular at contemporary masquerades. Reynolds had used the device recently in his portrait of Lord Henry and Lady Charlotte Spencer, the two younger children of the Duke of Marlborough (Huntington Art Gallery, San Marino).

79 *The Fortune-Teller* (Plate 56)
JOHN RUSSELL (1744-1807)

Pastel on paper, 91.4 x 70.5 cm
1790. Signed '*J. Russell, R.A. pinxt.*'

Tate Gallery. Bequeathed by Lionel Wormser Harris through the National Art Collections Fund 1940

Provenance: William Russell, younger brother of the artist; by descent to the Revd E.J. Russell of Todmorden; Lionel Wormser Harris; bequeathed to the Tate Gallery by Lionel Wormser Harris in 1940
Exhibited: Royal Academy 1790 (242)
Literature: G.C. Williamson, *John Russell, R.A.*, London, 1894, pp. 113, 163

John Russell was among the most prolific British artists of the eighteenth century, and exhibited no fewer than 329 works at the Royal Academy between its foundation in 1769 and the end of his career in 1806. Of these works many were portraits in pastels (or 'crayons' as they were known). Increasingly, during the late 1770s, the fancy picture too became a mainstay of his art.

The Fortune-Teller, exhibited in 1790, as with so many of Russell's fancy pictures, capitalised on a popular trend. In Russell's picture a young girl's fortune is by told by an old bearded man who reads her palm. The future he foretells concerns her love life, and presumably involved the arrival of a tall handsome stranger, or some such like. The figure of the laughing girl strongly recalls Reynolds's *Fortune-Teller* of 1777 (cat. 78) and the grizzled old fortune-teller the same artist's numerous depictions of his model, George White, although the similarity is generic rather than specific.

Russell was a curious character. He first emerges in the 1760s as a pupil of Francis Cotes, from whom he learnt the art of pastel. From the accounts contained in his own diary and the comments of Cotes, it is clear that Rusell was an absolute pain, inflicting his religious mania on his master and upon sitters alike. Yet, he attracted numerous fashionable patrons, wrote an important technical treatise on pastels, and in 1785 became 'Crayon Painter to the Prince of Wales'. Himself highly idiosyncratic, Russell delighted in portraying miscellaneous beggars, ferret handlers, and ballad singers. To these can be added his portraits of colourful characters such as 'Smoaker', the Prince of Wales's bather at Brighton, and Charles Cranmer, the porter and sometime model at the Royal Academy.

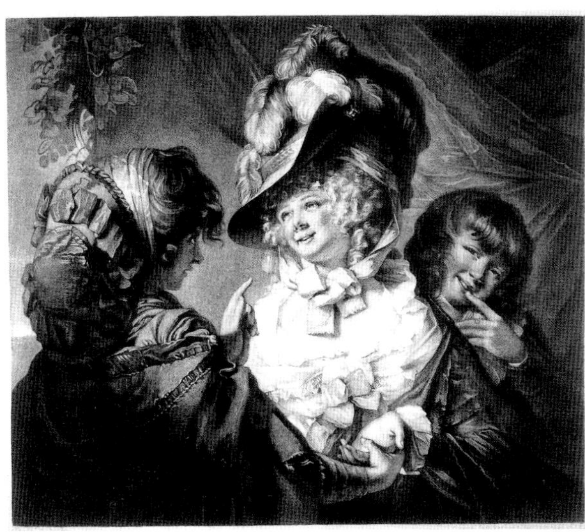

80 *The Fortune-Teller*

JOHN RAPHAEL SMITH (1752-1812), after the Revd Matthew William Peters

Mezzotint, 38.3 x 44.2 cm
LETTERED: '*Painted by the Rev M Peters RA/Engrav'd by JR Smith Mezzotinto Engraver to* [the Prince of Wales]'
The Trustees of the British Museum

Literature: Chaloner Smith, 1883, vol. 3, p. 1314, no. 186

Matthew Peters exhibited *The Fortune Teller* at the Royal Academy in 1785, by which time he was an ordained priest, and chaplain to the Academy. The image, which looks back to Reynolds's picture of the same title, is in some ways closer in style to Copley, who exhibited his group portrait of the three Royal Princesses at the Royal Academy in

1785. *The Fortune-Teller* was only one of two subject pictures shown following his ordination, the other being *An Angel Carrying the Spirit of a Child to Paradise* (Burghley House), of 1782. In 1788 Peters resigned from the Royal Academy to concentrate on his career in the Church, although he continued to exhibit occasionally and contributed paintings both to Boydell's Shakespeare Gallery and to Woodmason's Irish Shakespeare Gallery. In 1811, when in his seventies, Peters exhibited a *Fortune Teller* at the British Institution.

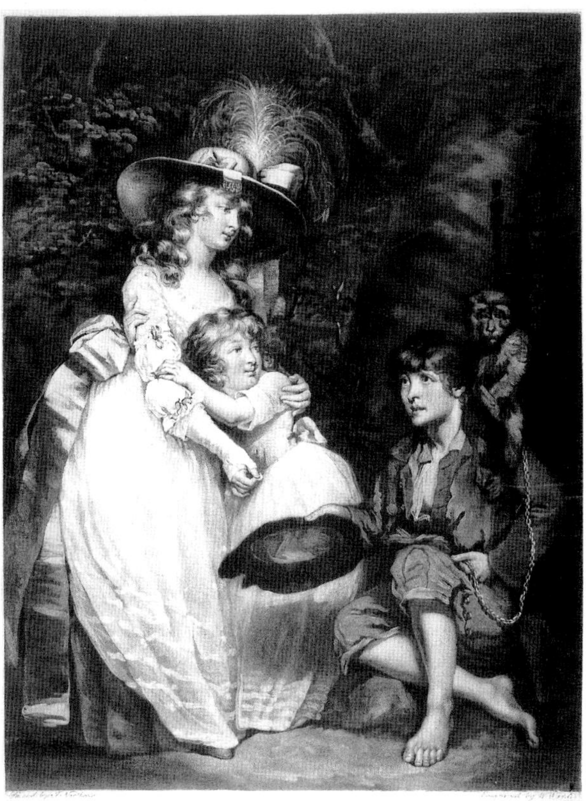

81 *A Young Lady Encouraging the Low Comedian*

WILLIAM WARD (1762-1826), after James Northcote

Mezzotint, 55.5 x 40 cm
LETTERED: '*Painted by J. Northcote/Engraved by W. Ward/A Young Lady Encouraging the Low Comedian*'
The Trustees of the British Museum

Like Beechey's portrait of Sir Francis Ford's children relieving a beggar boy, Ward's engraving after Northcote's painting of 1784 shows two well-dressed bourgeois individuals ostentatiously dispensing charity to someone less well off than themselves. The 'low comedian' is seated deferentially while the younger girl clings to her elder sister, both fascinated by, and afraid of, the rather lacklustre monkey seated upon his shoulder. The boy is recognizable as Jack Hill, the same model who sat to Gainsborough during the mid-1780s, notably for *A Shepherd* (see cat. 6) and the *Beggar Boys*, painted in the spring of 1785, and whom he had found begging near his house in St James's Street. As with Gainsborough's pictures of the same boy, Northcote's prime pictorial inspiration was derived generally from Murillo's paintings of street urchins, and possibly, in particular, that artist's *Three Boys* (Dulwich Picture Gallery), which it resembles compositionally (and which then belonged to the dealer, Noel Desenfans). *A Young Lady* was painted at a time when Northcote was beginning to turn his hand to fancy pictures and scenes drawn from contemporary literature. The painting upon which the present print is based (sold Christie's 5 June 1953 (96)), is on the scale of life, suggesting that it was, like Beechey's painting of the Ford children with a beggar boy (cat. 91) a commissioned portrait rather than a fancy picture made with to accommodate the furniture print market.

82 *Girl Gathering Mushrooms* (Plate 61)
THOMAS GAINSBOROUGH (1727-1788)

Oil on canvas, 127 x 101.6 cm, early to mid 1780s?
Henry E. Huntington Art Gallery, San Marino

Provenance: Sold Christie's 11 April 1797 (58); Francis Freeling sale, 15 April 1837 (59) bt. Prowett ; A Levy sale, 6 April 1876 (292) ; bt. Elliotson for Lord Dunmore; Anon. (Lord Dunmore) sale, 17 March 1877 (83) bt. Ross ; A. Levy sale, 3 May 1884 (19) bt. Grindlay; W.C. Alexander by 1887; bt. by Colnaghi 1905 ; Hon. Sir John Ward by 1932; by descent
Exhibited: Royal Academy 1887 as 'The Mushroom Gatherer'; Tate Gallery 1980 (138)
Literature: Whitley, 1915, p. 348; Waterhouse 1946, p. 140, no. 16; Waterhouse 1958, p. 104, no. 812 ; Hayes 1980, No. 138

This unfinished study probably dates from the mid-1780s, a time when Gainsborough was making extensive studies from young beggar children. The girl depicted here, with her mob of dark hair, is, for example, similar to the child in Gainsborough's *Girl with Pigs* (Simon Howard), exhibited at the Royal Academy in 1782 (see cat. 85), as well as a chalk study of a beggar child from the early 1780s, which shows a seated girl with short hair (Hayes, 1970, no. 836). The girl's kneeling figure also resembles that of the child holding a spoon and bowl in *Young Hobbinol and Ganderetta* (private collection), which Gainsborough exhibited at Macklin's Poet's Gallery in Spring 1788. Indeed, it is quite possible that *Young Hobbinol and Ganderetta* was worked up from a straightforward study of beggar children into a finished picture in order to satisfy Macklin's request for a suitable poetic subject.

83 *Girl with a Penny* (Plate 57)
THOMAS GAINSBOROUGH (1727-88), early to mid-1780s?

Oil on canvas, 127 x 101.6 cm
Private Collection

Provenance: Perhaps the Revd H.S. Trimmer sale 17 March 1860 (75), bt. Flack; Hon. Sir John Ward by 1932
Literature: Waterhouse 1958, p. 104, No. 1813

Although this painting, which has not hitherto been exhibited, is unfinished, and is of identical size to the *Girl Gathering Mushrooms* (cat. 82), it would be misleading to describe the works as pendants. Rather, they are both unusual examples in oils of child studies which might have been intended to serve as the basis for fancy pictures. And, although it has been suggested that the present work dates from the later 1750s (Waterhouse, 1958, p. 104) and is possibly a study of one of the artist's daughters, it is more likely to have been painted during the 1780s, at a time when Gainsborough was sketching extensively from child models. Gainsborough, we know, was fond of painting young beggar children, among his favourite models being a young boy from Richmond named Jack Hill, whom his daughter Margaret apparently wished to adopt (Whitley, 1915, p. 292-3).

The subject-matter of this painting, a girl holding a penny, acts as a reminder of the realities of life for beggar children who modelled to Gainsborough and others, highlighting the commercial relationship between artist and model. Towards the end of 1784 Gainsborough met a beggar woman with a small boy near his home in Pall Mall. Struck by the boy's good looks, he asked the woman to return to his studio with him. Gainsborough was apparently so taken with the child that he offered to adopt him. After considering his offer for several days the woman refused on the grounds that during the past year the child had earned some seven shillings a day by begging (Whitley, 1915, p. 232).

84 *Children by the Fireside* (Plate 58)
JOHN OPIE (1761-1807)

Oil on canvas; 127 x 99.5 cm
University of Manchester (Tabley House Collection)

Provenance: Thomas Lister Parker; purchased by Sir John Fleming Leicester, August 1808; by descent to Lt. Col. John Leicester-Warren; bequeathed by his executors in 1976 to the Victoria University of Manchester
Literature: Hall, 1962, p. 88, no. 144; Cannon-Brookes, ed., 1989, p. 56

Sir John Leicester purchased *Children by the Fireside* in 1808, the year after Opie's death. The painting bears an identical frame to Opie's *Calling of Samuel* (cat. 15), it being suggested that both frames were made by Opie's brothers with the intention of selling the works as pendants (Cannon-Brookes, op. cit., p. 56). Even so, *Children by the Fireside* appears on stylistic grounds to be an earlier work than the *Calling of Samuel*. It recalls in particular his *Children in the Wood* (Sotheby's, 13 July 1994 (57)), exhibited at the Royal Academy in 1797. Not only are both paintings nocturnes, but they feature two very similar young girls as models. The inspiration for the *Children by the Fireside* may ultimately have been a fancy picture by Gainsborough called variously *Jack Hill in his Cottage* and *Boy at a Cottage Fire and a Girl Eating* [sic] *Milk*, known now only from Charles Turner's mezzotint of 1809. This picture, which also shows two small children warming themselves by a fire, was painted by Gainsborough in 1787. It was sold in Gainsborough's posthumous sale, and was by 1807 in the collection of Richard Brinsley Sheridan. Apparently 'destroyed' in a restoration by William Redmore Bigg, the picture has been unlocated since the late nineteenth century.

85 *Girl with Pigs*
RICHARD EARLOM (1743-1822), after Thomas Gainsborough

Mezzotint
The Hon. Christopher Lennox-Boyd [Kenwood]
Gainsborough's House, Sudbury [Nottingham]

Gainsorough exhibited the *Girl with Pigs* at the Royal Academy in 1782, where it was immediately purchased for 100 guineas by Sir Joshua Reynolds. 'I think myself highly honour'd and much obliged to you for this singular mark of your favour,' Gainsborough told him, adding, 'I may truly say I have brought my Piggs [*sic*] to a fine market (Woodall, 1963, p. 127). Both the Queen and Samuel Johnson praised Reynolds's magnanimous gesture. Johnson, noting the rivalry that then existed between Reynolds and Gainsborough, stated that it was 'testimony of the improved moral advantages of the high civilization to which our age has attained' (Whitley, 1928, vol. 1, p. 378). Reynolds claimed that Gainsborough's *Girl with Pigs* was 'by far the best Picture he ever

Painted or perhaps ever will (Hilles, 1929, pp. 153-4). (He was then trying to swap it with the Earl of Ossory for a battered copy of a Titian.) Reynolds held on to it until 1790, when he sold it to Louis XVI's ex-Minister of Finance, reputedly for 300 guineas. The picture was sold on again five years later to Reynolds's friend and patron, the Earl of Carlisle, to whose family it still belongs. Robert Earlom had made a print of Gainsborough's *Shepherd* two years earlier (cat. 6).

It was claimed by Charles Robert Leslie in the nineteenth century that Gainsborough painted the girl with pigs from the same model who sat to him a few years later for the *Cottage Girl with Dog and Pitcher*, 'a portrait, and not of a peasant child but a young lady'. They do look alike. However, the resemblance is probably generic, irrespective of whether she was a genuine 'peasant child' or the daughter of a friend or sitter. Certainly, the pigs were real enough, as a visitor to the artist's studio recalled: 'Being acquainted with Gainsborough at the period when this work was in progress I have seen at his house in Pall Mall the three little pigs (who did not in the common phrase sit for their likenesses) gambolling about his painting room, whilst he at his easel was catching an attitude or a leer from them' (Whitley, 1915, p. 187).

Sir Ellis Waterhouse wondered whether Reynolds's interest in the *Girl with Pigs* was stimulated by the fact that the meditative attitude of the girl was reminiscent of the old masters, 'a sort of "Prodigal Son" with the gender transposed' (Waterhouse, 1958, p. 36). Gainsborough would not have known Murillo's *Prodigal Son Feeding the Swine*, then in a Spanish collection. Even so, like the *Cottage Girl with Dog and Pitcher* it is Murillo, more than any other, to whom Gainsborough was here paying homage.

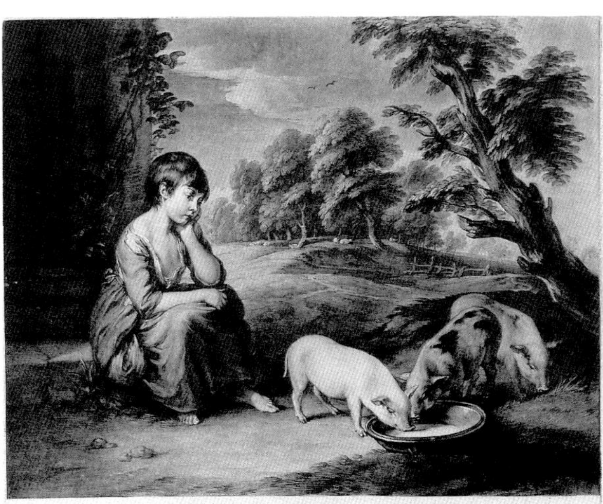

86 The Woodman, vide Cowpers Task Book V (Plate 63)
PETER SIMON (1764-post 1804) after Thomas Gainsborough

Stipple engraving, proof before title, 65 x 43.5 cm
LETTERED '*Painted by Thos Gainsborough/Engrav'd by Peter Simon/Publish'd June 4th 1790, by John & Josiah Boydell, Cheapside & at the Shakespeare Gallery Pall Mall London.*'
David Alexander

Literature: Horne, p. 87; Whitley 1915, p. 285

Gainsborough painted fancy pictures throughout his career and expected higher prices for them than his portraits or landscapes. In the 1780s he painted several pictures with either one or two figures, such as might have been staffage in earlier pictures, on a very large scale; one of the best known was the *Two Shepherd Boys with Dogs Fighting*

(see cat. 8). Pictures of literary subjects were painted in great numbers in the late 1780s, and it is possible that he may have had in mind Book v of William Cowper's poem *The Task* when he painted his large canvas of *The Woodman* in the summer of 1787; a reference to it was added to the lettering on this print. The model was a poor smith, whom Gainsborough rescued from destitution. The picture measured nearly eight feet by five feet, making it almost as large as the unfinished *Housemaid* (Tate Gallery). Gainsborough believed this to be his best picture; it stayed in his possession and in a letter written on his death-bed to his great rival, Sir Joshua Reynolds, he expressed his desire for Reynolds to see it. The picture was bought in the 1789 sale after his death by Sir Gerald Noel Noel, Bt, to whom Boydell must have applied for permission to have the picture engraved. Peter Simon was one of many stipple engravers working in London who came from from the Continent, in his case from France; he worked a good deal for Boydell.

DSA

87 A Peasant Family (Plate 62)
JOHN OPIE (1761-1807)

Oil on canvas, 153 x 183.5 cm, *c* 1783-85
Tate Gallery, London
Provenance: Palmer family by 1920s; Agnew; bequeathed, 1948, by Sir Otto Beit to the Tate Gallery

This picture, one of the most ambitious of its kind to have been produced in the eighteenth century, is remarkable because of the relative youth of Opie. John Opie was unleashed on the London art world in 1781 as 'the Cornish Wonder'. He had already, however, been producing character studies of great maturity, notably his study of a boy's head shown at the Society of Artists in 1780. He followed up this success in 1782 at the Royal Academy with a series of fancy subjects involving old men and women and rural children. Curiously, *A Peasant Family* was never shown at the Academy, although it is even larger than his Rembrandtesque painting of *A School* (private collection) shown in 1784.

A Peasant's Family is similar in scale and directness to Gainsborough's *Cottage Girl* of 1785 and Richard Morton Paye's *Sulky Boy* (Fig. 32) (Royal Academy, same year). All three acknowledge a common debt to Murillo. It is possible – given that we do not know exactly when Opie painted *A Peasant Family* – that he was responding to the work of the two elder artists. However, given his confidence in handling such subjects, and the circumstances surrounding Paye's picture, it is quite possible that Opie's *Peasant's Family* predates them. Like Gainsborough, Opie had a natural affinity with child sitters, the girls in *A Peasant Family* being reminiscent of Gainsborough's informal studies of his daughters of the 1750s.

88 The Return from Market (Plate 66)
FRANCIS WHEATLEY (1747-1801)

Oil on canvas, 74.9 x 62.2 cm
Initialled and dated '*F.W. px/1786*'
Leeds City Art Galleries
Provenance: A. McKay; Lord Northbrook; F.J. Nettlefold who presented it to Leeds in 1948
Exhibited: Royal Academy 1788 (37); 1877 (289); 1951-52 (40); Aldeburgh and Leeds, 1965 (14)
Literature: C.R. Grundy and F.G. Roe, *A Catalogue of the Collection of F.J. Nettlefold* vol. 4, 1938, p. 122; Webster, 1970, p. 74 (reproduced), p. 135, cat. 55.
Engraved: Stipple by Charles Knight, 21 April 1789

Wheatley, like Mercier and George Morland, is not an artist of the first rank. But he is, none the less, someone whose art deeply affected the popular consciousness in eighteenth-century England, and who made significant inroads into the genre of the fancy picture. *The Return from Market* is among his better works, both as a piece of painting, and as an example of the way in which he gave something fresh to the genre in question. It is superfically reminiscent of Gainsborough's pictures on the same theme of the late 1760s and early seventies, notably his *Peasants Returning from Market through a Wood* (Toledo), but the atmosphere could not be more different. Gainsborough's distanced figures drift like shadows through a hazy, idyllic landscape, without purpose or direction, creatures of the artist's imagination. Wheatley's woman peasant by contrast is a far more matter of fact, earthy presence. A stocky, yet pretty, figure in sensible shoes and apron, she makes her way along the road, counting the day's profits. Seated on her donkey is her small child, bundled up against the elements, alongside the empty bird cages, signs of a successful day at market. All these elements present an image of a happy hard-working rural labourer, content with her lot in life and a credit to her family. This reading is reinforced by the verses which were appended to Charles Knight's print, published the following year. While she may not be rich or titled, she is none the less invaluable to her husband for her simplicity and indeed her ignorance:

> To him, more dear for what she never knew,
> A prudent house-wife, virtuous, fond and true;
> And lo! the pledge of truth, a rosy boy;
> The father's opening form, the mother's joy.

The verses may have been composed after the image, but the sentiment expressed in them was pure Wheatley.

89 *Beggars on the Road to Stanmore* (Plate 65)
JOHAN ZOFFANY (1733-1810)

Oil on canvas, 74 x 63 cm, 1771
Private Collection

Provenance: Painted either for Andrew Drummond, or owned or given to his nephew, the Hon. Robert Drummond of Cadland; by descent
Exhibited: probably Royal Academy, 1771 (232); British Institution, 1840 (101); National Portrait Gallery, 1968, 1976 (55)
Literature: Manners and Williamson, 1920, pp. 193-4; Webster, 1977, p. 49

This is probably the picture exhibited by Zoffany at the Royal Academy in 1771 as *The Beggars Family*. It was painted either for Andrew Drummond, founder of Drummond's Bank, or his nephew, Robert Drummond. The present title of the picture derives from a family tradition that the beggars were painted on the road to Stanmore, Middlesex, where Andrew Drummond had an estate. Zoffany had recently painted a group portrait of the Drummond Family (Mellon Collection), whence the present commission may have sprung. Like the paintings of his pupil Henry Walton, *Beggars on the road to Stanmore* transcends the convention of the fancy picture. It is an extraordinarily graphic depiction of contemporary poverty couched in the language of sacred art. It thus forms a parallel with Joseph Wright's nocturnes of iron forges and blacksmith's shops of the early 1770s, where the creation of hot metal is likened to a Nativity. The resemblance of Zoffany's beggars to the Holy Family is enhanced by the kneeling figure of the boy, a surrogate John the Baptist, and the reverent attitude of the old man, a suitable substitute for St Joseph. Here the similarities

end. Zoffany's beggar family, unlike the Holy Family, consists of three generations, for the old man is surely intended to represent the woman's father rather than her husband, and the grandfather of the suckled child. The real father, we can assume, has departed leaving the family to survive on the charity of the parish and the beneficence of private citizens such as the Drummond family.

Although the beggar family's benefactors are not depicted in the painting their hovering presence is implied by the silver coin held by the young boy, its value underlined by the conrtast it forms with the single penny lying in the old man's upturned hat. The recent passage of their benefactors is also indicated graphically by the droppings of horse dung in the painting's foreground. *Beggars on the Road to Stanmore* is, in a sense, a more subtle treatment of a theme already addressed by Edward Penny in his *Marquis of Granby relieving a Sick Soldier* (Ashmolean Museum, Oxford), shown six years earlier at the Society of Artists. Here Lord Granby is portrayed dispensing charity to the soldier's family who stand begging by the roadside. Such pictures reflect a growing emphasis on the importance of being seen to perform charity and good works (Solkin, 1992, pp. 200ff). Their ownership of the picture confirms that the Drummonds, although they are wealthy bankers, wish to be considered humane and to display a concern for those less well-off than themselves. The Drummond family commissioned Zoffany to paint three generations of their own family: at the same time they purchased from the artist a painting depicting three generations of an indigent family from their own neighbourhood. Although the families led discrete lives their paintings hung together under one roof.

The individuals in *Beggars on the Road to Stanmore* were hired models and the young woman also appears in Zoffany's *Caritas Romana* of the same date where, rather than suckling a baby boy, she gives her breast to her father who languishes in prison (see Webster, 1976, no. 54). The two paintings, although they may not have been conceived as such (although they are identical in size) form compelling pendants on the theme of the receipt and giving of charity, using subjects from history and modern life.

90 *Charity Relieving Distress* (Plate 68)
THOMAS GAINSBOROUGH (1727-1788)

Oil on canvas, 99 x 76.2 cm, 1784
Private Collection

Provenance: Lord Robert Spencer sale 31.5.1799 (92) as *Italian Villa*, bought Bowyer; Walsh Porter sale 22.3.1803 (29), bought Marquis of Hertford: sold from Ragley *c* 1933 to Sir Felix Cassel, Bt., by descent
Exhibited: Schomberg House, 1784; RA, 1872 (206); Agnew, 1934 (7); Park Lane, 1936 (79); Arts Council, 1953 (48)
Literature: Whitley, 1915, pp. 228-8, p. 294; Waterhouse, 1958, p. 120, no. 988, p. 229
Engraved: Richard Banks Harraden, 1 February 1801

This painting was first exhibited as *The Beggars* at Schomberg house, Gainsborough's home in Pall Mall, in 1784, although as a report in the *Morning Herald* indicates Gainsborough reworked the composition in the autumn of 1787. After the artist's death the picture was cut down to its present size from a 'half-length' canvas (approximately 50 by 40 inches). A mezzotint engraving (Fig. 44) and a copy, perhaps by Dupont (F.C.F. Parker sale, 24 July 1936 (20)) both show the picture as it was before it was cut down. They include a figure on a donkey at the left, two extra figures at the right – a young lady and a maid – and a carved coat-of-arms above the door of the residence (which in the engraving appears to feature a unicorn). When it was exhibited at Gainsborough's house in July and August 1784, the picture was described by Henry Bate (later Sir Henry Bate-Dudley), Gainsborough's friend, in the *Morning Herald* in bucolic terms: 'This picture consists of an elegant building, in one of the approaches to which is an ascent of steps, and at a distance an arch through which a loaded mule is passing. The principal objects are a beggar woman, who is receiving relief from a servant belonging to the house. The beggar has an infant in her arms and one on her back, and is also surrounded by others, some of whom appear terrified at a dog who will not suffer their approach to the house. Two children on the steps of the door are represented making observations on the cirumstance. A very fine summer sky is introduced. A vine is represented against the side of the house; several pigeons, also, are descried fluttering about the building. The whole of which forms a beautiful assemblage of an interesting nature' (Whitley, 1915, pp. 228-9).

Strictly speaking the present work is not so much a fancy picture as a landscape with figures, in the same vein as the 'cottage door' scenes which Gainsborough began painting during the final decade of his career – although here poor peasantry are depicted by an imposing town house, rather than in a rural domestic setting. The dispensation of charity was an increasingly popular subject for artists in the second half of the eighteenth century, the present picture anticipating a similar painting by Francis Wheatley, reproduced as an engraving, and published in 1797, with the title *Rustic Benevolence* (Hayes, 1975, pl. 143; Webster, 1970, p. 182, repr.) When Gainsborough's own painting was engraved in 1801, it was entitled 'CHARITY sympathising with DISTRESS' and bore a dedication by the publisher Robert Bowyer to 'the Nobility & Gentry, whose humane exertions are employed in alleviating the distresses of the Poor' – a clear indication of the symbiotic relationship which the rich and poor were felt to enjoy.

One of the most curious aspects of the present work is the attitude of the peasant woman burdened with children, who resembles an allegorical figure of Charity. Most particularly, she resembles the figure of Charity designed only a few years earlier by Sir Joshua Reynolds for a painted glass window at New College, Oxford (Postle, 1995, pp. 167ff.). The attitude of the small boy tugging at his mother's skirts in Gainsborough's picture is identical to the small child in Reynolds's *Charity*. We cannot be sure, but the irony of adapting the high-flown allegorical figure of Charity to a peasant woman in receipt of charity would also have particularly appealed to Gainsborough – especially given his sceptical attitude towards Reynolds's pretentions as a history painter. It may also be relevant that the present work was displayed at the first exhibition in Gainsborough's house following his final secession from the Royal Academy only months earlier.

91 *The Children of Sir Francis Ford giving Coin to a Beggar boy*
SIR WILLIAM BEECHEY (1753-1839)   (Plate 69)
Oil on canvas, 180.5 x 150 cm
Tate Gallery

Provenance: Purchased with assistance from the National Art Collections Fund 1993
Exhibited: Royal Academy, 1793 (82) as 'Portraits of children relieving a beggar boy'
Literature: Roberts, 1907, pp. 40-41
Engraved: stipple by C. Wilkin, with the inscription '*Here Poor Boy without a Hat, take this Ha'penny*'

The picture was exhibited at the Royal Academy in 1793 as *Portraits of Children relieving a Beggar-Boy*. The children in question belonged to Sir Francis Ford, MP (1758-1801), who earlier that year had been created 1st Baronet, and who presumably wished to demonstrate his own philanthropic nature through the actions of his young offspring. Even so, Ford, a wealthy plantation owner, was not renowned for his interest in good causes. Following his election to Parliament he spoke only three times, once in favour of deferring the abolition of slavery. He stood down in 1796, and returned to his estates on Barbados where he died.

Beechey's supporters praised the picture, the *St James's Chronicle* taking the opportunity to press his claims for membership of the Royal Academy. He was duly elected ARA later that year. One critic, in search of increased pathos, felt that the beggar boy's 'shivering and starved appearance' would have been more plausible had the scene been set in winter rather than summer (Roberts, 1907, p. 41). The most telling comments, however, appeared in *The Oracle*. 'The Beggar Boy,' it stated, 'cheats the eye so singularly, that he appears to *tremble* as he sollicits alms. Your *Critic* here sensibly remarks, that Nature is violated, when we shudder amid a scene of foliage. Heaven keep POVERTY from thee, thou man of propriety! – it knows not the comfort of the seasons. – Want, ever cheerless, is usually cold, and supplication has not firm nerves.

"How should his houseless head, and unfed sides,
"His loop'd and window'd raggedness defend him
"From Seasons such as ours?"'

The quotation was adapted from *King Lear*, III, iv ('How shall your houseless heads and unfed sides,/Your looped and windowed raggedness, defend you/From seasons such as these?'). The allusion suggests that the critic had been playing close attention to exhibits at Alderman Boydell's Shakespeare Gallery and Macklin's Poet's Gallery – where this picture would have blended in nicely.

Unusually, for a piece of contemporary art criticism, *The Oracle* concluded with some comments on current social policy. Beechey's beggar boy, it stated, 'may suggest a Reform of our *Poor Laws*, and excite a temporary throb of pity in breasts, steeled, perhaps, against reality of distress'. The English Poor Law, which dated back to the reign of Queen Elizabeth, codified the duties of the parish towards to poor and the infirm; to care for those who through illness, old age or infirmity were unable to work; to provide work for children whose parents were unable to maintain them; and to provide work for unemployed adults (see Christie, 1984, pp. 95ff.). These Laws were reinforced in the 1660s by the passing of the Act of Settlement, which was intended to prevent the poor from leaving their own parish, and in turn ensuring that each parish carried its fair share of the burden. However, by the late eighteenth century the system was under increasing strain, as increasing numbers of unemployed men, women and children strayed with impunity beyond parish boundaries. This led in the south of England in particular to the rise of itinerant beggars – such as the boy depicted in Beechey's picture.

To some the relief provided by the Poor Law was sufficient to meet the demands, and it was claimed in 1793 that there 'is no country in the world where the poor are so amply provided for as in this... ' (Christie, 1984, p. 97). However, private concern over the inadequacy of public relief is reflected by the fact that between 1775 and 1796 over one hundred books and pamphlets were published over the need to amend the existing system. Beechey's picture, appeared at the very time when further Poor Acts were being added to the statute book, and may be seen as yet another manifestation of this concern.

92 *A Beggar* (Plate 64)
CHARLES TOWNLEY (1746-1800 or later) after George Dance

Mezzotint, 51 x 35.5 cm
LETTERED: '*Charles Townley fecit/Price 5 Shillgs/From an original Picture painted by* DANCE/*Publish'd according to Act of Parliament Oct. 23 1771; and sold by C. Townley, at Mr Hodgson's Greek Street,* SOHO.'
David Alexander

This study of a seated beggar shows him in the countryside: the sitter is identified in Henry Bromley's *Catalogue of Engraved Portraits*, 1793, as 'a Beggar who frequented the Bird-Cage Walk in St James's Park'. No publisher is named on the plate, but the wording of the publication line suggests that it may have been commissioned by Dance himself, with impressions being sold by Townley on his behalf. As it was issued in this way it probably did not sell very well, and is a rare print, which was not listed by Chaloner Smith in his classic catalogue of mezzotint portraits. The following year Townley engraved two mezzotints of portraits by Dance which were private plates, that is ones without the publication line necessary to secure copyright under the Engravers' Copyright act of 1735, which were for private circulation.

Nathaniel Dance (1735-1811), son of the architect George Dance, was in Italy between 1754 and 1765. He hoped to paint history pictures, and George III bought his neo-classical *Timon of Athens*; commissions for similar pictures did not follow and Dance, who was one of the original members of the Royal Academy in 1768, worked primarily as a portrait painter. This picture is unusual in his oeuvre, and it may have been painted as a speculation rather than as a commission; in this case having an engraving made may have been a way of helping to sell the canvas. Charles Townley was of a higher social class than most engravers: his father, the Revd James Townley, was Headmaster of the Merchant Taylors' School, which Dance attended. He was in fact a pupil there at the time of Charles Townley's birth.

DSA

93 *The Beggar and his Dog*
HENRY KINGSBURY (*fl* 1775-92), after John Kitchingman

Mezzotint, 60.6 x 45.7 cm
LETTERED: '*Painted by J. Kitchingman/Engraved by H. Kingsbury/*THE BEGGAR AND HIS DOG/*Vide Man of Feeling Chapter 14th, Page 31/Publish'd Octr; 25; 1775 by J.R. Smith, No 10 Bateman's Buildings, Soho Square*'
The Trustees of the British Museum

Literature: Chaloner Smith, 1883, vol. 2, p. 788, no. 16

The Beggar and his Dog is an episode from Henry Mackenzie's popular sentimental novel *The Man of Feeling* of 1771. Published when Mackenzie was only

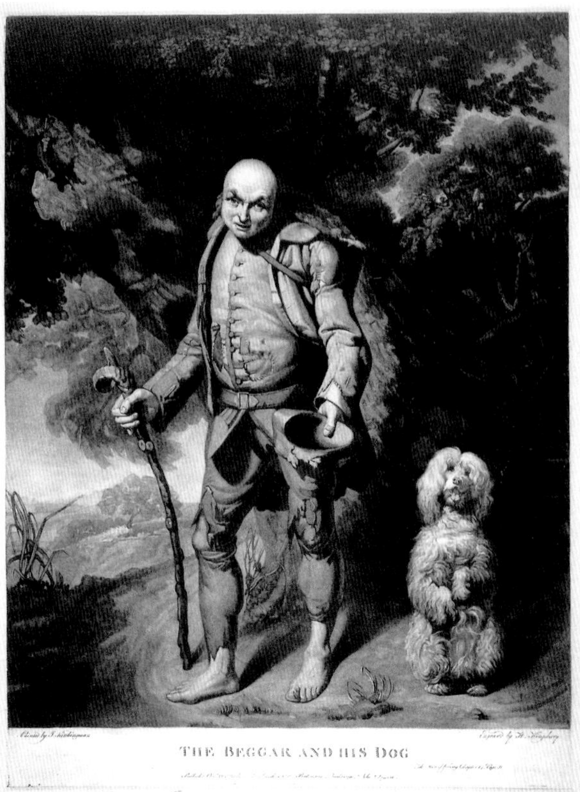

THE BEGGAR AND HIS DOG

twenty-two it became an overnight success and an emblem of Georgian sensibility. Walter Scott admired its 'moral pathos', while Robert Burns called it 'a book I prize next to the Bible'. In the present episode the novel's hero, Harley, befriends a worldly beggar as he sits by the roadside taking a stone from his shoe: 'The beggar had by this time come up, and pulling off a piece of hat, asked charity of Harley; the dog began to beg too:– it was impossible to resist both; and in truth, the want of shoes and stockings had made both unnecessary, for Harley had destined sixpence for him before.' Mackenzie's beggar, like the other characters encountered in the novel, excites at once compassion, amusement and active philanthropy. The beggar, although ragged and destitute, cheerfully accepts his lot, presenting no threat to Harley – or to the reader. Rather than dwelling upon his own woes, he has turned to telling fortunes, 'to prophesy happiness to others'. Written at a time when the appearance upon the country's roads of increasing numbers of rootless vagrants was a cause for private and public concern, Mackenzie's story, and its consequent visualisation by Kitchingman, reassured polite society that a suitably emotional response, reinforced by the gift of hard currency, was sufficient to maintain the status quo. Thus, the image both brings the audience into close contact with the deserving poor, while at the same time shielding them from less comfortable reflections on the harsher realities of life – was one of the leading functions of the fancy picture in the later eighteenth century. According to David Alexander, this print appears to be the first signed by Kingsbury. He exhibited it at the Society of Artists, 1776 (219)

94 *The Blind Beggar of Bednall Green*
WILLIAM WARD (1762-1826), after William Owen

Mezzotint, 56 x 48 cm
LETTERED: '*Painted by Wm Owen/Engraved by Willm Ward*

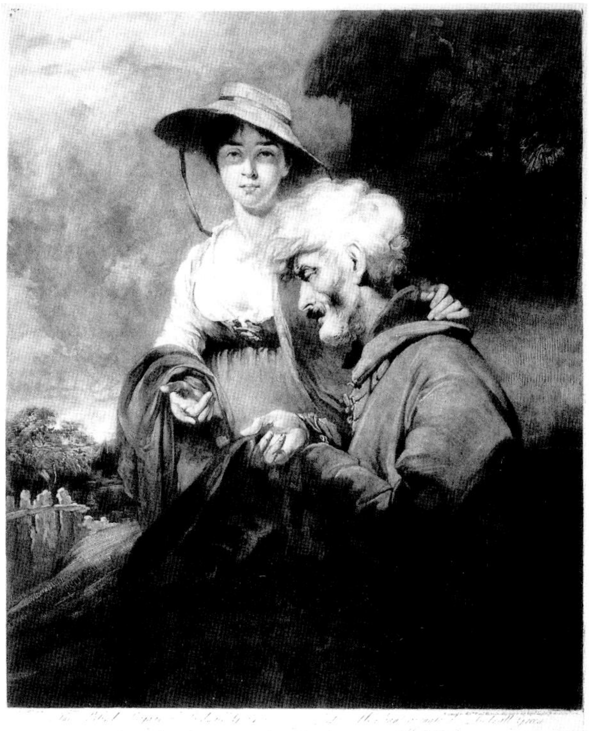

Mezzotinto Engraver to his Royal Highness the Duke of York/The Blind Beggar of Bednall Green/His reverend lockes/In comelye awls did wave/And on his aged temples grew/The blossomes of the grave/Le Mendicant Aveugle de Bednall Green/Ses Cheveaux venerables Pendolent en flocons/Ondoyants autour de/Son front ride/Vide Reliques of Ancient Poetry/LONDON Pub^d April 2 1804 by MESS^{RS} WARDS & Co. No. 6 Newman Street./Engraved from the Original Picture in the Possession of Thomas Heathcote Esqr. to whom this Plate is Dedicated by his most Obed^t. Humble Servt. W^m. WARD'

The Trustees of the British Museum

The legend of the Blind Beggar of Bethnal Green dates back probably to the reign of of Henry VI. It was revived in the eighteenth century through Thomas Percy's *Reliques of Ancient English Poetry*, published in three volumes in 1765. Percy, the friend of Reynolds and Johnson, did not initiate the eighteenth-century interest in the ballad so much as present the tradition in a well-informed and scholarly manner for an intelligent lay audience. Growing antiquarian interest in ballads and folk traditions was responsible in turn for the attention paid to contemporary characters and 'phenomena', who, it was felt represented a tangible link with the past. William Owen (1769-1825), a fashionable society portrait painter during the Regency, was also known particularly known for his fancy pictures depicting rural subjects, and which were extensively engraved.

95 *Crazy Kate*
THOMAS BARKER (1769-1847)

Oil on paper, laid on canvas, 106 x 77.5 cm, *c* 1795-1803

York City Art Gallery

Provenance: Purchased 1951 from messrs Appleby, London
Exhibited: Dijon, 1957, no. 19; Bath, 1986, no. 17

Literature: *Preview*, 17 (Jan. 1952), p. 197; ibid., 51 (July 1960), pp. 491-2; York, 1968, pp. 5-6; Bath, 1986, p. 31
Engraved: 1803 (with variations) by T. Burke

Barker's painting is based on an episode from William Cowper's poem *The Task* (1785). Here the poet describes a serving maid who, having lost her lover at sea, declines into madness:

> … and now she roams
> The dreary waste; there spends the livelong day,
> And there, unless when charity forbids,
> The livelong night. A tatter'd apron hides,
> Worn as a cloak, and hardly hides, a gown
> More tatter's still; and both but ill conceal
> A bosom heaved with never-ceasing sighs.
> She begs an idle pin of all she meets,
> And hoards them in her sleeve; but needful food,
> Though press'd with hunger oft, or comlier clothes,
> Though pinch'd with cold, asks never. – Kate is crazed.
> (*The Task*, Book 1, lines 546-56)

Cowper's poem deliberately broke with existing pastoral and Georgic traditions of depicting English rural life. Instead the author describes in an intensely personal voice scenes from everyday life witnessed in and around the town of Olney in Buckinghamshire – including Crazy Kate, who wanders across the common, oblivious to her wretched condition. Cowper's description of the impoverished and insane young woman is in marked contrast to the sentimentalised, picturesque beggar found earlier in the century in Mackenzie's *Man of Feeling* (see cat. 93). Rather, she resembles Beechey's shivering urchin of the mid-1790s (cat. 91) – although in Kate's case any attempts to relieve her condition through charity go unrecognized and unappreciated.

Although the precise date of *Crazy Kate* is not known, the stretcher was originally lined with pages of Barker's 1794 exhibition at Bath. It may predate Henry Fuseli's more famous painting of the same subject of about 1802 (Frankfurt-am-Main, Goethe-Museum), which was engraved by William Bromley for *Poems by William Cowper, of the Inner Temple, Esq*, published in 1806. While madness had an obvious appeal for Fuseli, poverty was also a natural choice for Barker, who had already begun to produce pastiches of Gainsborough's fancy pictures of the late 1780s – notably *The Woodman* (see cat. 86). Barker was one of a family of painters practising in Bath in the late eighteenth and early nineteenth century. Like Opie, he was promoted as a prodigy, his early career shaped by the shrewd patronage of the property developer Charles Spackman. In 1790 Barker, under Spackman's close guidance, held a one-man exhibition of his work in Bath – an exhibition which revealed at once his prococious technical ability (resulting from endless copying) and his bewildering eclecticism. Barker's large fancy pictures of woodmen and faggot gathers were quickly snapped up by wealthy collectors. In 1791 he was packed off to Italy by Spackman, who sponsored his travels. On his return two years later, Barker attempted to set up in London, although by 1800 he had returned to Bath where he lived out the remainder of his life. Barker's paintings were formulaic. Yet his lithographs, *Impressions of Rustic Figures after Nature*, published in 1813, reveal a lively and inventive draughtsmanship. Barker survived until 1847, his popularity gradually waning and his patrons deserting him. Ironically – for one who had profited so much from images of indigence – he died neglected and in poverty.

Textual References

Alexander 1992 David Alexander, 'Kauffman and the Print Market in Eighteenth-Century England', in W.W. Roworth, ed., *Angelica Kauffman: A Continental Artists in Georgian England*, London, 1992

Alexander 1993 David Alexander, *Affecting Moments: Prints of English Literature made in the Age of Sensibility, 1775-18*, exhibition catalogue, City Art Gallery, York; revised edition, 1993

Allen 1995 Brian Allen, ed., *Towards a Modern Art World. Studies in British Art 1*, New Haven & London, 1995

Andrew 1989 Donna T. Andrew, *Philanthropy and Police: London Charity in the Eighteenth Century*, Princeton, 1989

Armstrong 1913 Sir Walter Armstrong, *Lawrence*, London, 1913

Asfour et al 1997 Amal Asfour, Paul Williamson, Gertrude Jackson, '"A Second Sentimental Journey". Gainsborough abroad', *Apollo Magazine*, vol. CXLVI, August 1997, pp. 27-30

Barrell 1980 John Barrell, *The Dark Side of the Landscape*, Cambridge, 1980

Bath 1986 *The Barkers of Bath*, exhibition catalogue, Victoria Art Gallery, Bath, 1986

Beckett 1949 R.B. Beckett, *Hogarth*, London, 1949

Bermingham & Brewer 1995 Ann Bermingham & John Brewer, eds., *The Consumption of Culture 1600-1800. Image, Object, Text*, London and New York, 1995

Bindman 1981 David Bindman, *Hogarth*, London, 1981

Boucé 1982 P.G. Boucé, ed., *Sexuality in Eighteenth-Century England*, Manchester, 1982

Brewer 1997 John Brewer, *The Pleasures of the Imagination. English Culture in the Eighteenth Century*, London, 1997

Bristow 1977 E.J. Bristow, *Vice and Vigilance: Purity Movements in Britain since 1700*, Dublin, 1977

Bromley 1793 Henry Bromley, *A Catalogue of British Engraved Portraits*, London, 1793

Broun 1987 Francis Broun, 'Sir Joshua Reynolds's Collection of Paintings', unpublished PhD thesis, Princeton University, New Jersey, 1987

Cannon-Brookes 1989 Peter Cannon-Brookes, ed., *Paintings from Tabley. An Exhibition of paintings from Tabley House*, The Heim Gallery, London, 1989

Castle 1986 Terry Castle, *Masquerade and Civilisation: The Carnivalesque in Eighteenth-Century English Culture and Fiction*, Stanford University Press, 1986

Chaloner Smith 1883 J. Chaloner Smith, *English Mezzotinto Portraits*, 4 vols., London, 1878-83

Charrington 1923 John Charrington, *A Catalogue of the Mezzotints after… Rembrandt*, Cambridge, 1923

Collins Baker 1907 C.H. Collins Baker, 'Notes on Some Portraits in Mr John Lane's Collection', *The Connoisseur*, vol. XLVIII, July 1907, p. 136

Collins Baker 1912 C.H. Collins Baker, *Lely and the Stuart Portrait Painters*, 2 vols., 1912

Connell 1957 Brian Connell, *Portrait of a Whig Peer. Complied from the Papers of the Second Viscount Palmerston 1793-1802*, London, 1957

Cormack 1970 Malcolm Cormack, 'The Ledgers of Sir Joshua Reynolds', *The Walpole Society*, vol. XLII, 1970, pp. 105-69

Cotton 1856 William Cotton, *Sir Joshua Reynolds and his Works. Gleanings from his Diary, unpublished Manuscripts, and from other Sources*, ed. J. Burnet, London, 1856

Cotton 1859 William Cotton, ed., *Sir Joshua Reynolds's Notes and Observations on pictures … extracts from his Italian sketchbooks, also the Rev. W. Mason's Observations of Sir Joshua's method of colouring*, London, 1859

Cross 1980 A.G. Cross, *By the Banks of the Thames. Russians in Eighteenth-Century Britain*, Newtonville, Mass., 1980

Crown 1984 Patricia Crown, 'Portraits and fancy pictures by Gainsborough and Reynolds: contrasting images of childhood', *British Journal for Eighteenth-Century Studies*, vol. VII, Autumn 1984, pp. 159-67

Cunningham 1991 Hugh Cunningham, *The Children of the Poor. Representations of Childhood since the Seventeenth Century*, Oxford, 1991

Cunningham 1995 Hugh Cunningham, *Children and Childhood in Western Society since 1500*, 1995

Davies 1959 Martin Davies. *The British School. National Gallery Catalogues*, revised edition, London, 1959

Dulwich 1993 *Rembrandt van Rijn. Girl at a Window. Paintings & their Context IV*, Dulwich Picture Gallery, 1993

Einberg 1997 Elizabeth Einberg, *Hogarth the Painter*, exhibition catalogue, Tate Gallery, 1997

Farington Kenneth Garlick, Angus Macintyre & Kathryn Cave, *The Diary of Joseph Farington, July 1793 - December 1821*, 16 vols., New Haven & London, 1978-84

Farrer 1909 Revd E. Farrer, 'Henry Walton, Artist', *The Connoisseur*, vol. XXV, 1909, pp. 139-47

Farthing 1944 Cecil Farthing, 'George Morland's Father. A Neglected Painter', *The Connoisseur*, vol. XXV, 1909, pp. 101-4

Frankau 1902 Julia Frankau, *John Raphael Smith*, London, 1902

Garlick 1954 Kenneth Garlick, *Sir Thomas Lawrence*, London, 1954

Garlick 1989 Kenneth Garlick, *Sir Thomas Lawrence. A Complete Catalogue of the Oil Paintings*, New Haven & London, 1989

Gower 1900 Lord Ronald Sutherland Gower, *Sir Thomas Lawrence*, London, 1900

Gowing 1971 Lawrence Gowing, *Hogarth*, exhibition catalogue, Tate Gallery, 1980

Graves & Cronin 1899-1901 Algernon Graves, & William Vine Cronin, *A History of the Works of Sir Joshua Reynolds, P.R.A*, 4 vols., London, 1899-1901

Grundy & Roe 1938 C.R. Grundy & F.G. Roe, *A Catalogue of the Collection of F.J. Nettlefold*, IV, 1938, p. 122

Hall 1962 Douglas Hall, 'The Tabley House Papers', *The Walpole Society*, vol. XXXVIII, 1962, pp. 59-122

Hamilton 1884 Edward Hamilton, *The Engraved Works of Sir Joshua Reynolds*, London, revised ed., 1884

Hayes 1970 John Hayes, *The Drawings of Thomas Gainsborough*, 2 vols., London, 1970

Hayes 1975 John Hayes, *Gainsborough. Paintings and Drawings*, London, 1975

Hayes 1980 John Hayes, *Gainsborough*, exhibition catalogue, Tate Gallery, 1980

Hayes 1982 John Hayes, *The Landscape Paintings of Thomas Gainsborough. A Critical Text and Catalogue Raisonne*, 2 vols., London, 1982

Hecht 1956 J.J. Hecht, *The Domestic Servant Class in Eighteenth Century England*, 1956

Hill 1897 George Birkbeck Hill, *Johnsonian Miscellanies*, 2 vols., 1897

Hill 1994 Bridget Hill, *Women, work & sexual politics in eighteenth-century England*, 2nd edition, London, 1994

Holburne 1979 *A Guide to the Collections*, Holburne Museum, Bath, 1979

Kenwood 1978 *The Iveagh Bequest, Kenwood. Catalogue of Paintings*, 3rd edition, London, 1978

Ingamells & Raines 1978 John Ingamells and Robert Raines, 'A Catalogue of the Paintings, Drawings and Etchings of Philip Mercier', *Walpole Society*, vol. XLVI, 1978

Ingamells 1997 John Ingamells, *A Dictionary of British and Irish Travellers in Italy, 1701-1800*, New Haven & London, 1997

Laing 1995 Alastair Laing, *In Trust for the Nation. Paintings from National Trust Houses*, London, 1995

Langford 1989 Paul Langford, *A Polite and Commercial People: England 1727-1783* Oxford, Clarendon Press, 1989

Launay 1991 Elizabeth Launay, *Les frères Goncourt, collectionneurs de dessins*, 1991

Leslie & Taylor 1865 Charles Robert Leslie and Tom Taylor, *The Life and Times of Sir Joshua Reynolds with Notices of his Contemporaries*, 2 vols., London, 1865

Lindsay 1977 Jack Lindsay, *Hogarth. His Art and his World*, London, 1977

Lugt 1921 Frits Lugt, *Les Marques de collections de dessins & d'estampes*, Amsterdam, 1921

MacLaren & Braham 1988 Neil MacLaren, revised by Allan Braham, *The Spanish School. National Gallery Catalogues*, London, 1988

Malone 1819 Edmond Malone, ed., *The Literary Works of Sir Joshua Reynolds*, 3 vols., London, 1798, 5th edition

Manners 1913 Lady Victoria Manners, *Matthew William Peters*, London, 1913

Manners & Williamson 1920 Lady Victoria Manners & George C. Williamson, *John* [sic] *Zoffany R.A.*, London, 1920

Mercier 1969 *Philip Mercier 1689-1760*, exhibition catalogue, York City Art Gallery & the Iveagh Bequest, Kenwood, 1969

Millar 1951 Oliver Millar, *Southill, A Regency House. The Pictures*, 1951

Millar 1978 Oliver Millar, *Sir Peter Lely*, exhibition catalogue, National Portrait Gallery, London, 1978

Murillo 1982 *Bartolomé Murillo 1617-1682*, exhibition catalogue, Museo del Prado & Royal Academy of Arts, London, London 1983

New Haven 1980 *Painters and Engraving. The Reproductive Print from Hogarth to Wilkie*, exhibition catalogue by David Alexander and Richard T. Godfrey, Yale Center for Studies in British Art, New Haven, 1980

Nichols 1781 John Nichols, *Biographical Anecdotes of William Hogarth; with a Catalogue of his Works chronologically arranged; and Occasional Remarks*, 1st edition, London, 1781 (2nd edition 1782, 3rd edition 1785)

Nichols & Steevens 1817 John Nichols & George Steevens, *The Genuine Works of William Hogarth*, 3 vols., London, 1808-17

Nicolson 1968 Benedict Nicolson, *Joseph Wright of Derby*, 2 vols., New Haven and London, 1968

Northcote 1818 James Northcote, *The Life of Sir Joshua Reynolds*, 2 vols., London, 1818

Paulson 1971 Ronald Paulson, *Hogarth: His Life, Art and Times*, 2 vols., New Haven & London, 1971

Pennant 1811 *Pennant's 1780 Journey from Chester to London*, London, 1811

Penny 1986 Nicholas Penny, ed., *Reynolds*, exhibition catalogue, Royal Academy of Arts, London, 1986

Pointon 1993 Marcia Pointon, *Hanging the Head. Portraiture and Social Formation in Eighteenth-Century England*, New Haven & London, 1993

Pope 1960-63 Willard Bissell Pope, *The Diary of Benjamin Robert Haydon*, 5 vols., Cambridge, Mass., 1960-63

Postle 1988 Martin Postle, 'Patriarchs, prophets, and paviours: Reynolds's images of old age', *The Burlington Magazine*, vol. CXXX, Oct., 1988 pp. 735-44

Postle 1995 Martin Postle, *Sir Joshua Reynolds. The Subject Pictures*, Cambridge, 1995

Raines 1964 Robert Raines, 'Philip Mercier's later Fancy Pictures', *Apollo*, LXXX, 1964, pp. 27-32.

Raines 1967 Robert, 'Philip Mercier, a little-known eighteenth-century painter', *Proceedings of the Huguenot Society of London*, vol. XXI, 2, 1967, pp. 124-37

Roberts 1907 W. Roberts, *Sir William Beechey, R.A.*, London 1907

Rodgers 1949 B. Rodgers, *The Cloak of Charity: Studies in Eighteenth-Century Philanthropy*, 1949

Rousseau & Porter 1987 G.S. Rousseau & Roy Porter, eds., *Sexual underworlds of the Enlightenment*, Manchester, 1987

Rule 1980 J. Rule, *The Experience of Labour in Eighteenth Century Industry*, 1980

Schama 1991 Simon Schama, *The Embarrassment of Riches. An Interpretation of Dutch Culture in the Golden Age*, London, 1991

Shesgreen 1990 Sean Shesgreen, *The Criers and Hawkers of London. Engravings and Drawings by Marcellus Laroon*, London, 1990

Simon 1987 Robin Simon, *The Portrait in Britain and America*, London, 1987

Slack 1990 Paul Slack, *The English poor law, 1531-1782. New Studies in Economic and Social History*, Cambridge, 1990

Sparrow 1931 Walter Shaw Sparrow, 'New Light on Morland', *The Connoisseur*, vol. LXXXVII, February 1931, pp. 71-79

Spicer & Orr 1997 Joanneth A. Spicer & Lynn Federle Orr, eds., *Masters of Light. Dutch Painters in Utrecht during the Golden Age*, exhibition catalogue, New Haven & London, 1997

Tinker 1938 Chauncey B. Tinker, *Painter and Poet. Studies in the Literary Relations of English Painting*, Cambridge, Mass., 1938

Thomas 1971 Keith Thomas, *Religion and the Decline of Magic. Studies in Popular Beliefs in Sixteenth- and Seventeenth-Century England*, London, 1971

Toynbee 1928 Paget Toynbee, 'Horace Walpole's Journals of visits to Country Seats', *Walpole Society*, vol. XVI, 1927-28

Vertue 1934 'The Note-Books of George Vertue relating to Artists and Collections in England', Vertue III, *The Walpole Society*, vol. XXII, 1934

Waagen 1857 G. Waagen, *Galleries of Art in Great Britain*, London, 1857

Walton 1963 *Paintings by Henry Walton (1746-1813)*, exhibition catalogue by M. Rajnai, Norwich, 1963

Ward & Roberts 1904 Humphry Ward & W. Roberts, *Romney. A Biographical and Critical Essay with a Catalogue Raisonne of his Works*, 2 vols., London, 1904

Wark 1975 Robert R. Wark, ed., *Sir Joshua Reynolds. Discourses on Art*, New Haven & London, 1975

Waterhouse MS notebooks Ellis K. Waterhouse, 'A record of Pictures Seen, beginning 1924' (72 MS notebooks, Getty Center Library, Santa Monica, California)

Waterhouse 1941 Ellis K. Waterhouse, *Reynolds*, London, 1941

Waterhouse 1946 Ellis K. Waterhouse, 'Gainsborough's "Fancy Pictures"', *Burlington Magazine*, vol. LXXXVIII, June 1946, pp. 134-40

Waterhouse 1952 Ellis K. Waterhouse, *National Gallery of Scotland. Catalogue of Paintings and Sculpture*, Edinburgh, 1952

Waterhouse 1953 Ellis K. Waterhouse, *Painting in Britain 1530 to 1790*, London, 1953

Waterhouse 1958 Ellis K. Waterhouse, *Gainsborough*, London, 1958

Waterhouse 1973 Ellis K. Waterhouse, *Reynolds*, London, 1973

Webster 1970 Mary Webster, *Francis Wheatley*, London, 1970

Webster 1976 Mary Webster, *Johan Zoffany 1733-1810*, exhibition catalogue, National Portrait Gallery, London, 1976

White et. al. 1983 Christopher White, David Alexander & Ellen D'Oench, *Rembrandt in Eighteenth-Century England*, exhibition catalogue, Yale Center for British Art, New Haven & London, 1983

Whitley 1915 William T. Whitley, *Thomas Gainsborough*, London, 1915

Williamson 1894 George C. Williamson, *John Russell R.A.*, London, 1894

Williamson 1904 George C. Williamson, *George Morland*, London, 1904

Winter 1977 David Winter, 'George Morland (1763-1804)', Unpublished PhD thesis, Stanford University, California

Woodall 1961 Mary Woodall, *The Letters of Thomas Gainsborough*, London, 1961

Wynne 1972 Michael Wynne, 'Thomas Frye (1710-1762)', *The Burlington Magazine*, vol. CXIV, February 1972, pp. 79-84

York 1968 *Catalogue of Paintings. City of York Art Gallery*, York, 1968